Roland Barthes, Phenomenon and Myth

Roland Barthes, Phenomenon and Myth

An Intellectual Biography

Andy Stafford

Edinburgh University Press

For, to and with C.

Edinburgh University Press
22 George Square, Edinburgh

Transferred to digital print 2007

Typeset in New Baskerville
by Hewer Text Ltd, Edinburgh, and
printed and bound in Great Britain by
CPI Antony Rowe, Eastbourne

A CIP record for this book is available from the British Library

ISBN-10 0 7486 0867 2
ISBN-13 978 0 7486 0867 6

Contents

Acknowledgements

I WOULD LIKE TO thank the British Academy for its financial support for the original research, and also Lancaster University for help with further work. I am indebted to the following for their sparing time to answer questions: Philippe Rebeyrol, Louis-Jean Calvet, Maurice Nadeau, the late Bernard Dort, Jacqueline Fournié and Edgar Morin. My research would have been almost impossible without the help of Sophie Choisnel and Marie-Claire Chalvet at Les Éditions du Seuil in Paris and the expertise of Dr Lindsay Newman, Assistant Librarian at Lancaster University. I am grateful to John Parkin for allowing me to present Chapter 1 at the 'Barthes: retrospective' conference held at the University of Bristol in November 1992. Colleagues in the Department of French at Lancaster University, in particular Terry Keefe, the late Ralph Gibson, David Whitton, David Steel and Françoise Coquet, were patient and supportive with earlier drafts.

Many other people have helped with the preparation of this book, in both profound and incidental manners: Paul Stafford, Cathy and Valéry Fabing, Rami Mekdachi, Marie and Alain Guillot, Hajer Weslaty, Rosemary Chapman, Sally Johnson, Frank Finlay, Peter Wilkin, Nick Hewitt, Brian Rigby, Mary McAllester-Jones, Parry and Roxane Jubert, Roger Little and Charles Forsdick. Above all, Michael Moriarty and

Jackie Jones have given precious encouragement in their respective ways. Finally, Diana Knight, supervisor and friend, inspired my interest in Barthes; and maybe our approaches were not so different in the end, except perhaps in the conclusions drawn.

Note on Abbreviations

WHEREVER POSSIBLE, I HAVE used the three volumes of Barthes's *Complete Works – Oeuvres complètes* (Paris, Seuil, 1993–5). I have put all references to Barthes's works in the text itself and between brackets (OCi, OCii, OCiii) followed by the standard abbreviations for translations, listed below. Where the original published product has been edited (a significant number of examples mainly in the early work), I have used the original articles, listed separately in the bibliography. All translations are my own, though existing published translations are given a reference for further reading; where there is only OCi or ii, and so on, it is assumed that no translation exists.

Books (in translation)

BR *A Barthes Reader*, ed. Susan Sontag (New York, Hill and Wang, 1982).

CE *Critical Essays*, trans. Richard Howard (Evanston, Northwestern University Press, 1972).

CL *Camera Lucida: Reflections on Photography*, trans. Richard Howard (London, Fontana, 1984).

CT *Criticism and Truth*, trans. Katrine Pilcher Keuneman (London, Athlone Press, 1987).

ES *Empire of Signs*, trans. Richard Howard (London, Jonathan Cape, 1983).

ESem *Elements of Semiology*, trans. Annette Lavers and Colin Smith (London, Jonathan Cape, 1967).

ET *The Eiffel Tower and Other Mythologies*, trans. Richard Howard (New York, Hill and Wang, 1979).

FS *The Fashion System*, trans. Matthew Ward and Richard Howard (London, Jonathan Cape, 1985).

GV *The Grain of the Voice*, trans. Linda Coverdale (New York, Hill and Wang, 1985).

I *Incidents*, trans. Richard Howard (Berkeley and Los Angeles, University of California Press, 1992).

IMT *Image, Music, Text*, trans. Stephen Heath (Glasgow, Fontana, 1977).

LD *A Lover's Discourse: Fragments*, trans. Richard Howard (London, Jonathan Cape, 1979).

M *Mythologies*, trans. Annette Lavers (London, Jonathan Cape, 1972).

MI *Michelet*, trans. Richard Howard (Oxford, Blackwell, 1987).

NCE *New Critical Essays*, trans. Richard Howard (Berkeley and Los Angeles, University of California Press, 1990).

OR *On Racine*, trans. Richard Howard (New York, Performing Arts Journal Publications, 1983).

PT *The Pleasure of the Text*, trans. Richard Miller (London, Jonathan Cape, 1976).

RB *Roland Barthes by Roland Barthes*, trans. Richard Howard (London, Macmillan, 1977).

RF *The Responsibility of Forms: Critical Essays on Music, Art and Representation*, trans. Richard Howard (Oxford, Blackwell, 1985).

RL *The Rustle of Language*, trans. Richard Howard (Oxford, Blackwell, 1986).

SC *The Semiotic Challenge*, trans. Richard Howard (Oxford, Blackwell, 1987).

SFL *Sade, Fourier, Loyola*, trans. Richard Miller (Berkeley and Los Angeles, University of California Press, 1976).

SW *Sollers Writer*, trans. Philip Thody (London, Athlone Press, 1987).
SZ *S/Z*, trans. Richard Miller (London, Jonathan Cape, 1975).
T 'Theory of the Text', trans. Ian McLeod, in R. Young (ed.), *Untying the Text: A Post-Structuralist Reader* (London, Routledge & Kegan Paul, 1981).
WDZ *Writing Degree Zero*, trans. Annette Lavers and Colin Smith (London, Jonathan Cape, 1967).

Journals

LLN *Les Lettres nouvelles*
NRF (sometimes *NNRF*) *La Nouvelle Revue Française* (sometimes *La Nouvelle Nouvelle Revue Française*)
TP *Théâtre populaire*
TQ *Tel Quel*

Introduction

I claim to live fully the contradiction of my time, which might make sarcasm into the condition of truth.

Roland Barthes

ANYBODY WHO CAN BEGIN their first book by describing how the dramatic changes of the French Revolution were epitomised linguistically by the use of 'damn' and 'hell', and then go on to become an influential theorist and writer, must be worthy of our attention. References to the name and the ideas of Roland Barthes return with surprising regularity, and in a wide range of contexts, in Anglophone humanities and social sciences: it is quite clear that, as the French critic Pierre-Jean Faunau pointed out in 1973, we 'have to live' with Barthes.

As early as 1955, Jean Paulhan, the influential publisher at Gallimard, had foreseen the fame that the name Barthes now enjoys. Those people who talk in a left-wing manner, he wrote, always end up in a well-respected position in society:

> Monsieur Barthes is held in high regard by a bourgeois society which never fails to give him financial support. The way things are going, in fifteen years time, he will be Minister for Education; and he won't make a bad Minister.[1]

Now Paulhan was not entirely accurate in his prediction – Barthes did not follow his 'Marxist' predecessors into political office. But he was given a chair at the prestigious Collège de France in 1977, and invited around the same time to dine with French presidents and to appear on French television. Was this the same Barthes as the scourge of the post-war literary and university orthodoxy in the heated dispute with a Sorbonne professor, the staunch critic of 'recuperation' by the social 'doxa', the key player in the militant defence of Brecht's revolutionary popular theatre, the arch critic of bourgeois myth? How *did* a victim of tuberculosis at the age of 18, starting his publishing career only at the age of 38, and from a provincial, middle-class but impoverished background, become a touchstone of cultural theory and practice? How *could* a writer who never managed to win a prize for his writing become the prime theorist and practitioner of *écriture* ?

Given the recent publication in France of his *Complete Works,* one can now chart Barthes's unorthodox, if not meteoric, rise to prominence. This book will set out the conditions in which this 'outsider' to the academic and intellectual world become feted as one of France's most important post-war intellectual figures. This will require not so much a textual – though this is, by definition, the only manner in which we can 'know' Barthes today – as an intellectual biography. It will seek to redress an imbalance in accounts of Barthes which have tended to see all of his writing career refracted through his 'late' work. It is perhaps inevitable that we read dead writers 'backwards', and consider their last pronouncements as final. But surely, this refraction needs to be confronted with a description which moves in a different, if not opposite, direction. So, though not claiming any superiority or greater accuracy, this intellectual biography will start from the beginning, to allow the plurality of views on Barthes to continue, and (if anything) explain the 'late' by an earlier Barthes.

A Biography of Barthes?

> One day I would like to write a biography.
> Roland Barthes

Surely to write a biography of the very person who proclaimed the 'Death of the Author' is not in the Barthesian spirit? Despite recent attempts to announce the 'return' of the author,[2] would Barthes not escape such a 'resurrection'? Louis-Jean Calvet's recent biography of Barthes has been subjected to acerbic criticism. But though the objections misunderstood or even ignored Barthes's own interest in writing biography,[3] they did point to a general crisis of attempts to write a life, in relation to Barthes in particular.

There is, it seems, a biography published every fifty-four minutes of the British working day.[4] Yet, though contemporary theory has undertaken the study of *auto*biography, biography, as Laura Marcus has recently noted, 'remains very largely untheorised'.[5] The only successful attempt to counter the excesses of the biography industry in recent years, in English at least, appeared in a novel: A. S. Byatt's 1990 Booker Prize winner *Possession* manages brilliantly to combine a critique of academic biographical enquiry with barely camouflaged Barthesian themes.[6]

As a hugely popular form, biography raises numerous theoretical and practical difficulties. The first and most obvious is rather banal: if there are forty-three accounts of Lawrence of Arabia's life, which is/are correct? What access to historical knowledge has the biographer used, and is it ideologically constructed? Some may even suggest that biography tells us more about the biographer (and the reader too, perhaps) than the subject. But there are deeper and more perplexing levels at which the biographical *genre* seems to unravel.

Sharon O'Brien has recently described how the writing of most biography has not changed since the heyday of nineteenth-century realism, suggesting that traditional biographers' scepticism of biographical theory is related to fears that their 'pretence of objectivity' might be exposed.[7] She points to four pitfalls in biography. First, language is treated as a 'transparent medium capable of representing the world'; second, the character and the self are deemed 'knowable'; third, 'the cause-and-effect linearity' of a chronological plot is considered 'a reliable way of ordering reality'; finally, the author is assumed to be a 'trustworthy narrator who understands the relationship between the private self and the public world'. Add these to the fact that Barthes too is an author – and a complex one at that – and the problems of biography are greatly multiplied. The *undecidability* of influences and weights (the number and nature of choices, unconscious desires, etc.) that face each individual is intensified for biographers trying to consider somebody else's range or lack of 'options' (let alone their own); and, of course, there will always be deferred evidence: new material such as correspondence (especially in the case of Barthes, we hope) will appear to undermine and contradict the biography's assertions.

A number of these critiques have been borne in mind in relation to Barthes. Philippe Roger has suggested that there is no 'itinerary' to be traced in Barthes's work; and for Andrew Brown, there is only 'drift'.[8] In Yves Velan's view, Barthes (in the 1950s at least) was working 'backwards'.[9] There is another problem. The tendency, evident in his later career, to undermine any fixed 'image' of himself means that the biographer's task is more difficult. Of course, this trait can itself be cited as a biographical element; however, it still leaves inconsistencies. This *undecidability* was evident, for example, in Barthes's attitude to psychoanalysis, as Contardo Calligari underlined.[10]

Like his contemporary Marguerite Duras, Barthes was a skilful performer in interviews. Though not all of these have been republished in the *Complete Works*, Barthes was a prolific interviewee. Both playful and bored, affirmative and provisional, Barthes's interview 'performances' underlined the deep contradictions confronting the intellectual becoming a media star. Above all for the intellectual biographer, there was a 'performative contradiction' at the heart of Barthes's pronouncements.

The Barthesian view (reminiscent of Nietzsche's, as Douglas Smith has recently shown)[11] that language was, in many ways, flawed in its attempt to communicate pointed to a paradox: how could he tell anybody this? If the writing in the second half of his career was predominantly concerned with undermining the 'signified' of language and promoting the 'signifier', surely he needed to use a signified meaning to tell us this? How do we then write the intellectual life of a writer whose major occupation (at the end of his career, at least) was to undermine any image of himself which might take hold, whose own use of language was forced into the 'performance' of a communicative contradiction? How *do* we place writers in relation to their moment of living?

Phenomenon and Myth

> I have been carried, enthused, by my life-time and I have been able to insert myself in such a way that one cannot say whether I have been constructed by it, or if I have in small way been involved in shaping it.
>
> Roland Barthes

In an early 'mythology' called 'Phenomenon or Myth?', Barthes himself treated this dilemma, with respect to the *enfant terrible* of French poetry, Arthur Rimbaud. Barthes regretted that a recent book by René Etiemble concentrating on the 'myth' of Rimbaud – how the poet had been 'received' since the 1870s – had been rejected by *Les Nouvelles littéraires* as pure 'mystification'.[12] Etiemble's 'crime', complained Barthes sarcastically, had been to ignore Rimbaud's 'extraordinary work' and produce 'interpretations' which were now being deemed 'abusive'. Barthes had nothing but contempt for the reviewer of Etiemble's study:

> For *Les Nouvelles littéraires*, the Sun stopped years ago, when the Poet was a 'phenomenon': devoid of causes and finalities, detached from all History (whether before or after), and functioning like a celestial voice reaching the individual ear of a reader also devoid of history and society. (p. 952)

In Barthes's view the 'classical taboo of inspiration' had prevented the reviewer of Etiemble's book from seeing that there were *two* sides to Rimbaud: his 'noble Muse' *and* 'the avid and large number of people, anonymous and above all daft', who had read his poetry since. Since Rimbaud's poems were now well known, Barthes wanted to see a redress of the imbalance. Like Etiemble, he wanted to know how the reading public had 'consumed' Rimbaud, how the 'myth' of the poet had been constructed.

Despite readers' lack of awareness of this article on Rimbaud, there have been a number of attempts to use 'myth' in relation to writing about Barthes. In line with his literary self-presentation, *Roland Barthes*, a number of friends and critics produced, following his death in 1980, highly literary portraits of him. With the exception of Philippe Roger, these portrayals have erred towards the 'myth' pole set out in Barthes's own dilemma with Rimbaud. Barthes's favoured approach, the 'biographeme' technique of presenting 'fragments' (rather than a linear narrative), has led to a romanticised picture. The 'myth' has, in many ways, overtaken the 'phenomenon' in Barthesian studies (if 'Barthesian studies' is not a contradiction in terms).[13] For a later generation (including me), barely linguistically conscious during Barthes's lifetime, this mythical tendency has obscured his actual significance. If we want to know, as Sunhil Khilnani has put it in relation to Sartre and Althusser, what Barthes 'was actually doing',[14] this imbalance needs to be redressed (if only temporarily). Rather than as *either* a phenomenon *or* a myth, we need perhaps to place Barthes in his context *and* to suggest the manner in which he has been received: we must consider him then as both phenomenon *and* myth.

Such a biographical approach may well be purely 'parametric': suited to the object of study only. As an avid reader of the press and 'supple' dialectician, Barthes was aware of his image and perception by others. So confronting his ideas with their reception might not only enlighten us on their content's significance but also suggest their (and other) future developments in his writing, and let us see him in 'dialogue' with his age. His belief in the Brechtian idea that we should think through other people's minds and they through ours is well suited to this approach: this 'dialogue' between Barthes and French culture emphasises the *circulation* (rather than ownership) of ideas which he favoured.

Clearly, this dialogic approach cannot produce a comprehensive account. Barthes's impact, for example, on literary theory was immense in France, particularly after *S/Z*. Also, what happens in this 'dialogue' to anything written on Barthes after his death? The post-1980 reception falls outside the phenomenon/myth structure; but, of course, there is no more powerful constructor of 'myth' than a posthumous account, if only because there is no chance for the subject to reply. Furthermore, important work on Barthes, both in France and outside, has taken place *since* his death.[15]

However, the benefits of a dialogic approach seem to outweigh the shortcomings. Though not claiming to avoid all the pitfalls set out above, a 'dialogic', Bakhtinian account will allow us to appreciate the imponderables of a given life, within a semblance of order; to overcome a crude determinism, without overplaying its voluntarist counterpart; to deny a certainty of explanation, in favour of seeing an existence ultimately as a 'trace', contradictory but none the less tangible. By considering both the phenomenon and the myth we might be able to find Barthes *somewhere* between these two poles.

Spiral of Biography

Within this 'parametric dialogue', we could consider Barthes's career under his favoured figure of the *spiral*, in which a phenomenon moves upwards but remains, paradoxically, in the same position. It develops but is subject to the circularity of repetition. Indeed, the themes of his earliest published work – Nietzsche and Gide, the literary diary, classical music, Michelet – seemed to return with a vengeance in the 'late Barthes'. His very first writing – a pastiche of Plato's *Crito*, written in 1933 as an adolescent – was published for the first time in 1974 (OCiii 17–20); it is perhaps no coincidence that one of his first published articles, 'On Gide and his Journal', from a student magazine in 1942, was republished a year later in 1975 (OCi 23–33/BR 3–17).

Thus, Barthes's politically 'detached' years post-1975 seemed to be prefigured by the apolitical considerations of the 1942–6 writings. The broadly political period from 1947 to the early 1970s appeared, by the time of the rediscovery of his earliest writing phase in the mid-1970s, to be a kind of radical 'blip' between his highly literary and detached musings on life and culture pre-Liberation and post-1975. Barthes's thirty years of radical polemics matched almost exactly those of Fourastié's 'trente glorieuses' of the post-war thirty-year boom.

There are dangers in using a spiral in this way to consider Barthes's move from an apolitical period through a much longer radical phase, and finally 'back' to a 'detached' aestheticism. It hints that *by any standards* Barthes was a political writer and activist during long phases of his career. This could not be further from the truth in many ways, as his dislike of the 'hysteria' of political militancy showed. However, to deny the 'political' in Barthes is equally absurd. His militant defence of popular and then Brechtian theatre is evidence enough of a deeply politicised consciousness. So we could note how, for example, Barthes during May 1968 was highly marginalised and irrelevant to the events, as Calvet has suggested; or we could say that his attitude was very little different from that of Duras, Dionys Mascolo and Maurice Blanchot – a 'refusal which affirms' – which challenged, in Leslie Hill's words, 'all definitions of what constituted politics'.[16] Is there no way out of the contradiction of portraying the political in his work either as an internal *structural* development, or in an external and comparative manner which loses the specificity of Barthes? Such is the difficulty of choosing any structure in which to write the life of a writer. Therefore the structure of this study, outlined below, may be considered provisional, if only because each of the three elements of Barthes's career is, to lesser or greater degrees, present in the other two:

1. *Journalist.* The three books from 1942–60 – *Writing Degree Zero, Michelet* and *Mythologies* – all started from Barthes's work as a journalist for a diverse range of left-wing publications, with the exception of a brief period during the Occupation. The work resulted from both 'militant' journalistic *praxis* and financial expediency.
2. *Academic.* After Barthes's appointment in 1960 to an academic post, *On Racine* placed him in opposition to a Racine specialist. Barthes's seminars became a 'space' in which to develop the semiological approaches to *The Fashion System*, and close analyses of literary texts and their rhetoric. At the same time, his journalistic training allowed him to balance sociological research in *Annales* and *Communications* with a more adventurous, theoretical avant-gardism in the influential journal *Tel Quel.*
3. *'Novelist'.* Though not producing any 'novel', the last decade of

> writing was marked at the start by the development of a 'writerly' political strategy (*Empire of Signs*; *Incidents*; *Sade, Fourier, Loyola* and perhaps even *S/Z*), which initiated the radical and material pleasures of reading-as-writing in *The Pleasure of the Text*. The ironic presentation of the self in *Roland Barthes* and the novelistic fragments of *A Lover's Discourse* prompted at the end of his life a Nietzschean 'Life as Literature' and a romantic search for the lost past in *Camera Lucida*.

Though not arbitrary, the divisions make no claim for any major epistemological or political 'breaks' in Barthes's work. If 1966, as commentators have suggested, is a crucial date for French thought, then we can invoke the Barthesian idea from *Writing Degree Zero* that this 'revolution' has been 'overstated'. For, even though Barthes himself (in the 1971 preface to the *Critical Essays*) located 1966 as a crucial date, much of the shift that took place was merely a continuity in his own work.

The Foucauldian idea that rupture and continuity are not necessarily mutually exclusive suggests that none of the three categories excludes aspects of the other two. Just as Barthes continued his essayistic journalism throughout his career and, conversely, was attached (albeit temporarily) to academic institutions during the 1950s, so the 'novelist' was still in academic posts, and the journalist displayed both a literary essayism and an interest in academic performance. Using the figure of the spiral, these three divisions suggest only what seems to be the main activity at any one time.

By the same token, I will consider Barthes's posthumously published work, *Incidents* above all and pieces now appearing in the *Complete Works*, in relation to their time of penning; and, though outside of the 'reception' in the phenomenon/myth structure, their significance will be suggested. For there is a sense in which writing and publishing are dependent on tactical decisions: namely those of selection and omission. Barthes's propensity towards collections of essays is a good example. On the one hand, those selected for inclusion are significant, indicative of his 'intentions' at the time of editing; on the other, the omissions and acts of editing – the 'silences' – are of interest too, since they form part of Barthes's retrospective view of his own work. In this way, rewriting, choosing, discarding all become part of the phenomenon/myth dialogue. Since it was, ultimately, Barthes's own choice which brought many of his articles and pieces to prominence and left others in the shadows, this book will try to strike a difficult balance between acknowledging the fundamental importance of better-known writings and trying to reveal other lesser-known aspects: this is not only publishing- but also editing-as-event.

Biographer's Silences?

There is a danger of only presenting 'my Barthes'; and, of course, as I have suggested, all biography could be more about the biographer than its subject. *Mythologies* politicised me in the 1980s at a time when Barthes's critique of 1950s petty-bourgeois mentality seemed to have become relevant once more in Britain. Therefore this study will *tend* towards the political in Barthes's work. However, this will not be at the expense of the 'literary'. On the contrary, it is my view that the political and the literary sit in Barthes's work in a tight tension. Though sexuality is a political issue, I shall not consider Barthes as a specifically gay writer; a task which has already been begun.[17] I have also tried to avoid following the indiscriminate tendency in cultural studies to redefine what is 'insignificant' and 'significant'; I shall not discuss, for example, at which gym Barthes worked out.[18] Instead, I wish to set out the three crucial areas of Barthesian thought for us at the end of the twentieth century.

First, Barthes often cited Marx, Nietzsche and Freud as the key moments in modern thought. The battle between this triumvirate as the great thinkers of our age does not prevent their coming together in one view of humanity: for all three, we are not where we would like to be. This critique of alienation suggests that utopia, as Diana Knight has shown, is a central element of Barthes's work.[19] The dialectics of history and order, totality and singularity, modernity and classical culture, determinism and freedom, are all part of the 'space' in which Barthes was writing. His ambivalence towards all cultural phenomena was mirrored by the view that writing – creativity – was the only recourse against the deep *angst* and boredom of existence.

Second, Barthes is often held up today as a harbinger of *post*modernity, that rather vague time when modernity and Marxism are surpassed, and *historical* materialism is replaced by the *cultural* variety. Since it is both bogus (in my view, all of postmodernism is contained in modernism) and nonetheless evident (invoked endlessly in academic circles), 'postmodernity' requires a dialectical attitude of debunking and historical explanation: it does not exist, but is talked about by everyone. It is in this spirit that the history of its provenance acts as the subtext of this book. Furthermore, as intellectual biography, this study will not contain another detailed explanation of the three Ss – Saussure, semiology, structuralism,[20] and I will not treat in detail the work of Lévi-Strauss, Derrida, Foucault, Lacan. Rather, following what J. G. Merquior has called the 'literarisation of thought', I will consider current talk of *post*modernity as a return of Nietzscheanism.[21] Like that of Edgar Morin, described by Myron Kofman as a 'smuggler' carrying 'contraband' ideas and methods across epistemological borders, Barthes's thought will be seen as an effort to destroy traditional academic barriers.[22] What Bernard Comment has seen as the 'neutral' in Barthes's work, this study will consider as a mobile, and highly eclectic, *swinging* between opposing and contradictory positions.[23]

Third, the 'political' – with all its tensions with the 'literary' – suggests a dialogue between Barthes and today, a dialogue which undermines the purely textual parameters of biography. Though I am not proposing to study Barthes's life or writing like a text, Barthesians might want to think of the study in this way. The 'resurrection' of a Michelet, the living nature of theatre, the dialectics of criticism, all aspects of Barthes's interests rarely touched on hitherto and dealt with here, suggest a real relation with the present. It is a 'generous', but by no means complete, link to the past in all its contradictions, an attitude which will form in my conclusion a consideration of a (re-?) definition of the *post*-romantic.

Finally, a word about translations. Barthes was obsessed by language, and, naturally, by words in particular. Therefore, in translating Barthes into English, I have encountered the usual difficulties and no doubt performed travesties of translation. The key concept and practice in the Barthesian world *Écriture* (meaning 'writing' but also scripture) will be retained in the French, illustrating what Raymond Jean described in Barthes's study of Japan as 'an excellent travel guide for the country of *écriture*'.[24] My only hope is that, by placing certain key words in French in parentheses, usually words with an English cognate, I have managed to some extent to write 'with' Barthes.

PART ONE

JOURNALIST

IN HIS INTRODUCTION TO the writing of Roland Barthes, Jonathan Culler described Barthes as a 'Man of Parts'. Literary historian, mythologist, critic, polemicist, semiologist, structuralist, hedonist, writer, Barthes defied a simple definition (and indeed, continues to do so).[1] One important aspect of his activities was nevertheless overlooked in Culler's list, one which encapsulated and helped formulate, as well as explain, the overall diversity of his writing. Between 1942 and 1960, Barthes published over 200 pieces, some long, others brief, in over forty different publications. A way of overcoming a number of obstacles in his early life – financial difficulties in his family, protracted illness and resultant professional instability – journalism was to become also a central aspect of his formative years.

Though Barthes was part of the same generation as important post-war intellectuals such as Jean-Paul Sartre, Simone de Beauvoir, Albert Camus and Maurice Nadeau, his illness had played a crucial role in undermining his career. In a sanatorium for tuberculosis throughout most of the war, he had been absent from the combat against the Nazi occupation of France.[2] He had struggled to complete his classics degree, and watched his childhood friend, Philippe Rebeyrol, enter the prestigious École Normale Supérieure. Whilst intellectuals played an important role in the liberation and reconstruction of France, and friends forged careers at university, Barthes sat in sanatoria in south-east France and Switzerland, and arrived back in Paris in 1947, frankly, irrelevant.

However, it had been precisely during this relative isolation that his writing career had begun. For the next eighteen years he steadily increased his flow of articles, reviews and editorials, reaching a high point between 1953 and 1956, during which he produced over 130 pieces. As British academics would today consider twelve pieces a year very satisfactory, Barthes's output was that of a professional journalist. Though employed at various points – teaching abroad between 1948 and 1950, and working in an office in Paris between 1951 and 1952 – and briefly supported by meagre research grants from the Centre National de Recherche Scientifique (CNRS) in 1953 and 1956, he had nevertheless, as Calvet's biography insists, to endure an embarrassing penury. He might have held a part-time position as 'literary consultant' for the publishing house L'Arche for two years, but it seemed that his own publishing was providing an important source of income.

Indeed, writing was such a bread-and-butter issue for Barthes in the 1950s that he could see a 'proletarianisation' of the writer taking place. Referred to humorously in his early mythological study 'The Writer on Holiday', published in September 1954 (OCi 580/M 29), the idea of the exploitation of writers was suggested more seriously by him at a conference on Franco-German literature in the Black Forest a few months later.[3] This consideration of the social status of the writer underlined the political manner in which he viewed the act of writing and being published.

If journalism was a way to supplement a meagre income, it was also to be Barthes's 'training'. Though writing for a wide range of publications brought in extra money, it also encouraged him to theorise and practise a politics and an ethics of writing which were to dominate the rest of his career. The ability to turn a wide number of varied social phenomena into critical and politicised insights was to become the Barthesian hallmark: his 'style' and brilliant 'essayism' were indebted (paradoxically perhaps) to his 'exploitation' as a journalist in the 1950s.

There is a final reason for a consideration of 'Barthes the journalist'.

As an intellectual writing in journals, he displayed an ambivalent relationship to French academic inquiry. François Dosse has shown how the early structuralists in France set themselves up in contrast to the stifling orthodoxy and methodological complacency of the French academic system typified by the Sorbonne.[4] This academic scepticism was evident in Barthes's interest in popular culture. Reviewing a study of leisure in the popular theatre in 1954, he criticised the 'academic allure' of the book, which impeded a real understanding of the contemporary sociological importance of theatre. Why, he wondered, having provided an impressive 'social snapshot' of crowds in ancient Greek theatre, could not 'the academic approach' provide a similar analysis for contemporary drama culture (OCi 387–8)? Doubtless, his suspicion was related to the abrupt manner in which illness had excluded him from the academic world. It was also a reflection of his experience of working to widen the popular theatre movement, which, though primarily state-funded, vaunted its autonomy from the educational establishment. Yet by 1960 Barthes had joined this 'academism'. Indeed, the first full-time post of his career, in the newly created sixth section of the École Pratique des Hautes Études (EPHE), was located in the grounds of the Sorbonne itself.

In the preface to the English edition of *Homo Academicus,* Pierre Bourdieu suggested that, thanks to his 'marginal' position at the EPHE, Barthes (and others, such as Althusser, Deleuze, Derrida and Foucault) had 'strong connections with the intellectual world, and especially with avant-garde reviews (*Critique, Tel Quel* and so on) and with journalism (especially the *Nouvel-Observateur*)'.[5] But Bourdieu's main point was that to understand Barthes's strong views in the famous dispute in the 1960s with Sorbonne Professor Raymond Picard, we needed to take account of his place on the margins of the academic institution. Though undoubtedly correct – Barthes continued to rely on these publications throughout his academic career – Bourdieu's assertion paints only half of the picture.

To see Barthes simply as a minor, marginalised but nevertheless integral part of 'Homo academicus' is to misunderstand the conditions of his entry into the academic sphere. Barthes relied on 'non-academic', avant-garde and intellectual journals, throughout the 1960s and 1970s, *precisely because* he had been a journalist in the 1950s. Thus, in its haste to set out the relational and structural activities of university intellectuals, Bourdieu's synchronic account underestimates (perhaps inevitably) the *diachronic* dimension: Barthes the academic was a product of the 1950s intellectual, cultural and political milieu, outside of the academy. The vital question for a more comprehensive explanation of Barthes's actions and views is this: with what experiences as an intellectual journalist and popular theatre activist did he become a 'marginal' academic actant?

As we shall in these first two chapters, an ambivalent relationship to academic inquiry, and the combination of political and expedient journalism, meant, on the one hand, that Barthes appreciated the importance of writing as a strategy and the appropriate tactics with which to 'fit in' with a wide range of publications. On the other hand, he had a space within which to question the accepted disciplines and barriers of research culture: away from formal academic constraints, he could begin to transgress and undermine the epistemological bases of traditional inquiry.

1

Strategies and Tactics

'To have been challenged', wrote Victor Hugo in 1869, 'is to have been noticed.' Barthes quoted this maxim in 1955, whilst promoting the theatre and theories of Bertolt Brecht. Though referring to an initial success in this, it could apply equally to Barthes's own situation at the time; for it summed up the distinctly polemical fashion in which he made his name.[1] If, as Philippe Roger has described in his recent article 'Barthes in the Marx Years',[2] Barthes's popular theatre activism led to his most political and militant writings, then it is no coincidence that his 'discovery' of Brecht in July 1954 heralded his period of intense journalistic activity. The period 1953–6 saw a significant shift in his preoccupations, standing and notoriety. Barthes later claimed (OCiii 1320–2) that he rarely wrote an article without being asked to do so; it is probably in this early period that we can locate the beginning of the 'commissioning' ethos in his publishing. These three years proved of fundamental importance to his future writing and academic career.

However, this does not mean that we should overlook the first pieces written in the sanatorium a decade before. Chapter 2 will consider these half-dozen articles in some detail. That they did not contribute in any directly meaningful way to his rise to prominence in the 1950s in no way discounts their significance. In a sense, though, Barthes was right in his later life to downplay these writings, since from a 'Barthes myth' point of view they were relevant, at their time of appearance, only to a relatively narrow section of the population, namely the fellow consumption sufferers who would have read the journal in which they were published.[3]

Underlining the centrality of 1953–6 does not reduce either the importance of Barthes's work from 1947 to 1952. The publication in 1953 of his first book, *Writing Degree Zero*, and the study of the nineteenth-century historian Jules Michelet the following year, were the fruit of over seven years' work, and they were published largely because they had appeared as articles in this immediate post-war period. Indeed, it was precisely in the immediate aftermath of the Liberation that Barthes's first journalistic break came.

Despite severe paper shortages, the post-war period in France saw a veritable explosion of new publications. This was reflected not only in the rise in prominence of intellectuals and writers, but also in the thirst for new ideas in the euphoria of liberation. Sartre launched *Les Temps modernes* in 1945; intellectuals flocking to the Parti Communiste Français (PCF) began writing in *Action* and *Les Lettres françaises*, more moderate writers in *Gavroche* and *Terre des hommes*. The 'black years' of the Occupation also inspired the Catholic trade-union weekly *Témoignage chrétien* and *Réforme*, its Protestant counterpart. Though all left-wing in this period of desire for social change, none was able to rival the prestige of *Combat, the* pre-eminent paper of the French Resistance; and it was here that Barthes began his writing career proper.[4]

It was a significant place to be first published for two reasons: *Combat* was a daily newspaper read avidly by intellectuals, and though on the radical left, it declared itself independent in the partisan politics of the Cold War. Writing for *Combat* also cemented his relationship with the publisher and literary critic Maurice Nadeau.

When the latter left *Combat* in 1950 to edit the cultural pages of the new weekly newspaper, left-wing but also independent, *France-Observateur* (the forerunner of today's *Nouvel-Observateur*), Barthes was invited to follow. Then, when Nadeau set up a new a monthly arts and culture journal *Les Lettres nouvelles* in 1953, Barthes was again a significant participant. With a regular slot to publish his monthly mythological studies, Barthes could begin his analysis of French society, the fruits of which formed his best-selling book *Mythologies.* Furthermore, it was whilst working for *France-Observateur* that he met Edgar Morin, with whom he launched the 'New Left' journal *Arguments* in 1956, and who helped Barthes obtain his post at the EPHE in 1960.

At a time when one nailed one's political colours to a particular publication's mast, Barthes was beginning to write in a variety of different journals. Though on the left, the prestigious Catholic journal *Esprit* was not at all of the same political or ideological persuasion as *Combat* or *France-Observateur.* Published by Les Éditions du Seuil, a small publishing house also on the Catholic left which had emerged from the Resistance, the April 1951 number of *Esprit* gave Barthes the opening pages in which to publish the results of his work on Michelet.

The interest of the Catholic journal in Barthes's article had been encouraged by the Catholic novelist, poet and concentration camp survivor Jean Cayrol. He was a figure at Seuil, who was to play an important role in the launch of *Tel Quel* in the late 1950s. Having commended Cayrol's work in *Combat* in 1950 (OCi 88), Barthes and Cayrol had become friends. A lengthy study of Cayrol's novels appearing in *Esprit* in 1952 (OCi 115–31) gave Barthes a regular slot in *Esprit*: an account of a visit to the *Folies Bergère* (OCi 195–202) and then a wrestling match (OCi 569–76/M 15–25), and a sociological study of the human face (OCi 224–32), all followed in 1953. The depth and breadth of the analyses not only foreshadowed Barthes's later illustrious career, but also convinced Seuil to become his principal publisher for the rest of his life.

The articles in *Esprit* were important for another reason. The two pieces on popular entertainment – *Folies Bergère* and the wrestling match – opened other doors. In 1953 Barthes was invited to join the editorial board of a new popular theatre journal. *Théâtre Populaire* wanted to support the thirst for theatre evident in post-war France, spearheaded by Jean Vilar and the Théâtre National Populaire (TNP). Barthes's critique of the bourgeois aesthetic of the cancan on the one hand, and his empathetic reading of wrestling as a form of people's theatre on the other, fitted with the political and cultural perspectives of the post-war popular theatre movement in France. His involvement was to be a crucial part of his activities in the prolific period of journalism.

Between 1954 and 1956, the writing for, and editing of, *Théâtre Populaire* was complemented by a series of articles on theatre and literature for *France-Observateur.*[5] On the left wing of the popular theatre movement, Barthes gained an experience of writing by arguing and politicising, the intensity of which was matched by the ironic and detached essayism of the regular monthly mythological studies in Nadeau's *Les Lettres nouvelles.* These two spheres – activity in the popular theatre and theorisation of social mythology – operated at exactly the same time and for the same period (1954–6); and though different in many ways, they were to become a crucial aspect of French intellectual life at a time of political and cultural polarisation. A growing radicalism gave Barthes the space to prove Victor Hugo's maxim correct.

In the period 1947–56, then, we can see emerging a wide network of friends, colleagues, comrades. This was doubtless a function of the growth in the publication industry, particularly in specialist and cultural journals. But it was also evidence of Barthes's ability to connect with a range of debates and ideological positions. This chapter will discuss the manner in which he could fit into the myriad of left-wing milieux.

Literary History and the Non-Communist Left

> Marxism alone can explain why and how a given tendency in art has originated in a given period of history.
>
> Leon Trotsky

By his own claim (OCiii 1310), Barthes emerged from the Occupation period a 'Sartrian and a Marxist'. Neither of these political affiliations is of any great surprise, of course. Sartre was *the* pre-eminent figure for an intellectual generation for at least a decade after the war. The growth of interest in Marxism in a period of radicalisation and militancy was exemplified by the rapid expansion of the Communist Party at the

Liberation; and not only was the PCF largely untarnished by collaboration with Fascism, it was seen also to be defending France against a perceived annexation by the United States. But things were more complicated.

Emerging from the Second World War as the dominant left-wing political ideology, Marxism was soon compromised and profoundly indicted by the revelations about the Gulag in the Soviet Union. Made in 1949 primarily by David Rousset, himself a Marxist who had returned from a Nazi concentration camp, they precipitated a slow but steady haemorrhage of intellectuals out of the PCF. Second, and rather confusingly, Sartre was now moving slowly but surely *towards* the French Communist Party. These were difficult times indeed for somebody claiming to be a Sartrian and a Marxist. However, unlike a Sartre or a Morin (and even a Foucault, it seems), Barthes's understanding of Marxism had not been mediated by the French Communist Party or Stalinism. A number of years before Rousset's revelations, Barthes had appreciated a Trotskyan critique of the Soviet Bloc.[6]

Georges Fournié, deported by the Nazis with Rousset in 1943, had contracted tuberculosis in the Buchenwald concentration camp. As an anti-fascist in the 1930s and veteran of the Spanish Civil War, he was a Marxist of Trotskyist persuasion. The encounter and subsequent friendship with Fournié in the sanatorium in Leysin, Switzerland, in 1945 had two important effects on Barthes's future career. First, Barthes was fascinated ('séduit') (OCiii 1309–10) by Fournié's Trotskyism. In his youth, Barthes had been 'left-wing', according to his life-long friend Philippe Rebeyrol, and a fervent admirer of the socialism of Jean Jaurès.[7] Long discussions with Fournié offered an alternative view of socialism. Second, Fournié was to provide him with useful left-wing connections in Paris.

After his discharge from treatment and return to Paris in 1947, Barthes met up with Fournié, who introduced him to Maurice Nadeau. Nadeau had spent much of his youth reading avant-garde works of art, and during the Occupation, he had befriended various surrealists and published an important study of surrealism.[8] On the editorial board of the *Revue internationale* at the Liberation, Nadeau had conceded that the Communist Party had the upper hand: Trotskyism had been temporarily defeated.

Barthes had read and been inspired by Nadeau's articles in the 'cultural page' of *Combat* - ' "I am one of your readers" ', Barthes had apparently declared at their first meeting.[9] Applauding the role of *Combat*, led by Nadeau, in defying the French state's attempts to censor the erotic writings of the American author Henry Miller, Barthes welcomed 'the routing of the "moralisers" '. Nadeau's influence on Barthes was such that, when he sent him a collection of his articles from *Combat*, soon to be published in book form, Barthes said that he agreed entirely with Nadeau's views on literature. Nadeau has not hidden Barthes's influence on his own view of the importance of the literary critic.[10] Thus a strong literary and political relationship was formed between the two.

The historic irrelevance of Trotsky's Marxism in post-war France[11] did not seem to deter Barthes from using historical materialism in his early writings. Returning from temporary posts in Romania and Egypt to Paris in 1951, he published three book reviews in *Combat* (OCi 103–7). In the first, he praised recent anti-racist publications by Michel Leiris and Daniel Guérin, putting forward a distinctly historical materialist explanation of racism by relating it to the development of slavery and early capitalism. Then the attempt by the Vietnamese Communist Tran Duc Thao to marry phenomenological and dialectical materialist analyses drew his praise. Finally, his disparaging review of Roger Caillois's account of the unmerited popularity of Marxism, *Description du marxisme*, represented a defence of a non-Stalinised, tacitly Trotskyist version of Marxism.

In response to Caillois's description of Marxism as 'muscovite dogmatism', Barthes asserted the existence of a 'certain number of men' whose Marxism was impermeable to the Moscow version:

> For many dissidents for whom Marxism continues to provide a rich individual destiny, muscovite dogmatism is not a scandal: it is a tragedy, at the centre of which they still try, like an ancient Greek chorus, to maintain an awareness of misfortune, a taste for hope

> and the desire to understand. To them, the description by Roger Caillois will look like one of the many mind-numbing attacks on the salutary disturbance of the world which Marxism, despite its zealots and its sceptics, continues to inspire. (OCi 104)

Though six months later he published a less acerbic criticism of Caillois's book in *Esprit*, Barthes's attack in *Combat* would have done little to ingratiate him with Caillois's publisher, the prestigious Gallimard. Indeed, despite the efforts of Raymond Queneau, Gallimard rejected the manuscript of *Writing Degree Zero.*[12] However, it was a version of Marxism which was to place him in opposition, in historical and aesthetic terms at least, to the important figure of Sartre.

When asked in 1971 what his literary influences on the 'degree zero' thesis were, Barthes replied that he 'knew Marx, a bit of Lenin and a bit of Trotsky and all the Sartre one could read'. Calvet has pointed to Sartre's influence on Barthes with respect both to Camus's novel *The Outsider* and to a 'synthetic' and 'total' anthropology.[13] Indeed, the vocabulary of 'responsibility' and 'generosity' of intellectuals and writers in Barthes's early writing was clearly Sartrian. However, Barthes also claimed in 1971 to have 'marxianised' Sartre's views on literature: the reference to Trotsky gives us perhaps the key to this view.

Barthes's early writings on the 'degree zero' of literature were asking different questions to those of Sartrian literary theory, particularly in relation to language, literature and revolution. For example, at the end of his first article in *Combat* in 1947, he wondered whether it was possible to 'liberate language before History', a question, which, as Diana Knight has shown in her book on Barthes's utopianism, was to return continually in his work, and to remain largely unanswered.[14] This first article generated a flood of letters; and 'Do We Need to Kill off Grammar?', published seven weeks later, was Barthes's reply to this 'abundant' correspondence.[15] What had prompted a considerable number of letters from readers to this 'unknown' writer?

The search by certain contemporary authors for a neutral style of writing was akin, began Barthes, to a 'zero degree' in linguistics. Neither 'subjunctive' nor 'imperative', this new literary style was 'flat and neutral', rather like a journalistic form of writing. Though, like a newspaper reporter, in the thick of the 'shouting and opinions', these new authors were not actually taking part in them. With all judgements and opinions absent – in Camus's *The Outsider*, for example – this new writing style was not so much 'impassive', for it was still located *amidst* 'the cries and judgements', as 'innocent'. This 'suspension' of judgement would be crucial in Barthes's later career, but, for the moment, it implied an oblique critique of the literary theory of Sartre, who had recently published in *Les Temps modernes* in May and June 1947 his series of essays 'What is Literature?'.[16]

Through praising Sartre's 'perspicaciousness' in his novels' attempts to escape literary rhetoric and establish a 'degree zero', Barthes was clearly ignoring Sartrian 'commitment' in the novel. By allowing his vocabulary the power to describe, Sartre avoided a crucial element of old-fashioned writing; rhetoric, said Barthes, had relied on the 'disjunction' of size between thought and form. In direct contrast to Sartrian strictures on the novel, he described Sartre's literary writing as the opposite of classical realist writing, in which reference to a 'secret universe' was a 'constant feature'; and in contrast to Sartre's view that language was 'transparent', Barthes concentrated on Sartre's style. Though he described how Sartre avoided gratuitous and 'guilty' forms of literature, this was still to consider form and use of language in the Sartrian novel. For though Sartre avoided both the literary forms of sumptuousness and simplicity and retained only the spirit of 'get-up-and-go' ('it was undoubtedly a victory that no one had ever said that Sartre wrote well'), Barthes's view that Sartre's 'seemingly innocent writing allowed his thought to come into play without cluttering it up with stylistic distractions' was used to show, *pace* Sartre, that 'form' was unavoidable in writing literature.

Not content with applying the strictures of form and language to a writer whose principal idea at the time was precisely to avoid these questions, Barthes now showed the limits of form and language in Sartre's writing. Sartre (and Camus), he concluded, had the same strategy for reaching a language of universality: removing from literary language everything which was part of convention and fixed and replacing it with 'a kind of immediate norm of language'. But the problem was, Barthes suggested, the prevailing historical conditions of literature meant that this 'victory' was unsure. No sooner had the perfection of an absence of style been achieved than the use of language – literature – turned this absence 'necessarily' into a new literary form which was no longer 'innocent', because it became reinserted into the myth of literature. Here, said Barthes, was the 'tragic aspect' of literature: 'Try as [the writer] might to remove pitilessly any temptation towards emphasis, in doing so he cannot but create a new form of preciosity, i.e. concision.' Here was the nub of Barthes's disagreement with Sartre: literature was as a variable as the language which composed and described it.

The reference to the seventeenth-century literary phenomenon 'préciosité' was to be, as we shall see in a moment, an important element in the divergence between Barthes's and Sartre's view of literary history. It was informed by an eschatological view of language. Since the standard language of literature was like a dialect, quickly becoming anachronistic, the only way to 'revolutionise' it was to make it 'historical' – to make it keep up with the times. The question now, in Barthes's view, was not how but whether it was writers alone who could provide this solution. If any attempt to criticise a non-universal literary language was turned back on the writer by itself becoming a new form of literary language, then language became 'closed off' by the enormous 'influence' ('poussé') of all those people who did not use it. This was a social, rather than strictly literary, problem: 'the impasse of style' was 'the impasse of society itself, [. . .] there can be no universal language outside of a concrete universality in civil society – and not this mystical or token universality'.

The Marxian (not to mention Hegelian) vocabulary of the 'universal' and of 'civil society' betrayed the distinctly materialist implications behind Barthes's view of language. Though Sartrian literary theory had lamented the lack of universal access to literature, it had seen this on a purely sociological, and not linguistic, basis. Literary exclusion for Sartre was based on social realities, for Barthes on the question of language. In the second article, Barthes justified this view historically.

He began by setting out how, up until recently, writing had been considered an artisan skill, for which the writer had a special tool: French grammar. Like a plastic substance, its form could be worked into different shapes, thereby revealing the 'possibilities of an art for art's sake'. In his view, this 'formal work' was indicative of a much wider significance of language's history: 'To believe in a unique grammar, to practise a *pure* French language was to prolong the famous myth of the clarity of French, the fortune of which is closely linked to French political history.' Barthes now provided the details of this political history. In 1647, it was decreed that the clarity of French was that spoken at the court, by the group of people closest to political power. But after 1660, as 'cynicism gave way to hypocrisy' and monarchical power became absolute, the clarity attributed to those at the court was soon posed as 'universal' – as exemplified by Port-Royal Grammar's justification of grammatical rules, not by usage, but by the logical agreement between rules and the requirements of classical wit ('l'esprit'). Barthes's historical account had important implications for a class-based analysis of the development of language:

> All commentators even in modern times go on about the reforms of this period which led to a language that was so clear that it could be understood by everyone. But this 'everyone' was never anything but a tiny section of the nation. What's more, it was in the name of universality that those words and sentence structures intelligible to ordinary people (those relating to work and movement) were excluded from language. Doubtless there was a certain universality of writing which stretched across to the elite elements of Europe living the same privileged life-style, but this much-prized communicability of the French language has never been anything but horizontal; it has never been vertical, never reached the depths of the masses. (OCi 79)

In pointing to the centralisation of power by the ruling class of seventeenth-century France (typified here by the control of language), Barthes wanted to challenge the Sartrian and common sense view of the French Revolution as a *decisive* break in literary history:

> It must be said that, since the elaboration of this policy in our classical language, no serious revolution in rhetoric, be it romanticist or symbolist, has been able to undermine this language which put itself forward as universal but is only for the privileged. Revolutions in language, all exclusively literary, are very overstated; they boil down to waves of decency or of infatuation, with a bearing on certain minor literary procedures. They have been nothing but a storm in a teacup. (OCi 80)[17]

This 'long view' of historical change was to become typical of the *Annales* historians at the end of the 1950s, and it had been central to Trotsky's Marxist account of cultural history.

In 1923, in response to the 'shallow' analogies which tried to see the historical development of the bourgeoisie as similar to that of the working class, Trotsky had insisted – in contrast to the 'spontaneous' revolution by the proletariat – on the long accession to power of the bourgeoisie across the seventeenth and eighteenth centuries.[18] Indeed, Barthes's early use of this 'long view' of history stood in marked contrast to the cultural nationalism of the Communist Party which prevailed on the left after the Liberation. As Sunhil Khilnani has shown, the 'ultramontane' position which the Communist Party developed after the Occupation involved showing itself as the inheritor of Jacobin revolutionary patriotism; and raising the Great Revolution's historical and material significance also fitted into the popular front politics which the PCF had operated since the mid-1930s.[19] The 'long view' was also a direct response to Sartrian literary history.

Though Barthes had welcomed the attempt by Sartre the novelist to find a 'degree zero' of literary writing, he seemed to disagree with Sartre the literary historian; or rather, as Roland A. Champagne has suggested, perhaps Barthes was simply 'refining' Sartre's ideas on committed literature.[20] Indeed, Sartre's literary history in 'What is Literature?' appears rather contradictory, if not hasty, in its argument. On the one hand, Sartre had argued, like Barthes, that the bourgeoisie as an ascending class was 'quietly gaining economic pre-eminence' before the Revolution, and that, because it already possessed 'money, culture, leisure', it had to endure only 'political oppression'. On the other hand, Sartre's history of literature had also suggested that the political triumph of the bourgeoisie at the Revolution 'dramatically changed from head to toe' the writers' condition and questioned the very essence of literature.[21] Though borrowing much from Sartre's ethos of committed literature in the 'degree zero' thesis, Barthes wanted, it seems, a much more consistent, less contradictory, view of the effects of the bourgeoisie's rise to power on literature. Thus, for Barthes, it was not the French Revolution which was of crucial importance in literary history but the revolutionary period of 1848–51. In the first of his second series of articles for *Combat*, 'Triumph and Rupture of Bourgeois Writing', he set out this alternative view of literary history.[22]

The years around 1850 saw three important factors coming together, suggested Barthes: drastic changes in European demography, the replacement of the textile industry by metal, and the division of French society into three enemy classes. Rather than the French Revolution heralding modernity – it had simply formalised the hegemony of a class ascendant since the seventeenth century – modern capitalism was born when the bourgeoisie's troops turned on striking workers in the June days of 1848, ruining the Liberal illusions of a continuation of the worker–bourgeoisie alliance against the church and the monarchy. It was this event, not the French Revolution, which had serious repercussions for writing and language in France:

> These conjunctures threw the bourgeoisie into a new historical situation. Until then it was bourgeois ideology which was itself the measure of the universal, claiming to be so without contest; the bourgeois writer, the sole judge of the misfortune of other men, and having no-one else before him to look at him, was not torn between his social condition and his intellectual vocation. [But] from that point on, this same ideology appeared to be only one amongst others; the universal eluded him, bourgeois ideology

> could only surpass it by self-condemnation; the writer became prey to an ambiguity since his conscience no longer fitted neatly with his condition. (p. 4)

The events of 1848 shattered a literary monolith into a galaxy of forms, to the extent that it was the existence of literature which was in question each time a writer created. The 'tragic' status of literature resulting from the 'pluralising' of writing meant that the 'universal' would evade Sartrian attempts to write committed novels.

Though Sartre had been conscious that 1848 was significant for literature, he considered that it had encouraged writers to play 'abstract games', and that after 1848 writers had failed to 'rally the proletariat' and no longer had 'a direct grip on reality'. His contempt stood in marked contrast to Barthes's view of the 'plurality' of writing in the period following 1851. Though unsure about the possibilities of liberating language before history, Barthes was certainly not condemning the Flauberts and Mallarmés of French literature in the Lukácsian fashion that Sartre wanted to. He saw post-1848 formalist and avant-garde writing as attempts to come to terms with a highly fragmented and complex social and linguistic reality.[23]

The disagreement with Sartre hinged not only on literary history and the 'long view' of social change, but also, as we saw earlier, on the attitude to language. For Sartre, language was translucent, for Barthes opaque. For the latter, the problem of literature was not so much the author's political stance *vis-à-vis* the readership and a view of art and politics, but the limits and constraints on language versus its freedoms. Though it is clear that the literary history Barthes put forward, with its explanation of the standardisation of language, was linked to his view of language's opacity, it would be difficult to suggest which, if either, came first. What can be said is that this view of modernism had deep implications for one's views on art and aesthetics.

As Jacques Lehrmann has pointed out, the 'degree zero' thesis articulated a crucial point on art made by Trotsky in the years following the October Revolution: art could not be approached like politics, and it was impossible to superimpose 'term for term [. . .] bourgeois culture and proletarian culture, politics and artistic creation'.[24] Maurice Nadeau's review praised *Writing Degree Zero* for showing that, 'contrary to what the contemporary fans of historical materialism [i.e. the Communist Party] say', the relationship between writing and history was not 'mechanical'; but also that, unlike economic systems, each of which destroys the previous one, literature contains in it all of the 'problems of its history'.[25] Indeed, the book contained stringent and ironic criticism of the petty-bourgeois nature of Stalinist literary writing in the works of André Stil and Roger Garaudy (OCi 175–6/WDZ 77).

However, Barthes's overt rejection of a 'socialist realist' aesthetic – itself a direct result of the political ethos of *proletkultism*, criticised by Trotsky in 1923 – had not been present in any of the earlier articles later incorporated into the book. There is a real sense in which the experience of the questionnaire on left-wing literature which Barthes and Nadeau organised at the end of 1952, and published in *France-Observateur*, had encouraged Barthes's critique of Stalinist literature. Though his articles on the 'degree zero' thesis were published after the promulgation of the 'socialist realist' doctrine, they still contained no reference to this. It was clearly reading the responses to the questionnaire, particularly Edgar Morin's, which encouraged Barthes to look at the products of socialist realism; for his conclusion was that progressive literature was ultimately that which 'questioned' social, including literary, reality (see OCi 132–3, 191–4).

Though Barthes's interest in literary forms put him in opposition to Sartre's rather hasty discounting of avant-garde literature (a stance which would play into PCF 'socialist realist' policy, which began soon after 1947), it did not mean at all that Barthes had answered 'yes' to the question of whether it was possible to 'liberate' language 'before history'. His ambiguous attitude to Sartre's own prose was mirrored by his ambivalence towards the avant-garde.

Nevertheless, *Writing Degree Zero* was distinctive and polemical enough to gain Barthes crucial critical attention. It merited, as Calvet points out, a serious review by Jean-Baptiste Pontalis in *Les Temps modernes* – though Calvet is incorrect to say that Pontalis made no attempt to relate Barthes's book to Sartre's views: the opening paragraph set out the

Sartrian objective 'reception' view of literature in opposition to Blanchot's subjective view of language generation in literature and suggested that Barthes's study aimed to reconcile these two perspectives.[26] Maurice Blanchot's own review in the *NNRF*, seemingly inspired by Barthes's study, saw the author as the 'other' of the reader, and the degree zero as the 'neutrality' of literature, good or bad. Making only one direct comment on Barthes's enterprise, in a footnote, he suggested that Barthes was doing to literature what Marx had done for society.[27] Jean-Marie Caplain, writing in *L'Observateur*, remembered the first article in *Combat* in 1947.[28] He characterised the starting point of social and economic conditions – political classes and organisation of society – as part of a 'Marxist analysis of literature', and he predicted with uncanny accuracy Barthes's success: in the same way as 'existentialism' had become synonymous with Sartre and 'gratuitousness' with Gide, so *écriture* would be 'attached' to Barthes.

It is a testament to the success of Barthes's first book that the term 'degree zero' began to enter the literary vocabulary of the time. Writing in *Critique* in May 1954, Gabriel Venaissin wrote a review of Cayrol's award-winning novel *Je vivrai l'amour des autres* under the title 'Jean Cayrol, novelist of the zero degree'.[29] Jean Piel's review of Barthes's book had recently appeared in a general article on the social role of the critic and literary criticism.[30] In a rather traditional humanist piece which justified the critic's function (and thereby, no doubt, the journal in which he was writing), Piel made some important points about the four books under review. Besides works by Nadeau and Jean Paulhan, Piel noted the significance of a recent study of Albert Thibaudet's views on creative criticism, which suggested that the critic worked with a piece of literature as if 'organising a game of whist in which the author is dead'. Not only was Piel thereby obliquely pointing to future developments in Barthes's views on the author, he also underlined the central concern of Barthes's 'brilliant' first book, which was to try to insert literary history into 'history *tout court*', an attempt 'to elucidate the relationship between the acts of social consumption and lonely individual creation'. Thus impressed, the editorial board of *Critique* asked Barthes to write his first piece for the journal, in the July/August number of 1954, on Alain Robbe-Grillet. 'Literal Literature' became his first clear statement on the *nouveau roman.*

Writing Degree Zero was indeed reviewed widely, and favourably by Dominique Arban in *Le Monde.* But for Claude Mauriac, one-time secretary to De Gaulle, and son of the best-selling author and writer François, the 'degree zero' thesis was indicative of a school 'which had arrived at the freezing point of literature'. How could Barthes use his praise of Blanchot, Queneau, Cayrol, Sartre and Camus to denigrate such stylists as Gide, Valéry and Breton? Here, concluded Mauriac junior, was an example of the 'terrorist' attitude towards literature typical of the Communist thoughts of a Dionys Mascolo, whose book on intellectuals and writers, *Le Communisme,* had been just published. Mauriac was, after all, writing in *Preuves,* the CIA-funded French counterpart of *Encounter.*[31] Though misunderstanding Barthes's attitude to Gide (as we shall see in Chapter 2) and to literary history in general, Mauriac was to find his view of a 'freezing' of literature reinforced in the five years to come. His review of *Writing Degree Zero* became a chapter in his 1958 book *L'Alittérature contemporaine,* which attacked the *nouveau roman* and other modernist writings for their coldness and lack of humanity.

Barthes's association with a Trotskyan and avant-gardist conception of literary freedom was soon confirmed by his involvement with Nadeau's new cultural and literary monthly journal. Launched in March 1953, *Les Lettres nouvelles* took up the conclusions of the questionnaire by Nadeau and Barthes published two months earlier. The journal stated in the first number its aim of walking a fine line between, on the one hand, traditional and often conservative literature and, on the other, the propagandist use of literature by Sartrian 'engagement' and Stalinist socialist realism. It drew its inspiration from a left-wing and politically independent line. By publishing and advertising a 'literature which was on the move' it was to be this spirit which helped encourage Barthes's awareness, in the decade to come, of a *nouveau roman.*[32]

It was therefore curious and perhaps surprising that, the same month, Barthes should be invited to join the editorial board of *Théâtre Populaire.* Though in no way controlled by the Communist Party, it was nevertheless set up by a fellow-traveller of the PCF, Robert Voisin.[33] Barthes's active and politicised involvement with the journal and in the wider popular theatre movement was, in contrast to his view of the essentially questioning nature of progressive literature, a distinctly militant and Marxist one. Before we consider the 'militant' phase of Barthes's journalism, we must underline his attachment to a highly 'voluntarist' view of history in this period.

History and its (Dis)Contents

> History, the science of humanity; History, the work of humanity.
>
> Jules Michelet

> I believe that one of the reasons for the present fascination which Sociology can have over us is precisely that it poses itself frankly and openly as a demand for explanation; and it is because it wants to explain that it can be part of a certain polemical and politically committed current [. . .]. It fits with the situation of those people who want to explain or demystify the totality of social relations in which they find themselves.
>
> Roland Barthes, in 1956

As noted in the discussion of the 'degree zero' thesis, Barthes's thought was concerned fundamentally with 'History'. The use of a capital 'H' belied a deeply historicist reasoning. This was a form not only of determinism (such as history's effect on literary writing which followed 1848) but also of voluntarism.

Barthes's first writing specifically on history was a review in 1950 of a book by André Joussain on the 'law of revolutions'. Joussain's 'comparative history' of revolutionary moments angered Barthes not only with its formalist search for a 'law of revolutions', which managed to equate Hitler's 'revolution' with that of Spain in 1936 or Russia in 1917, but also with Joussain's implicit denial that humans made history. Preferring to speak of 'Man' rather than 'men', Joussain's approach, said Barthes, had neglected the history-makers:

> [N]o-one has the right to take History from those men whose daily lives, attached to a particular time, place and condition, have made this History [. . .]. Every fact and every man in history is inalienable. And we should send the law of revolutions back to its rightful place within an ambiguous mythology which thinks about history only so as to take it away from the men who make it. (OCi 86)

Then in his 1951 review of two books on anti-racism he linked the voluntarist and determinist view of history to the political power of explanation.

Setting out in historical materialist fashion how racism was linked to the development of capitalism, Barthes insisted that since (almost) 'nothing escaped History', then any historical explanation of racism must put its abolition 'into the hands of men'. It is worth quoting the final paragraph of the review in full:

> It is because nothing in the past exists outside of historical reasoning that the future can become the complete property of men who will make it. The *cultural* explanation of facts normally considered *natural* is therefore a profoundly humanist step, possibly even the most concrete form of humanism; because, with it, hope is not some messianic postulation, but a virtue of the truth. At the same time, this hope contains its own weapons: with regard to a cultural fact such as racist feelings, explanation is the first, if not the only, authentic act in its destruction. (OCi 106)

Not only was 'History' crucial in explaining the development of a 'plurality of writing' after the socio-economic and political events of 1848, it was fundamental, Barthes seemed to be suggesting, to the intellectual's actions in explaining the reality of the world and exposing its myths. What inspired this deep attachment to 'History'?

Commenting on Barthes's conclusion, in his first review of Caillois's book, that an account of Marxism was 'premature' before 'History' had taken its course, Philippe Roger describes this argument as typical of remnants of post-war Trotskyism and Sartrianism, a view which mixed 'voluntarism' with a Hegelian sensitivity to teleology.[34] This seems plausible given Barthes's knowledge of Sartre and his Trotskyan initiation into Marxism; but we must insist also on the influence of Michelet.

Indeed, Barthes had been recommended by his friend Fournié to Nadeau for his knowledge of Michelet, and, at their first meeting, had been asked to write a piece for *Combat* on Michelet, which was never published.[35] His knowledge of Michelet was, by all accounts, phenomenal. Lucien Febvre, eminent historian in the *Annales* group and specialist on Michelet, considered Barthes's book 'one of the most vivid writings' on Michelet.[36]

Barthes's attitude to Michelet was highly contradictory. In Barthes's article on Gide's diary in 1942, Michelet had been cited favourably for his awareness (like Gide's) of the self-referential and self-constructing nature of his writing; and in 1944, prefiguring the 'degree zero' thesis view that bourgeois control of language had excluded the masses and displaying a concern for 'refinding' past human objects in history, Barthes had praised Michelet's 'solidarity' with past lives in writing as if one of them (OCi 30, 46). But after his 'initiation' into Marxian and Sartrian perspectives at the end of the war, Barthes began, it seems, a political critique of Michelet's writing of history, evident in his critique of Joussain's 'law of revolutions'. Praising the synthetic use of 'economic, social and intellectual' dimensions by the *Annales* historians such as Febvre and Bloch, Barthes criticised the romantic tendency of both Joussain and Michelet to develop a philosophy of history which saw a 'mechanism, a 'thread' in history (OCi 85). But it was Michelet's formalist use of analogy which Barthes criticised most.

This came across in his second review (for *Esprit*) of Caillois's book on Marxism, called 'Using a Metaphor (Is Marxism a "Religion"?)'. Published six months after his important essay on Michelet in the April 1951 number of *Esprit* (see Chapter 2), this second review of Caillois's *Description du marxisme* continued the philosophical vein which had begun the first review for *Combat*. There, as noted above, Barthes had put forward a (tacit) defence of Trotskyan Marxism against Caillois's conflation of Marxism with Stalinism. However, this was only the second half of that review. It began by criticising the manner in which Caillois had analysed Communism. Barthes complained that Caillois had simply described the doctrine of Marxism and its Stalinist orthodoxy in such a way that each discredited the other. Rather than judge the 'form and the content' of Marxism, regretted Barthes, Caillois had simply underlined its inflated importance around the globe; and, in distinctly Hegelian terms, Barthes rejected the 'quantitative' – as opposed to qualitative – manner in which Caillois had assessed Marxism (OCi 103). In his second review of Caillois's study, Barthes now continued this style of analysis. 'Using a Metaphor' picked up on Caillois's equation of Marxism with a form of religion (OCi 111–12). Noting how Caillois imputed the 'hierarchy, dogmatism and infallibility' of religion to Marxism (based on his analysis of Stalinism), Barthes traced this form of analysis back to the nineteenth century. Following German philosophers of history, opined Barthes, echoing his criticism of Joussain's 'law' of revolutions, certain French nineteenth-century historians began to consider history as having a 'direction and a meaning'; this meant that their writing of history needed to 'construct' 'History' by 'bringing together elements which looked similar'. This 'non-Cartesian' method, concluded Barthes, was based on 'analogy':

> Michelet thus reconstituted the origins of Rome using a series of analogies, inducing the unknown from the known. History then found itself penetrated by a multitude of themes which joined distant points in Time and introduced into the mass of the past a calming familiarity. For historians of the day this security was that of a science: analogy was a scientific method *par excellence*, because nineteenth-century science [. . .] could not limit itself to a pure description of historical phenomena; it needed at all costs to find [history's] secret order and motor, its reason, law, spirit, *organisation.* (OCi 111)

In formal terms, he concluded, this romantic historiography, dominant in the period 1750–1850, relied on the metaphor of the 'chain'. This 'equational series', postulating an organic, natural development in history, allowed, at one and the same time, for 'an identity and a variation in its contents'. But, Barthes pointed out, historical method in the nineteenth century soon realised that there was a problem with using analogy.

Historians recognised that the *character* of a particular event was actually unable to take into account its *content*. The form of an event might *look* like another at an entirely different point in the past, but its content was tightly tied to its own particular moment in history:

> History contained a contradictory postulation: an irreversible development *and* a linear stability, an absolute disparity of content *and* a community of forms. The problem for modern historiography is how to account for both the structure *and* flow of Time, how to organise the past in such a way as to establish a link between facts which have occurred only once. Thus, all scientistic History explains nothing, and all analogic History sacrifices the content of a fact: History is inalienable but also explicable, this is the dilemma. (OCi 112)

Countering the formalism of both Michelet's writing of history and Caillois's description of Marxism, Barthes now suggested that it was Marx in the nineteenth century who had resolved the contradiction of stability and movement in history. Marx's 'class struggle' was not an analogy but 'an organisational principle' which did not undermine 'the inalienable content' of each of its episodes. It was a 'hypo-phenomenon', a 'constant', which could be applied to the singularity of a historical event: rather than considering the 'surface' links between facts (as Michelet's analogic method might), the class struggle view of history placed analogy at the 'root' of them. Barthes now likened Marx's conflict-based and synthetic account of history to the developments taking place in contemporary French social sciences:

> [S]ocial sciences are slowly but surely transforming the very notion of a historical fact, so that, for example, a numerical method of analysis such as statistics can be applied to it. Facts for a modern

> historian are gradually losing their isolated nature and the dilemma of an ordered movement in History is moving towards a resolution; we are reaching a new notion of History, which will be a science of both the irreversible and the repeated. (*ibid.*)

For us, at the end of the twentieth century, such a historical method is taken for granted. But in the middle of this century, it was (in France at least) only the *Annales* which had begun to synthesise social sciences and history. Clearly, the social history which they initiated broke down the rigid barriers between sociology and history. This ground-breaking redefinition of disciplines was, as shall see in the next chapter, to inspire an epistemological adventurism in Barthesian method.

It has been worth quoting these passages at length not only because they show the origins of Barthes's dislike of analogy and his subsequent preference for the 'literal', evident in his 1950s views on the theatre and literature, but also because a sensitivity to the unrepeated/repeated was a central feature in his later writings. It was quite clearly Michelet and (a Hegelian) Marxism which attuned him to this crucial dilemma of historiography. The problem of how to portray both change and structure in history will return when we look at his move towards structuralism in Chapter 3. For the moment, it is the insistence on the content of history which we must retain, for it was this which dominated the political phase 1953–6.

Militancy and Politicisation

Eric Marty has pointed to the surprising 'violence' in Barthes's writings on the popular theatre.[37] I have argued elsewhere that Barthes's dogged defence of Brecht was, in large part, inspired by his disappointment with the mainstream popular theatre's inability to provide for the masses a theatre which was on a par with the historical events of the time.[38] Nevertheless, it was via Brechtian theatre that his most radical and Marxist ideas emerged. Brechtism was to play an important role not only in forming him intellectually for years to come, but also in bringing him into the intellectual spotlight. That

Eugène Ionesco in 1956 should write and produce a satirical play on the Brechtians of the time, *L'Impromptu de l'Alma*, in which the dogmatic theorists of theatre were called (in mimicry of Barthes's name) Bartholoméus I, II and III, was indicative enough of the impact of Barthes's activities in the 1950s.

It was above all in his editorials that Barthes was crucial in the politicisation of *Théâtre Populaire*. Written without exception in the first person plural ('nous'), these put forward the collective and militant point of view of the journal. His first editorial in January 1954 spoke of the need to 'vomit' bourgeois theatre; the editorial in September 1954, of the 'combat' against the 'gangrene' of bourgeois theatre (OCi 381–3, 438–9). However, these embattled manifestos were but a prelude to the polemic over Brechtian theatre which ensued.

Given over in its entirety to a study of Brecht, *TP* 11, published in January 1955, was the 'spark' (in Bernard Dort's words) to the arguments over the worth of Brechtian theories.[39] It was this number which provoked Jacques Lemarchand, drama critic for *Le Figaro littéraire*, to accuse *TP* of having developed a dogmatic defence of epic theatre. Published in the *NNRF* in May 1955, 'The Narrow-minded Schoolchild and the Short Organon' was an ironic and generally light-hearted reaction to *TP*'s promotion of Brechtian theatre; according to Dort, the 'schoolchild' comment was aimed at himself and/or Barthes.[40] Lemarchand had been theatre critic for *Combat* until 1950 and had made a drastic shift of readership by moving to *Le Figaro littéraire*. Daniel Mortier underlines, nevertheless, his open and avant-gardist tastes; Lemarchand's great interest in the new, post-war theatre after the Liberation could be contrasted with the notoriously traditional drama critic for *Le Figaro*, Jean-Jacques Gautier, savaged by Barthes in 1953 (OCi 432–4).

It was Barthes who, in the following number, defended the journal against Lemarchand's criticisms. His editorial in *TP* 12 became a defence of the record of the journal, to counter the accusations that its number 11 smacked of 'messianism', that the journal was a 'totalitarian organ of Brechtism'. The journal's crime, in Barthes's view, was simply to have expressed 'an ideological sympathy for Brecht'. It was in the wake of the heated debate over Brechtian theatre that Barthes's views undoubtedly hardened.

In the next number of *TP*, he defended Sartre's latest play *Nekrassov*, which had been roundly criticised by nearly every drama critic; and, despite a number of formal reservations, the play was worth defending: '*Nekrassov* is an overtly political play', he declared (OCi 494). This was an important development in Barthes's attitude to political and avant-garde theatre.[41] It also proved that Vilar's TNP, which had so inspired him in 1953, was by 1955 failing to provide a political theatre for the popular masses now visiting the theatre. But what was it that the popular theatre was not reflecting? This question can be answered by a look at the manner in which *Les Lettres nouvelles*, the other sphere of Barthes's concerns, became politicised.

The routing of the French army at Dien Bien Phu in Indochina in May 1954 had ended the nine-year-long colonial war there and badly dented French colonial authority; the defeat had encouraged uprisings in Tunisia and the civil war in Morocco against French rule. The concessions made by Prime Minister Mendès-France to these countries in August 1954 was a spark for the All Saints' Day uprising in the Aurès mountains in Algeria, the beginning of the bloodiest war in French colonial history. As *LLN* followed these events, its political shift was noted by the journal's rivals and opponents, in particular the *Nouvelle nouvelle revue française.*

The *Nouvelle revue française* had been an important journal before the war, but had been tarnished by collaboration with the Nazis. Banned after the war, it was not relaunched until 1953, under the (playfully) altered name the *Nouvelle Nouvelle revue française.* Its editor was Jean Paulhan, important literary adviser to Gallimard, and it quickly became the rival to Nadeau's journal *LLN.* In the January 1955 edition, writing under the *nom de plume* Jean Guérin, Paulhan pointed out that, after the departure of Maurice Saillet from the editorial team of *LLN,* Nadeau seemed 'disposed to increase its political content'.[42] As we shall see, Barthes played a crucial role in this.

Barthes's first 'petite mythologie du mois' ('little monthly mythology') had been published in November 1954, the same month as the uprising in Algeria. But it was in the December 'mythology' that he had begun to attack the ideologies which maintained the colonial status quo. As well as ridiculing media representations of marital values and religious and newspaper beliefs in Martians, he attacked the church, the monarchy and, most importantly, the army.[43] The first paragraph of 'Perpetual Mythology' read:

> The Army, the Church, the Monarchy. That's about as good as the entertainment gets for French people [. . .]. Turn to this or any other month's tabloid press: more flags (the departure from Hanoi), clergy (Monsignor Villot, the bishop's secretary), and royalty [. . .] Quite clearly, Voltaire, Stendhal, Vallès and Michelet are writers of the future. (p. 944)

Having shown in the three preceding mythological studies how 'order' was being maintained by myth, in 'New Mystifications' Barthes now singled out the army for criticism:

> Take an army; show openly the petty officiousness of its officers, the narrow-minded, unjust nature of its discipline, and into this stupid tyranny throw your average person, fallible but nice, your archetypal viewer. Then, at the last moment, pull the rabbit out of the hat, and produce the picture of a triumphant army, flags blowing adorably in the wind, and which [. . .] could only inspire your faith, even after a beating. [. . .] Take another army: show the fanaticism for science of its engineers, their blind devotion; show how men and couples are destroyed by this strictness which is so inhuman. And then get your flag out, save the army with a bit of progress, and put the greatness of one army together with the triumph of the other. (p. 947)

These 'mythologies' were putting into practice what Barthes theorised in 'Phenomenon or Myth?', the 'mythology' which ended the December 1954 column. His 1953 view that '[b]ringing explanation into myth is the only efficient way for an intellectual to be politically active' (OCi

211) was to become, by the end of 1954, a serious and reasoned political strategy. 'Phenomenon or Myth?' did not simply attack the manner in which literary critics denied the importance of the 'myth of Rimbaud', it also treated the overall dilemma of the left-wing critic faced with the urgent task of explaining the emerging mass culture and consumer society as well as the 'high culture' of Rimbaud. Barthes began: 'That these objects of consumption urgently need the critic's attention, even when they concern phenomena reputed to be more noble than a film star, is what the dogmatic [''immobile''] press cannot quite understand' (p. 951). The irony, he suggested, was that denying the myth of Rimbaud was itself part of an enormous 'murderous myth': to separate 'Literature' from its history was to 'exorcise the intellectual', to deny intellectuals a 'critical power', their 'only generosity', said Barthes in Sartrian terminology. Presenting 'an innocent world of inspired art' which allowed ' ''feeling'' devoid of danger' was an act which was 'the least ''humanist'' ', because it denied 'History'; the very fact that Rimbaud's 'revolt' had been switched to become a myth of social order was a 'fact of human history' which was far more important than Rimbaud's poetic skill. Thus, the act of demystifying, Barthes stressed, was not so much one of principle as one which was linked to the historical moment: 'All that counts is the general historical reality in which the myth appears; it is in the name of this History that we must judge this myth, and not at all based on an essence of Rimbaud: we judge the harm caused by the myth, and not at all its error' (*ibid.*).

This 'mythology' suggested that, in 1954 at least, Barthes firmly believed that he had a political mission in his monthly column. Whenever he saw a new myth (he cited the examples of Martians and Brando's marriage), he knew that he had to counter these attempts to maintain 'Order', by denouncing and explaining them. But here, he conceded, was the dilemma of this political act; this denunciation could only ever be an explanation. He recognised the inadequacy and limits of such an act: the nature of human alienation and social mythology was such that he must have a dialectical love/hate relationship with these myths, what he called the 'dialectique d'amour':

> [B]ut such exposing is really only explaining; and I find myself more than ever tied to my time by a real dialectic of love ['dialectique d'amour']. For in so far as every mythology is the palpable surface of human alienation, it is humanity which I see in all myths: I hate this alienation, but I realise that for the time being this is the only way I can locate ['retrouver'] my contemporaries. (p. 953)

Paulhan's view that Nadeau was increasing the political nature of *LLN* was clearly a reaction to these first two 'monthly mythologies' by Barthes. Furthermore, as the war in Algeria intensified, Barthes's mythological studies became part of a generalised political critique by *LLN*.

Nadeau had published in March 1955 an article by André Calvès which exposed the colonial discourse used by the French government in Indochina. An ironic 'A to Z' of the vocabulary used during the war in North Vietnam, 'Short Lexis to act as a History of the North Vietnam War' exemplified *LLN*'s political stance on the colonial question.[44] Calvès's study was a first-hand account of his two-year service as a soldier, and bears a strong resemblance to Barthes's mythological analyses of colonial discourse in Morocco, 'Moroccan Lexis' and 'Moroccan Grammar', published six months later.[45] Not only did Barthes use the very same title-word ('Lexis'), but similarly his article exposed the hypocrisy of colonial discourse; just as Calvès's article had reacted to the French colonial tactics in Vietnam and the language used, so Barthes criticised the double standards of the French government and press in their attitude to the civil war in Morocco. Following this, Nadeau published in December 1955 a manifesto against the Algerian war which had been signed by 300 intellectuals.[46] It was a reaction to the 'turning point' of autumn 1955, when the French government discussed the need for a 'state of emergency' in Algeria. Since the signatories were not listed, it is difficult to know whether Barthes had participated. Nevertheless, his 'lexis' of colonial language in Morocco in the previous number of *LLN* was an important contribution to the journal's anti-colonial stance.

This can be seen in the similarity of concerns in Barthes's and Calvès's articles. In the July/August 1955 number of *LLN*, Calvès began a regular column of political satire which directly preceded Barthes's 'monthly mythology'. Many of Calvès's short pieces were criticisms of French policy in Algeria and Morocco; and Barthes matched these with '*The Lost Continent*' and his study of French government language concerning Morocco. As in Calvès's column, Barthes's main political points were against the Algerian war; and both reacted, in their own fashion, to the draft of reservists in summer 1955.[47]

But it was not simply the colonial situation which both covered in their own, ironic ways. The 'monthly mythology' and Calvès's column showed a similarity of themes outside of colonial conflict. For example, Calvès criticised Billy Graham and the *Figaro* visit to Moscow, as Barthes had done in 'Billy Graham at the Vel'd'Hiv' and in 'The Cruise of the *Batory*' respectively. Calvès had denounced the lynching of Emmet Till, just as Barthes was to in 'The Great Family of Man' in March 1956. 'The Blue Guide' in October 1955 ended by condemning the guide's bias towards 'Francoism'; the month before, Calvès had denounced the French government's attitude towards Spaniards who had fled Franco's regime. The same month as Barthes's 'The User and the Strike' satirised *Figaro* readers' reactions to the transport strike in Paris, Calvès published an article in his monthly column which criticised the Communist trade union, the Confédération Générale du Travail (CGT), for its role in preventing a general strike.[48]

In the increasing politicisation of *LLN* Barthes and Calvès provided each other's regular columns with information to analyse, a duet which continued until the end of the 'monthly mythology' in April 1956. Yet, in the political battle between *LLN* and *NNRF*, it was Barthes, not Calvès, who was singled out for criticism. As Phillipe Roger has pointed out, Barthes had already been seen to criticise Camus for his failure to write a novel with a 'historical materialist' account of resistance to oppression.[49] Then, in the June 1955 edition of *NNRF*, following Lemarchand's accusation of messianism in the Brechtian stance of *TP*, Paulhan too attacked Barthes.[50]

Paulhan explained how he had read assiduously the 'monthly

mythologies' through the seven months they had been published, quoted a number of paragraphs of Barthes's analyses and commented upon them. Having likened the royals to a set of pug-dogs in a reserve ('The "Blue Blood" cruise'), proclaimed that the world was 'malleable' in the final passage of 'Paris Not Flooded', exposed the myths of black Africans ('Bichon'), the avant-garde ('The Vaccine of the Avant-garde') and the liberal nature of the church ('A Nice Worker' and 'The Iconography of the Abbé Pierre'), Barthes had rounded off with a complex study of the myth of Rimbaud ('Phenomenon or Myth?') by announcing his strategy of the 'dialectique d'amour'. As far as he could understand the reasoning, wrote Paulhan, everything for Barthes was 'myth'. Completing his dissection of the first seven months of the monthly column, Paulhan quoted the stern final paragraph of 'Blind and Dumb Criticism', in which Barthes had asserted that, though critics had understood nothing of Henri Lefebvre's play on Kierkegaard and existentialism, Lefebvre the Marxist understood them perfectly. Paulhan now accused Barthes himself of being a Marxist and asked why he did not just admit it.

Barthes's reply to Paulhan's invitation in the July/August number of *LLN*, 'Am I a Marxist?', likened Paulhan's question to the recent McCarthyite trials in the United States and accused Paulhan of performing a witch hunt (OCi 499). Furthermore, Barthes suggested, Paulhan did not understand the term 'Marxist'. In order for it to be applied to people, opined Barthes, they had to have a theory and a practice. His conclusion was that, since the poser of the question could neither understand what being Marxist meant, nor see it other than as a profession of religious faith, Paulhan and his journal must be 'completely reactionary'. In a clever twist, he added that, in order to know this, *he* did not need any further declaration than the question he had been asked: the naiveté of Paulhan's question underlined his reactionary political ideology.

Is there any significance in this caustic exchange? Calvet has suggested that, intimidated by the publication of his letter to Camus in which he had stressed the virtues of historical materialism, Barthes now wanted, in this mythology, to back away from the 'Marxist' label that suddenly seemed to be sticking to him.[51] It also showed that Barthes's political viewpoint in the 'monthly mythologies' had been singled out above and beyond that of Nadeau and Calvès as the example of the contemporary French Marxist; this was underlined by Paulhan's reply to Barthes in the October 1955 number of the *NNRF*.[52]

Paulhan reminded readers how his earlier comment on the 'monthly mythologies' had been written with 'great esteem'; he had simply asked Barthes to say what was *not* 'mythical'. Asserting the innocence of his questions, he noted also how he had asked 'by chance' whether the writer of the 'mythologies' was using 'man', 'human' and 'dialectique d'amour' in the Marxist sense: 'I could easily have asked if he meant them in the Nietzschean or Bergsonian sense.' In an attempt to bring goodwill to the argument, Paulhan suggested that Barthes's question about Paulhan's knowledge of Marxism had been 'friendly and flattering'. Why, he asked, could not Barthes have been more 'sensitive' to the 'praise' that his first assessment of the 'monthly mythology' had represented? What was he so scared of? The Third and Fourth Republics of France had produced no McCarthyists, continued Paulhan, but plenty of Marxists, such as Maurice Thorez and – rather problematically, it has to be said – Léon Blum; like them, Barthes would no doubt go on eventually to hold a ministerial position. Furthermore, Barthes's view that the *NNRF* was 'completely reactionary' was 'curious', opined Paulhan: it was typical that the *NNRF* should be considered 'reactionary' by 'Progressives', whilst 'revolutionary' by 'Conservatives'. With memories of collaboration by the *Nouvelle revue française* in mind, Paulhan defended his journal against Barthes's accusations. Perhaps, he said, 'Mr Barthes' had failed to read or even misunderstood the journal's 'explanations', which were the opposite of Barthes's 'conventions' and 'trickery': these were the source of the 'smear' in which *NNRF* looked 'reactionary to Marxists' and 'Marxist to reactionaries'. Then again, sniped Paulhan, Barthes was not 'averse to a certain smearing'.

It is difficult to draw conclusions on Paulhan's view of Barthes in 1955. Paulhan's rather maverick account of Marxists in French history and the prediction of Barthes's future career were provocative if not playful. But clearly this rather caustic exchange was to be highly instructive –

Paulhan's claims of 'disinterested expression [. . .] spontaneously thought out [. . .] and with an attitude of both passionate [. . .] and respectful questioning' was a perfect example of the 'liberal myth' of impartiality which Barthes analysed in 'Myth Today'.

I have found few other significant reactions to the militant Barthes to give an idea of his standing in the period 1954–6.[53] However, these exchanges are interesting in as much as we can see that Barthes was considered, by a minority of critics at least, to be on the offensive before and during the 'monthly mythology' period. This was not a mere coincidence, or an idiosyncrasy on the part of Paulhan. Barthes's mythological intervention fitted into the politicisation of *LLN*.

These experiences for Barthes were also lessons in tactics and strategies; and it was precisely this self-awareness that he began to develop in his writing. Indeed, a notion of his dialectical sensitivity throws new light on his writings of the period. The 'dialectique d'amour', the love/hate relationship with myth that he evinced in 1954, may help to explain the apparently conflicting attitudes between a number of the 'mythologies'. Andrew Brown has sought to resolve Barthes's contradictory attitude to the floods of Paris, for example, by seeing the 'duplicity of response' as typical of Barthes's 'drift'.[54] Surely however, the 'dialectique d'amour' is a crucial element in an explanation of Barthes's attitude towards the abundance of myths that the floods generated in the press and media. Brown's point that, in depicting the scene of the floods 'with the care of a Dutch landscape-painter', Barthes's mimicry 'enables us to enjoy the floods as an aesthetic object as well as understand them as an example of how myth works' also needs a notion of his dialectical strategy.

The analysis of Rimbaud in 'Phenomenon or Myth?' not only helped to explain Barthes's contradictory attitude to a particular myth, but also pointed to a general strategy in his analysis: the dilemma of whether to consider Rimbaud as a phenomenon or a myth was resolved by looking at the general historical situation in which the demystifier was operating. For example, Barthes's view here that the myth of Rimbaud needed to be demystified could be seen as contradictory to his later use of Rimbaud the 'phenomenon' (the poet) as a corrective to the novels of

Jules Verne, in 'The *Nautilus* and the Drunken Boat'. To consider the invocation of Rimbaud's poem simply as typical of Barthes's 'drift', as Brown does, is to misunderstand Barthes's original political project. It was his dialectical understanding of his acts of demystification which informed his use of Rimbaud as phenomenon *in this particular case.*

Another example may make my point clearer. Barthes's critique of those who would deny the explanatory role of the critic (in 'Blind and Dumb Criticism' and 'Racine is Racine') stands in direct opposition to his view in 'Adamov and Language' that bourgeois critics were doing *too much* explaining. In Richard Klein's view, this contradiction was indicative of Barthes's move from a thematic to a structuralist mode of criticism.[55] Again, it was indicative rather more, it seems, of Barthes's view of the demystifier's historical and dialectical relationship to myths: if bourgeois critics were stressing one aspect of a work (the ineffable and inexplicable nature of Racine's theatre), then Barthes's historical understanding of myth pushed him to oppose the 'admirable security derived from a void' by supplying the historical content effaced by bourgeois ideology.[56] But if bourgeois ideology was trying to impose meaning and derive security – for example, in the case of Adamov's play *Le Ping-Pong*, by calling up the 'enormous cavalry of the symbol' (OCi 615 / ET 55) – then Barthes's understanding of the historically specific nature of demystification meant that he needed to stress *precisely* that which he had criticised in 'Racine is Racine': the ineffability and inexplicability of a work. For, as in the theatre, his mythological studies had a strategy, which was always to take the opposing view to that of bourgeois critics.

So the dialectical strategy set out in 'Phenomenon or Myth?' explained not only the contradictions within certain mythologies ('Paris Not Flooded'), but also the apparent contradictions *between* mythologies.[57] We will look further at the significance of his mythological analyses in the next chapter; but Barthes's sensitivity to dialectical acts of criticism also had implications for his journalism.

His dialectical strategy suggested, above all, that he had an acute awareness of tactical journalistic moves: he could work in different circles – from the politically independent *LLN* and *France-Observateur* to the militancy of *TP*, from the secular intellectualism of *Combat* to the Catholic personalism of *Esprit* – and move quite freely between them. When, in 1971, he spoke of the 'suppleness' of the dialectic in Marxist thought that his Trotskyist friend Fournié had shown him, it could easily have been a reference to the ease with which he, in Gidian and 'Protean' fashion, had maintained a number of political and ideological allegiances, juggling a range of positions on the French left in this early period of his career.

However, as we shall see, this was not without its contradictions. The dialectical strategy could not cover *all* his opinions on French culture. How, for example, did Barthes square his militant activity in the popular theatre with support at the same time for the politically detached and somewhat elitist intellectualism of a Robbe-Grillet novel? Could the concern for an objective 'History' in the theatre be squared with an explanation of contemporary subjective reality in the novel?

2

Disciplines and Barriers

Woe be to him who tries to isolate one department of knowledge from the rest. All science is one: language, literature and history, physics, mathematics and philosophy; subjects which seem the most remote from one another are in reality connected, or rather all form a single system.

Jules Michelet

All generalisations are dangerous.

Alexander Pope

BARTHES'S RISE TO PROMINENCE in the 1950s was reflected in the huge attention given to *Mythologies*. This was recognition not only of the book's audacity and humour, but also of its theoretical and methodological originality in the final essay, 'Myth Today'. If many of the reviews attempted to draw the political conclusions of his best-known book, this was due to the totalising and historical methodology which Barthes seemed to be advocating.

Annette Lavers has argued persuasively that 'totality' was a central concept in post-war left-wing thought, starting with the discovery of Hegel, running through Sartre and Marxism, to influence one of the most important groups of historians and social scientists in post-war Europe, the *Annales* school.[1] The importance of this group was, in part, due to France's relative backwardness in sociology, despite being the country of Auguste Comte and Emile Durkheim. Before the war, sociology was not considered in any sense a separate discipline; and, according to François Dosse, the immediate post-war period saw an 'explosion' of interest in this subject.[2]

Barthes was clearly caught up in this 'explosion', as the late Julien Greimas, great linguist and friend of Barthes, has noted:

> In his first [phase], he believed in the necessity and possibility of creating a science of humanity. In the same way that the natural sciences were formed in the nineteenth century, would not the twentieth century be the century of the human sciences?[3]

Indeed, Barthes's early writings made regular references to not only the *Annales* group but also other social scientists and sociologists: Werner Sombart, Georges Friedmann, Marcel Mauss, Gilberto Freyre, Georges Gurvitch.

However, Barthes's interest in a 'total' explanation of humanity must not obscure his sensitivity to the pitfalls of synthetic explanations. To totalise is, by definition, to generalise; and it runs the risk of not only overdetermining but also overlooking the singular, the particular. Thus, there was for Barthes a danger of explanation ignoring the exception. His example was commonly taken from natural science. The difficulty that the eighteenth-century natural scientist Linnæus had in classifying the duck-billed platypus appeared, on a number of occasions in Barthes's writings, as an illustration of the ability of phenomena to escape classification, from revolutions in 1950, to human faces in 1953, to the *fait divers* in 1962 (see OCi 85, 198, 1181, 1309/CE 185). If, as Lavers suggests, totality is a crucial concept from post-war Hegelian Marxism through to structuralism, then the modest 'paradoxa' of the platypus, stupid but scandalous, constantly tugs at the totalising tendencies of 'committed' explanation.

Barthes's interest in the 'scandalous' exception derived in part from his concern with the exclusion operated by language. This was soon linked to a more general social alienation. In his first sociological writing, 'Features and Faces' published in *Esprit* in 1953, Barthes investigated the lack of variety in the everyday human face. The poetic and moving description which ended the article of a poor woman avidly reading a cinema magazine exemplified to Barthes the alienation of the face taking place in a culture dominated by film stars. Her obvious destitution stood in glaring contradiction to her fascination with the faces of the rich: it was as if her own face, her individualism, had been 'stolen' by an alien(ated) culture of glossy life-styles and magazines (OCi 232).

This acute concern with poverty and alienation – doubtless drawn from his close reading of Michelet – suggested an appreciation of both an objective and a subjective experience of social reality. 'Totality', in the face of the contradictory nature of human experience, was confronted with the dilemma of representing both the general and the 'particular'. The positivism of generalisation typical of a totalising epistemology could lead to further exclusion. If a 'totalising' explanation risked ignoring the subjective and daily alienation of social (and linguistic) exclusion, then the conclusions of 'Myth Today' displayed Barthes's growing sensitivity to the analyst's (i.e. Barthes's) own subjective position in all attempts to demystify. It was no coincidence that Michelet, as H. Stuart Hughes has pointed out, was an important influence in the post-war challenges by the *Annaliste* historians to positivism's dominance of the social sciences. Michelet had been praised by the *Annales* historian Lucien Febvre in a post-Liberation rediscovery of national pride, but he had been largely ignored since the rise of German positivist historical methodology in the wake of the Prussian defeat of France.[4]

So, if Barthes did fit into the post-war left-wing use of totality in general, he had his own particularities. In Philippe Roger's view, he had developed a reading culture – not just Michelet, but Gide and Nietzsche – which was largely at odds with debates of the time.[5] As we shall see, he would use this both with and against the prevailing intellectual and academic trend. Michelet, Marx, Sartre, Trotsky, Gide and Nietzsche – one might also add Paul Valéry – made up a curious mixture indeed.

This reading culture was complemented by the closeted and intellectually intense nature of Barthes's stays in the sanatorium. In 1975 he suggested as much: 'whereas other illnesses desocialise you, tuberculosis would project you into a little ethnographic society which was like a small tribe, a convent or a phalanstery' (OCiii 119/RB 37). Calvet has described in detail the conditions of his early writing career: though detached from the debates around the Occupation and the Liberation and with his promising academic career in doubt, Barthes could receive in Saint-Hilaire-du-Touvet the benefit of companionship and the space within which to forge ideas, establish a reading culture and above all publish articles of a sophisticated nature.[6]

Long periods in sanatoria during the war saw Barthes operating then in a highly academic sphere but, paradoxically, far away from the academy. The closeting and the unorthodox reading diet allowed a freedom of learning which would encourage, at least, a disregard for traditional epistemological barriers, if not a pleasure in crossing them. It is thus to these early writings we must first turn. Needless to say, the sheer range of subjects of these earliest writings in the 'sana' – from modern and classical literature, literary theory culture and drama theory to film criticism, travel writing and music – prefigured the diversity of interests evident in his journalistic activism of the 1950s.

Gide and Nietzsche on Barthes's Magic Mountain

Having helped in the mid-1930s to set up an ancient Greek theatre group at the Sorbonne, Barthes displayed a fascination with ancient Greek culture which was already apparent in the first piece of writing he produced. When published for the first time in 1974 (forty years after being written), his pastiche of Plato's *Crito* was prefaced by comments on the narrowness of French secondary education in the classics in the 1930s. Language and grammar, he said, had been amply catered for, but if one wanted to know at that time about ancient Greek *culture*, then Nietzsche was the only option (OCiii 17). Indeed, his first published article of his whole career, 'Culture and Tragedy', was precisely a treatment of Nietzsche's views on ancient Greek tragedy (OCi 19–22). This fascination with ancient Greece was evident not only in the choice of classics as his degree subject, but also in his predilection for one of France's greatest literary Hellenists.

Published the same year as this article on Nietzsche, 'On Gide and his Journal' was above all a brilliant analysis of Gide's classical Greek roots;

and though its republication in 1975 was prefaced by Barthes's (reported) comment that the article betrayed a 'wishy-washy humanism', the contents were to become crucial elements in his writings of the late 1970s (OCi 23–33/BR 3–17).[7] This early article belied a deep affinity to Gidian thought, in both its writing strategies and its classical preoccupations.

Suggesting that Gide's own loves – Montaigne, Goethe – were not so much an influence as an 'identity', Barthes seemed to be saying the same about *his* own 'identity' with Gide. Indeed, he considered that Gide's preface to a collection of extracts by Montaigne told us 'as much about Gide as it does about Montaigne', a comment worth bearing in mind when we look at Barthes's own prefaces. Written in fragments, reminiscent of Nietzschean aphorisms and prefiguring his own fascination with this elliptical style, the article also attempted to situate the importance of the diary in relation to Gide's writing in general. It displayed Barthes's interest in biography. Having warned that Gide's *Journal* was of little interest to those in whom 'Gide's works had awakened no curiosity in the man', the article went on to study intricately the relationship and the passage between writer and work, Gide's 'ethic'. This covered Gide's image as a writer: 'many comments [. . .] will probably annoy people who have something against Gide', but, said Barthes, hinting at his own interest in the writer, 'the same comments may delight others who for some reason (secret or not) consider themselves similar to Gide'. This interest in the literary journal and the comments on the 'egotistical', corrective and self-searching nature of autobiographical writing would, as we shall see in Chapter 6, dominate the 'late Barthes'.

The influence of Gide's dialectical self-positioning on Barthes's own sensitivity to strategy and tactics, which we looked at in Chapter 1, was matched by the importance of Gide's penchant for the natural sciences. Quoting Nietzsche and Valéry on the usefulness of natural science, Barthes's noted their 'attentive interest in the world of forms'. Many thinkers used science for ontological problems, he said, by relating it first to themselves, then to their readers, a skill used by Gide in his novels. He concluded that the forms that the world's contents took were part of 'mythology'. As both allegory and symbol, mythology could explain life by making it appear 'a bit stronger and bigger': 'all mythology is a dream'. Myths were 'an equivalence between an abstract reality and a concrete fiction', wrote Barthes in a neat Gidian paradox. Already in 1942, we can see emerging the mythology of literary fiction in the 'degree zero' thesis, as well as the fictional nature of social mythology.

Gide's writing seemed to influence Barthes's other early articles written in the sanatorium. The similarity of 'In Greece', an account of a visit to Athens and a number of Greek islands, to Gide's aphorisms in *The Fruits of the Earth*, is more striking than Barthes has since suggested (OCiii 170–2/RB 99). It described in detail a climb in the midday sun which celebrated 'the conjunction of the sun, water and the earth', revelled in the slow intoxication brought on by the Greek way of drinking wine, and mistook a 'beautiful' 16-year-old shepherd, with his 'blond locks' and blue eyes, for an ancient Greek figure. Insisting on the physical sensations of heat in the hills, Barthes's account possessed a materialist and spiritual quality in its attachment to Greek history, a crucial facet of Gide's famous hedonist phase.[8]

Indeed, for Barthes, Gide stood 'at the cross-roads' of Christianity and Hellenism, receiving the benefit of both, straddling two different cultures and systems of thought. Receiving these 'two lights' meant not only bringing together different influences but also learning to set up new epistemological oppositions and combinations. This is best illustrated by Barthes's interest in Gide's notion of Goethe's '*schaudern*' ('trembling'). Combining wisdom and suffering, Gide was, said Barthes, a modern Greek: he had applied the central feature of tragedy to the contemporary world: 'the difficult thing – and one which the Greeks had achieved in the fifth century BC – was how to be wise without necessarily being rational, to be happy without necessarily renouncing suffering'.

Barthes had located this central element of tragedy originally in his reading of Nietzsche; and it was a view of tragedy in ancient Greece (as well as Elizabethan England and seventeenth-century France) which was to become important not only for the post-war popular theatre movement. Tragedy, Barthes believed in 1942, could help to pose the fundamental questions concerning human experience and existence:

> What the world needed [during the epochs of tragedy] was to obtain and provide above all a harmonious – though not necessarily serene – vision, which voluntarily abandoned certain nuances, questions, and possibilities, in order to show the enigma of humanity in its bare bones. (OCi 19)

Casting off the niceties of life in favour of the big question of human existence, tragedy displayed humanity's unique powers of thought; but this 'lesson' was necessarily accompanied by pain. Semi-godlike in its desire and capacity to know, but not divine in its form, humanity had to suffer with its knowledge:

> Tragedy in the theatre teaches us to contemplate suffering in the cruel light that it projects on us; or rather, to deepen this suffering by laying it bare and clarifying it, immersing ourselves in this pure human suffering in which we are physically and spiritually moulded; all this so that we find not our *raison d'être* (this would be criminal) but our ultimate essence and with it our full possession of human destiny. (OCi 21)

This juxtaposition of knowledge and suffering was central to Barthes's appreciation of Gidian *schaudern*, a tragic view of humanity which informs much of Barthes's work in the years following the war.

The ability of tragedy to connect with the fundamental questions of real life was mirrored in the post-war period's existential(ist) *angst* of self-awareness. Writing the prospectus for an exhibition by the puppet-theatre designer Dominique Marty in 1946, Barthes reiterated the relevance of tragedy to contemporary life.[9] Though evident in his theatre writings, the notion of tragedy disappeared from them when Brecht's epic theatre replaced tragedy as the appropriate theatre form, and Robbe-Grillet's new novel criticised tragedy's 'anthropomorphic' placing of humanity at the centre of the universe. But above all, *schaudern* appeared an important influence on the strategy of the 'dialectic of love' – finding knowledge of one's contemporaries at the heart of their social alienation.

There was a final crucial influence of Nietzsche and Gide from this period, which concerned the relationship with the past and the processes of cultural change. Following Nietzsche, Barthes considered that certain periods needed tragedy because it reflected the mental state of their inhabitants. This interest in the social conditions of the origins of the French classical theatre was matched by his insistence on the importance of Gide's 'dialogue with great French writers'. If Gide was for Barthes the arch-modernist – Gide showed 'confidence in the reader', and, like 'Poe's modernism', Gide had 'dismantled the procedures of creation, and was almost as interested in them as the work itself' – Gide had, Barthes concluded, also inspired a pleasure in classical literature. Following Gide, Barthes insisted on the classical rule:

> have the courage to say what is obvious, in such a way that it is never in the first reading that we gain pleasure; the pleasure will come from what is not said, which will only be discovered, because the signposting is there.

Prefiguring the critical debates of the 1960s, he concluded his early article on Gide thus: 'Classics are the great masters of the obscure', and they oblige us to think 'all alone'. This conclusion was the prelude to Barthes's 1944 article in *Existences*, 'Pleasures in the Classics' (OCi 45–53).

Despite the title, the article celebrated both modern *and* classical literature: 'Those who read only classics and those who do not read them at all', began Barthes, 'are both as narrow-minded as each other.' Now in 1944, he stressed that distinctly modern writers such as Valéry, Proust, Gide and Montherlant in fact greatly appreciated the distinctly personal pleasure of reading classical literature. 'This pure mirror, lit up by ourselves' was an 'arrow' which, aimed at us by a classical author, could not fail to allow us 'to see ourselves'. But the attraction, he stressed, was precisely that classical authors never actually spoke about themselves or 'us': despite its 'clarity', classical literature had these 'troubling gaps'. One was 'never sure whether they were left there on purpose or not'; they produced an 'unending darkness and [. . .] piercing silence', forcing the reader to think. The Classics offered us so many 'exquisite paradoxes [. . .] with such a disdain for self-explanation' – beneath 'cool reason', for example, there roamed the passionate desire to suppress passion, and dry maxims were nothing but 'hidden confessions' – that we were 'free to suppose anything of them'. In early deconstructionist fashion, he declared such works of classical literature 'public property' to which we could 'add indefinitely': like a chess-board where new moves always appeared, classical literature, reputed to be highly conformist, lent itself to 'the least conformist analyses'. To illustrate his point, at the end of the article, Barthes provided two dozen 'fragments' from French classical authors (from La Bruyère to Racine), which, like the 'mouth-watering morsels at the start of *A Thousand and One Nights*', would arouse the appetite for classical literature.

Not only did this article point to his later critical practice specifically in relation to classical literature, it suggested that Barthes could happily juggle the modern and the classical in such a way that the distinction between them was, at least, weakened. Indeed, the 'plasticity' of Barthes's early literary criticism was such that he was able to balance this 'plea' in favour of classical literature with his enthusiasm for Camus's modernist novel *The Outsider* the very same year (OCi 60–3). However, that his praise for Camus in 1944 (and in a second article in 1954) was to be radically undermined by the bitter debate with Camus over the latter's *The Plague* in 1955 showed, in Philippe Roger's view, that Barthes was learning to 'bend the stick'.[10]

Barthes's growing dialectical sensitivity would be applied also to the analysis of language in the 'degree zero' theory which we looked at in Chapter 1. For how – if not by a dialectical approach – could Barthes square his pleasure in 1944 in the classics with his view three years later that classical language, both excluding and exclusive, had been part of the centralisation and standardisation of language serving bourgeois hegemony? But can dialectical sensitivity explain fully Barthes's demand to Camus for a 'historical materialist' form of realism – not exactly what one might expect from the author of *Writing Degree Zero* and the champion of the avowedly apolitical *nouveau roman*? Also, surely Racinian tragedy was not only a product of Port-Royal's centralisation of the French language but also total anathema to a popular theatre audience in 1950s France? The apparent contradictions in Barthes's literary aesthetics were dependent on the manner in which he undercut the generic divisions between the theatre and the novel.

Critical Performance

Michael Moriarty has noted that theatre held a 'special position' for Barthes in the 1950s.[11] Yet, when the 1950s are considered, it is usually Barthes's championing of the *nouveau roman* which is underlined. There is a real sense in which his support for the new novel has been overstated (as we shall see in Chapter 3), to the detriment of his activities in the theatre. His passion for the popular theatre was influenced, no doubt, by his reading of Michelet and view of the exclusion of the popular masses from self-expression. It was an enthusiasm which, once dashed, was to have an important effect on his attitudes to social mythology when he came to write the concluding essay of *Mythologies*, 'Myth Today'.

His full endorsement of the aims of a popular theatre first appeared in a speech to the popular theatre association ATP ('Friends of Popular Theatre'), published just before the start of the 1954 Avignon Festival (OCi 430–1). His speech was inspired by the dramatic increase in interest in popular theatre; and from this point until the effective collapse of the ATP two years later in 1956, Barthes was an active and important member who spoke at numerous associations around the country. But before July 1954, his theatre writings betrayed a certain scepticism towards the possibility of a popular theatre in a class-divided society.

In line with the Trotskyan perspective described in Chapter 1, there was a distinct hesitation in his belief in the viability of a real popular theatre culture. In his first article on Jean Vilar in March 1953, Barthes had tempered his enthusiastic praise of Vilar's TNP production of Kleist's *The Prince of Homburg* with a caveat. It was premature to call Vilar's a 'people's theatre': it was 'non-bourgeois' only, he insisted. Since 'History' dictated that the people's aesthetic tastes were largely petty-bourgeois, Vilar's efforts could be nothing more than a challenge to bourgeois aesthetic hegemony:

> Vilar's is a people's theatre therefore only on the level of ideas, and to the extent – albeit decisive – that he breaks from the closed stage of bourgeois theatre, which serves classical ideology. On the sociological level, the persistent split in society means that [his theatre] can be nothing more than an avant-garde experiment, supported for the moment ['spontanément'] by the more advanced elements of the middle classes and the poorer elements [. . .] of the bourgeoisie. (OCi 208)

This pessimistic – some might say realistic – assessment of the possibilities of truly popular theatre in a class-divided society stood in marked opposition to the 'gradual levelling of the classes' that, the very same month, the first editorial of *TP* was glimpsing in post-war French society.[12] But, despite this early scepticism, his speech to the ATP in Avignon in July 1954 put forward a three-point plan which would lead to the establishment of a truly popular theatre. How did this change of perspective come about?

Barthes at first had insisted, as we saw above, that the popular theatre's only realistic goal in a class-divided society was that all manifestations of bourgeois theatre be combated; and his vitriolic first editorial for *TP* (in January 1954) argued forcefully that, before a society's culture could be 'reconciled', its economy needed to be so (OCi 381). But, in the same number, he began to see a possibility of a truly popular theatre. His review of the TNP's recent production of Molière's *Don Juan* – in *TP* and *LLN* the same month – insisted on the production's '*popular* success' (OCi 379, 384–6). He was also clearly inspired by the 'popular' make-up of the participants in the discussion day on *Don Juan* organised by the TNP.[13] The next two years saw an almost manic activity in the popular theatre movement. Between January 1954 and April 1956, Barthes produced over forty pieces on theatre (editorials, general articles and production reviews, which required visits all over France), and listed in *Bref* (a monthly journal for ATP members) were regular talks by Barthes to regional associations. In contrast to the indecision in his question as to the possibility of liberating language before 'History' at the end of *Writing Degree Zero,* he seemed to be adopting the view that liberation of the theatre was indeed possible before 'History'.

We might wish to explain this by insisting on generic differences. The theatre, Barthes stressed, had a definite 'sociality'. Unlike literature, it was a mass communion of ideas and images, which could inspire and challenge a popular audience (OCi 222). Barthes's interest in tragedy and praise of Brechtian theatre were informed by his insistence on the need for a 'voluntarist' theatre aesthetic, which showed first that history was full of potential, and second that the remedy for humanity's ills was 'in their hands'. One of the great things for Barthes about Vilar's production of *The Prince of Hombourg* had been that it had rediscovered the central feature of tragedy, which was to show humans in front of their destiny. The open, fresh-air aspect of Vilar's stage design, the opposite of bourgeois theatre's stifling 'essentialist' view of humanity, showed the mystery of the 'possible' in the face of the irremediable final event ('avènement') of tragedy. It was this 'greatness' of history that Barthes wanted on stage, a view evident in his 1942 article on Nietzsche and tragedy and in his first major article for *TP,* 'The Powers of Greek Tragedy' (OCi 216–23). The 'irremediable' nature of tragedy praised in Vilar's play in 1953 became, after the discovery of Brecht, an insistence on the 'remediable', a crucial component in Barthes's passage from tragic to epic theatre.[14]

Indeed, as Michael Moriarty has pointed out, the theatre 'offered a hope of escaping the impasse of literature so pessimistically diagnosed' in *Writing Degree Zero*: 'the most an avant-garde novel (as exemplified by Robbe-Grillet) can do', continues Moriarty, paraphrasing Barthes, 'is estrange the reader from the essentialist art of the bourgeois novel by subverting its own founding categories of character and plot'.[15]

Such a view, dependent on his second article on Robbe-Grillet, 'Literal Literature' published in September 1955, represented a development in his perspectives on the novel from his first writings on Robbe-Grillet in 1954. Whereas 'Objective Literature' (OCi 1185–93/CE 13–24) in July 1954 had ended on a positive note – Robbe-Grillet's aesthetic encouraged an earthly, not a demiurgic, vision of the world –, 'Literal Literature' (OCi 1212–17/CE 51–8) was more pessimistic about literature's ability to escape bourgeois recuperation, and concluded that the novel was a 'constitutively reactionary' genre (compare OCi 1193/CE 24, with 1217/58). Clearly, between these two articles, Barthes had undergone a change of heart on the role of the novel.

This shift is paralleled by Barthes's attitude to avant-garde theatre. In the first article, he considered Robbe-Grillet's effort to be the equivalent of the theatre of Beckett, Adamov and Ionesco (OCi 1192/CE 23). As his view hardened against avant-garde theatre in favour of political realism (Chapter 1 has compared his enthusiasm for Sartre's *Nekrassov*, a traditional play in formal terms, with his warnings about avant-garde theatre in 1956), so his view of the *limited* effect of avant-gardism in the new novel increased.

The tempering of his earlier enthusiasm for Robbe-Grillet was evident in his pessimistic conclusions in his sociology of the novel in January 1955. Underlining the persistent and rigid class divisions in the consumption of literature, this concluded that the 'alienation of society' put literature in a tragic contradiction: 'just as the world is revealing brilliantly the reality of History, the novelist is still obliged to take refuge in an "essentialist" view of the reader' (OCi 470). Then in 1956, 'New Problems of Realism' denied that showing the 'contingency of the object [in the new novel]' could be in any way part of the final goal of realism; it was but a stage towards it, the final goal being a 'total socialist literature' (OCi 549–51). And, just as he had seen a limited role for popular theatre *before* his enthusiasm took off in July 1954, he now replicated this perspective in 1956 in relation to the novel: literature could go no further than to reveal, and liberate itself from, the 'norms of bourgeois descriptions'. Placing the committed literature of socialist realism back to back with the *nouveau roman*, he concluded:

> So today we find ourselves confronted by two types of realism: a realism of depth, socialist in its structure, but bourgeois in form; and a realism of surface, free in its form but apolitical, therefore bourgeois in its structure. My personal feeling is that the major problem confronting our literature is how to join these two types to create a total realism. (OCi 551)

None of these comments suggested any deep attachment to the political and aesthetic efficacy of any novel, of the sort that Brechtian theories had encouraged him to form in the popular theatre, or as evidenced in his support for Philippe Sollers's novels in the 1960s. Indeed, his view in 1958 that 'There is No Robbe-Grillet School', though supportive of Robbe-Grillet in general, was, in the original article in *Arguments*, critical of this author's complicity in encouraging the press to see a new literary 'school'.[16]

If his general pessimism in 1955 about the novel had been engendered by his politicisation in general, and by his discovery of Brechtian popular theatre in particular, it should be no surprise that Barthes began to apply (particularly Brechtian) theatre categories to his literary criticism. Not only did 'estranging' – *the* pre-eminent Brechtian technique – become his buzz-word in 1955, but also categories of epic and historical theatre entered his literary criticism.

Nowhere in his writing on the novel had Barthes criticised a novel for not being a politically committed history. Indeed, *Writing Degree Zero*, as we saw, had been opposed to a Sartrian ethos of commitment. The public argument with Camus in early 1955 over the latter's allegory of the French Resistance, *The Plague*, was, as Roger points out, a curious episode in Barthes's 'Marxian' phase. Mildly contradictory in his attachment to Camus's style of blank writing between 1944 and 1954, there was a huge discrepancy between his criticism of 'Marxist tautologies' in *Writing Degree Zero* and of Camus's novel in the name of 'historical materialism'.[17]

Rejecting the symbolism with which Camus's novel was making Nazi tyranny into a metaphor, and invoking a 'literal art in which plagues are nothing other than plagues' in its place, 'Chronicle of an Epidemic, or a

Novel of Solitude?' (OCi 452–6) clearly prefigured his second article on Robbe-Grillet, which denied metaphor and promoted a 'literal' art. But how did this fit with historical materialism? Clearly, as Roger suggests,[18] there was an influence from the critique of Camus by Francis Jeanson which had heralded the famous split between Sartre and Camus in 1952. But to understand fully Barthes's criticism of Camus's novel, we must link the voluntarist view of history evident in his writing on theatre at this time to his views on *The Plague.*

The profoundly historical demand by Barthes appears throughout the article, from the first-paragraph explanation of how Camus's novel avoids the historical basis of the chronicle, to the final lines showing the gap between Camus's role as the 'first witness to our History' and his failure to assume this role by ignoring 'the solidarity of a combat'. The 'literal', non-symbolic and non-allegorical method was a realism, and, said Barthes in revolutionary mode, it had to be more fundamentally linked to a perception of the Resistance as '*all* of the Resistance'. The similarity of these last words to those used by Barthes in his criticism of Vilar, when he considered that certain TNP productions had failed to live up to their role of influencing French history in a progressive fashion (see for example OCi 389 and 740), reinforces the view that Barthes was applying theatre categories to Camus's novel. Furthermore, Barthes's regret that the 'tragic' element failed to emerge in Camus's novel, and that Camus preferred solitude to 'solidarity', stood in opposition to Robbe-Grillet's rejection of tragedy. All this was, needless to say, decidedly non-Robbe-Grilletian in its view of political commitment.

Brechtian theatre had achieved a way of showing the capacity of humanity to act, and Barthes saw this achievement as specific to the theatre. And yet he soon transposed this enthusiasm for theatre to the novel, in his critique of *La Peste*'s failure to show humans acting upon history. It was not simply that certain literature could be judged by a Brechtian theatre 'grid'. This worked both ways. As Barthes moved away from the theatre in the post-1956 period, plays became 'texts' for literary analysis.[19] We will see, in the next chapter, how *On Racine* was the best example of this trend: not only because it showed Barthes 'producing' Racine in a more contemporary manner, but also because it represented his demoralisation about the French theatre scene and a final episode in his disillusion with Vilar. This latter was linked to the perceived failure to provide a popular theatre culture which matched the dramatic events of French 'History'. Whether it was in the repertoire or in the production style, be it Balzac or Brecht, Racine or Jarry, the TNP and its director were seen to be ducking the responsibilities in 1957 and 1958 of challenging, amidst an air of censorship, polarisation in the Algerian war, possibility of a coup by the army generals, and De Gaulle's manoeuvring to seize power (see OCi 740, 1227, 775–7). Both in his fascination with Russian revolutionary history (in his 1954 desire to see Eisenstein's *Battleship Potemkin* in 'Cinemascope'), and in his 1957 analysis of history in the theatre, 'Brecht, Marx and History', Barthes was moving beyond a Marxian view of history (OCi 380).

I have suggested that Barthes, though apparently giving literature and theatre different status by virtue of their genre, could cross the barrier between them with impunity, aesthetically, politically and epistemologically. Now, for the second half of this chapter, we must look at this phenomenon in relation to Barthes's interest in sociology and social theory.

Sociology, Histor(iograph)y, Modernity

For Barthes in the early 1950s there seemed to be a link between the formalist, analogic methods of Joussain and Caillois and the denial that people made history. He countered this by postulating the modern synthesis of sciences used by *Annales* historians and the Marxian historical principle of class struggle. 'History' was at once for Barthes a highly determining force – as with 1848 and the history of forms – and an infinity of possibilities.[20] The manner in which his Brechtian voluntarism – humanity's control over human ills – sat with his Robbe-Grilletian critique of anthropomorphism – the *denial* of humanity's control and centrality in the world – might be explained by his dialectical attitude towards agency and determinism; but we might also explain it by looking at the manner in which he progressively removed the barrier between history and its representation.

What I have described above might be termed a 'firm' view of 'History' in Barthes's thought, be it voluntarist or determinist. This seemed to be softened by the 'suppleness' of the dialectical method, for which Andrew Brown has used the term 'drift'.[21] The notion of 'drift' might be useful to characterise the *result* of the combination of the firm and 'supple' in Barthesian historicism, but it does not suggest the manner in which this developed. For this, we must now look at Barthes's major article on Michelet, 'Michelet, History and Death'. It is crucial in showing how, within the swing between voluntarism and determinism (and perhaps as a function of it), there is a definite ambiguity – and perhaps a slippage – in his notion of 'History'.

Barthes's posturing in favour of a 'content' of history in his attacks on Caillois and Joussain stood in opposition to his interest in the history of literary forms and his study of fashion forms, which began in 1956. In one sense, Michelet, though analogic, was an excellent way to *counter* formalism. The 'historian from below' *par excellence*, according to Edmund Wilson, Michelet championed the excluded masses of history.[22] Similarly, Barthes's study of Michelet's historiography, 'Michelet, History and Death', published between his critiques of Joussain and Caillois in April 1951, focused in great part on the historian whose ultimate tribute to the silenced masses of history had been to prefigure his own death and dissolve his own life into theirs. However, if Barthes's aim at the end of the 1940s had been to write a thesis on Michelet's petty-bourgeois ideas, then by the time of his book on Michelet in 1954, with this critique contained in a brief two-page study, it seemed that, though critical of the romanticist and analogic method, his attitude to Michelet was ambivalent.

'Michelet, History, and Death' did seem critical of the nineteenth-century historian. Michelet's analogic method was based on a 'two-term' dialectic, said Barthes, which, showing history's development as a 'series of equations', failed to explain historical changes. In Michelet's history, 'causality disappears in favour of identity' (OCi 93); and, as Hubert Juin pointed out in a review of *Michelet*, there was a short step for Barthes to Hegel's critique of tautology.[23] This use of analogy was not only ahistorical, continued Barthes, it was also indicative of Michelet's inability to think and act outside of the mythology of the French Revolution. Seeing history as a steam-train hurtling teleologically and mythically towards the Revolution meant Michelet could see events afterwards only as a 'post-history'; and, concluded Barthes in seemingly critical mode, 'all history with an end-point is a myth'. His criticism of petty-bourgeois ideology's tendency to tautology in *Mythologies*, as well as his citing of Michelet's classic petty-bourgeois populist study *Le Peuple* in the same breath as the 1950s right-wing xenophobe Pierre Poujade (OCi 679–80/ET), suggested that he had definite criticisms of Michelet. It appeared to be *despite* his petty-bourgeois, populist politics and his romanticist view of the motor of history and consequent use of analogy that Barthes found Michelet of immense importance.

It was seemingly Michelet's *representation* of history that Barthes wanted to retain. Disappointment with Vilar's choice of the romantic play *Ruy Blas* for the 1954 TNP season was contrasted with Michelet's portrayal of history. Like Shakespeare, Michelet's history, decided Barthes before his discovery of Brecht, 'presented [an] epic transmutation which changed event into History and men into destiny'.[24] The same year, he praised the *nouveau roman* for its critique of the romanticist use of psychology and 'depth' of character (OCi 416–17), in a manner not so different from his 1957 belief in the modern aspect of Michelet's 'bird's-eye' view of both 'earthly and historical space' (OCi 726). Thus, there was clearly something in Michelet which redefined, even escaped, romanticism: call it post-romanticism, whatever, Barthes considered Michelet to be relevant to the 'modern'.

The best example of this breaching of the division between the romantic and the modern in Barthes's view of Michelet was his 1959 preface to *The Witch*. Here Barthes considered Michelet to be the first 'sociologist':

> What [in Michelet] was disdainfully called Poetry we can now begin to see as the precise outline of a new science of the social: it was because Michelet was a discredited historian (in the scientistic sense of the term) that he could be at once a sociologist, an

> ethnologist, a psychoanalyst, a social historian; although his thought and its form even contain large amounts of rubbish (whole areas of him could not get away from his petty-bourgeois background), it can be said that he really did anticipate the founding of a general science of humanity. (OCi 1259/CE 115)

An important part of this redefinition of the modern in relation to the romantic was the manner in which Barthes's own view of sociology had been distinctly poetic and literary in its origins.

In 1950, he had seen Jean Cayrol's new 'concentration camp' literary aesthetic (OCi 88) less as a 'testimony' than, like Theodor Adorno, as a central account of human alienation in post-war Europe. Barthes was inspired no doubt by his friendship with another camp survivor, Georges Fournié. Barthes's 1952 article in *Esprit* 'Jean Cayrol and his Novels' set out how literature, as shown by Cayrol, could be both an 'objective' account of 'humanity's new station', a 'sociology' (OCi 118), *and* evidence of the possibility of a 'warmth' in literature, a solution to the 'problematics of alienation' (OCi 125–6). Thus, Barthes's earliest account of 'objectism' ('chosisme') and critique of anthropomorphism, central features of his later views on the *nouveau roman*, pointed not only to the religion-like, Gidian *schaudern* in his view of literature – we had to know our new objective place in human society and suffer with it – but to the epistemological breakdown in his thought between sociology and literature.

Just as Cayrol's literary prose could point, objectively, to humanity's new station, make important sociological revelations and provide a human poetics to counter alienation, so Michelet's history of the witch, toing and froing between history and poetry, provided crucial sociological and scientific information. In both cases, the poetic/sociological mix allowed for treatment of a major epistemological difficulty, of how to take account of both the general *and* the particular. By presenting the witch as an 'intermediary generality', Michelet, the first sociologist, had 'reunited in her the general and the particular, the model and the creature: she was at once *a* witch and *the* witch'. In the same way, Cayrol's use of the first person solved the third person's inability to cover both 'personality and generality' (OCi 1253, 118).

The influence of Michelet's poetic sociology can be seen before 1959. Michelet's use of 'myth' in his mystical portrayals of childhood was appreciated by Barthes in 1955 in his 'History of Childhood'. The manner in which Michelet had shown the child to be 'other' to the adult might have been mystical and 'dreamy' ('rêveur'), but at least it could play a role in undermining bourgeois myth. Michelet might have been creating another myth but at least, suggested Barthes, the 'refugee' from bourgeois ideology was setting out how 'bourgeois mystifications' operate and suggesting subsequent attempts to 'expose' them (OCi 459). Thus, in the 'mythic' writing of Michelet (and Cayrol), the 'literary' could be a source of knowledge; and this science, corrected by poetic, mythical and human elements, could be (at least temporarily) a form of disalienation. Interestingly, this conversion of Michelet from simple petty-bourgeois historian into a sociologist by way of his literary/poetic and mythical tendencies was also a central feature of Barthes's appreciation of Brecht in the 1950s.

The central plank of Barthes's Brechtism was the strong approval which he gave to the manner in which epic theatre posed the problem of ethics, of political action in the face of human alienation. From his first review of the Berliner Ensemble in 1954, his writings on Brecht are concerned centrally with the ability to leave a space between a historical materialist explanation of alienation and the manner of overcoming it, a space which leaves the decision on the appropriate form of action with the (popular) audience. Preferring Brecht's portrayal of history to Marx's in 'Brecht, Marx and History' in 1957, Barthes wrote:

> Between the explanation and the expression of human alienation, Brecht develops an intermediary space, that of the problematics of lucidity; neither a historical theatre, nor a theatre of action, his work posits unceasingly both the History which explains, and the action which disalienates. (OCi 755)

Brecht's theatre was not, Barthes said, one of causality, as Marx might have advised, but a 'general category'. History 'is everywhere, but in a diffuse fashion, non-analytical; it is stretched, and glued onto human misfortunes, consubstantial with them, like the back and the front of a piece of paper'. Echoing his own 'dialectic of love' strategy, Barthes concluded that 'what Brecht allows to be seen and to be judged is the back of the paper, a surface sensitive to sufferings, injustices, alienations and impasses'. Though Brecht's turning history into this 'general demand on thought' was a highly voluntarist, Marxian category, Barthes's view of Brecht's 'bias' – presenting history as both alienation and action – was little different from the 'bias' we saw in his view of Michelet's poetic and total sociology. Michelet's writing of history, like Brecht's, did not preach, but placed partisanship at the centre. 'The innateness of Justice' in the people that Barthes found in Michelet in 1951 (OCi 94) was the same as the unspoken partisan nature of Brecht's 'space'.

Here was the 'modernity' of Michelet for Barthes. With his 'super-visibility' and his unspoken populism, he had provided and prefigured, in formal and aesthetic terms, Brecht's 'space' for popular action. This 'modern' aspect was important to a left-wing intellectual disappointed by facile and propagandist modes of art and political persuasion, particularly since the language of this was at best worn out, at worst that of the enemy. Barthes's early writings are saturated in general with a notion of intellectual 'commitment' (Sartre, Marx, theatre, etc.), but in particular with an acute perception of the difficulties of being a committed practitioner. This conflict, experienced first by Michelet, was evident in Barthes's 1958 article on Voltaire, 'The Last Happy Writer' (OCi 1235–40/CE 83–9).

In Voltaire's time, Barthes suggested, things for the progressive enlightened writer had been straightforward. Denouncing the excesses of the aristocracy and the church was an uncomplicated form of dissidence and opposition. However, were he alive today, stressed Barthes, Voltaire would have found himself on the other side to 'Marxists, progressists, existentialists, intellectuals'. In the original version of the article, Barthes underlined that it was the struggle between the bourgeoisie and the proletariat which would have put Voltaire on the side of reaction and split him from the left.[25] For Barthes, political and committed action had become, since the nineteenth century, far more complex for the intellectual. Here is where the 1850 theory in the 'degree zero' fitted in with his interest in Michelet.

The year 1850 was not simply the 'cut' which began the 'modern' period in literature and language, it was also both the ideological ruin of bourgeois and petty-bourgeois politics and the first defeat for an independent labour movement. Not only was literary language suddenly fractured, but the whole ideological belief in republican capitalism because unsustainable. Barthes's comment in *Writing Degree Zero* about Marxism being 'justified' after the events of 1848 (OCi 177/WDZ 79) was mirrored by his quoting at the start of his book on Michelet the latter's famous phrase about being born under 'the Terror of Babeuf' – the precursor of revolutionary Marxism in the French Revolution – and living to see the collapse of the First International (OCi 246/MI 5). Underlining the fundamentally *intellectual* and self-reflexive preoccupation of Barthes's interest in Michelet is the fact that the articles on Voltaire and *The Witch* were written and published at almost exactly the same time.

If the article on Voltaire stressed the simplicity of being effective in one's political action *before* 1848, then Barthes's preface considered *The Witch* as an allegory of the *modern* intellectual. Following Lévi-Strauss's view that finding an 'aberration' was the way for society to live out its contradictions, Barthes noted that the witch had an equivalent in modern French society. Tacitly, this included Barthes himself:

> In today's society the complementary role of the Micheletian Witch would perhaps be continued by the mythical figure of the intellectual, who, known as a traitor, is sufficiently detached from society to see it in its alienation, and drawn towards a correction of the real but powerless to achieve it: both excluded from the world and yet necessary to it, tempted by a praxis but only able to participate in it by way of the immobility of a langage, [the intellectual] is just like the medieval Witch who soothed human suffering only by using ritual and at the price of illusion. (OCi 1258/CE 113–14)

This study of the witch had been written by the detached and ironic Michelet of post-1851, now politically marginalised, stripped of his chair at the Collège de France for inciting his students to rebel, and with a petty-bourgeois political outlook unable to explain the new class split in post-1848 France. This condition of the first modern intellectual, which Michelet represented to Barthes, is mirrored in the fact that the vast majority of Michelet's writings chosen by Barthes for inclusion in *Michelet* are from post-1851.

This identification with Michelet's contradictory political position was evident in 'Myth Today'. Though born part of the 'people', Michelet had had to admit in 1869 that 'their language was inaccessible' to him, and he could not speak it for them. This was precisely the exclusion of the demystifier regretted by Barthes at the end of 'Myth Today': the semiologist as an intellectual had to suffer an exclusion from the very people who were deemed the victims of myth. To finish this chapter and to conclude this first section on Barthes the journalist, we must examine in detail the significance of *Mythologies* – looking at reviews of the book and suggesting its place in his career – to consider, in both myth and phenomenon terms, how he became this 'mythical intellectual figure'.

Mythologies *as Phenomenon and Myth*

This book is myself.
Jules Michelet

> Introduce into the citadel of objectivity the Trojan horse of subjectivity.
>
> Lucien Febvre

Mythologies has not only been successful since the 1960s, but had an impact at its time of publication. That it came second in the 1957 Sainte-Beuve Prize to Cioran's philosophical essays, *La Tentation d'exister*, barely testified to its commercial success. According to Jacques Bersani, it was 'the bedside book of many French students in the 1950s'; and, writing a similar kind of journalism in Italy at the same time, Umberto Eco had to stop, when he read Barthes's book, out of 'humility'.[26] Furthermore, *Mythologies* was reviewed in numerous publications across the political spectrum: the extremes of sympathy and antipathy that the book inspired were a tribute to its powerful effect, and particularly to its political (as opposed to literary or philosophical) approach. Though attitudes were divided along political lines – it was reviewed favourably in the left press and unfavourably on the right – some reviews were more equivocal than others. This was most notable on the left, which, despite broad support, was at times harshly critical. The interplay of Barthes's book with the press of the period was unmistakable. A number of reviews, particularly on the right, in the act of criticising actually confirmed some of the analyses of petty-bourgeois ideology that *Mythologies* had put forward.

A number of reviews propagated inaccurate myths about the author. Jean Cathelin in *Demain* thought that the use of linguistics was a result of Barthes's 'long months in isolation' perfecting a 'dialectical creation where post-hegelianism and neo-scholasticism met', typical of the generation reaching 30. Cathelin was unaware, it seems, both of Barthes's age in 1957 (42) and that his 'isolation' in the sanatorium had occurred more than a decade before.[27] Bernard Voyenne repeated this myth of youthfulness in *La Pensée française*. Barthes looked like 'a whippersnapper', who, '30 years old, perhaps, [. . .] has read, seen and understood everything, but was finally no more than a choirboy'.[28]

Friends, colleagues and ex-colleagues in the world of left-wing journalism were generally impressed by *Mythologies*. In *LLN* the Swiss novelist Yves Velan underlined its 'detergent power': the *Mythologies* were so politically accurate and ideologically powerful that they should be made into a 'hand-gun' format to be brought out 'at a moment's notice'.[29] For Maurice Nadeau in *France-Observateur* Barthes had shown that myths both oppressed and made people blind to their oppression. He had exposed the 'ruse of the bourgeoisie', which was to use the contradictory economic status of the petty-bourgeoisie to persuade 'the woman shop-assistant, office worker, high-store assistant, who live only just within their means' that 'there was, somewhere, a perfect world'.[30] Alain Bosquet in *Combat* considered *Mythologies* to be 'discomforting', with its 'corrosive and biting wit'; similarly, popular theatre enthusiast Claude Roy described the accurate account of the French government's doublespeak in colonial war situations as 'a bracing tonic'.[31] An ex-colleague from *TP*, Morvan Lebesque, writing in *Le Canard enchaîné*, underlined how Barthes's analysis of colonial language could be used on the most important *mana* of the day, that of 'Algeria is French'. Another contributor to the popular theatre journal, Michel Zéraffa, writing in *La Parisienne*, praised Barthes's attempt to 'expose the mystifications of one class by an other'; though lacking a definition of the relationship between bourgeoisie and petty-bourgeoisie, *Mythologies* would displease both of these classes, 'the former suspicious of radiography, the latter not knowing what it is'.[32]

It was not just friends and colleagues who noted the impressive political charge of the studies. Indeed, calling *Mythologies* a 'politically committed critique', *Cinéma 57* reviewer René Guyonnet spelled out the conception of 'political' as the 'whole of human relations in their real social structure, in their power of constructing the world'.[33] Jean Baumier in the Communist-leaning *Europe* believed, in contrast to Zéraffa's view that it was a book for intellectuals, that it could be popularised for the 'wider public' if the study showed that bourgeois myths were 'deliberately' constructed, the Fiat motor company's 1956 annual report being his example.[34] Nicole Vedrès used Barthes's studies to analyse further the oppressions which bourgeois myth attempted to hide; apologising to the *Mercure de France* for her praise, she defended Barthes's 'perfect little manual of iconoclasm'. As Baumier had done with the rhetoric of companies such as Fiat, she 'completed' the book's analysis of women writers by stressing the manner in which women's magazines ignored the class privileges of mother novelists. Rather than describing the lives of women novelists as 'Mrs X: two novels, three children, Mrs Y: one novel, two children', if one wanted to 'talk about Writing and Housework', suggested Vedrès, 'the following was more appropriate: Mrs X, two novels, one home-help, Mrs Y, three novels, two servants, Mrs Z, two collections of poetry, one do-it-all maid'.[35] Though Barthes's indictment of the minority control of society was not suggesting anything new, the originality for André Marissel in *La Revue socialiste* was to have shown 'the processes by which skilful creators of myths [. . .] manage to take advantage of our naiveté, whilst intellectuals, those who *look* and teach the exploited to *see* and *understand*, are constantly placed in the stocks'.[36] So not only was the left impressed by Barthes's studies of myth, it could use his insights for further political critique of the status quo. When reviewed by the right-wing press, *Mythologies* proved Marissel's view of the fate of left-wing intellectuals to be accurate.

The anonymous reviewer in *Pourquoi Pas?* considered Barthes 'a left-wing intellectual, or better still: terribly intellectual and of Marxist persuasion', displaying 'an unbearable and pedantic pretentiousness', to such an extent that his 'political views' blinded him to social reality. This was similar to the view in the *Croix du nord* of Henri Platelle, who, deeming Barthes's Marxist analysis 'typical of those who wrote for [the PCF journal] *Les Lettres françaises*', was drawn into an amusing, if not ironic, confusion: it was, of course, *Les Lettres nouvelles* which had published most of the 'mythologies'.[37] For *Le Monde*, it was Robert Coiplet who provided the first of three reviews of *Mythologies* in 1957. Despite misunderstanding the conclusion of 'The Poor and the Proletariat', Coiplet's review appeared nonetheless charitable, when one considers that he had been the brunt of a number of criticisms in the original versions of certain 'monthly mythologies'.[38] In 'Blind and Dumb Criticism' in November 1954, Barthes had cited Coiplet as an example of those who had quickly deemed a work ineffable and criticism therefore useless. Ironically, admitting that he did not feel qualified to discuss Barthes's use of psychoanalysis, Coiplet now placed himself neatly in the second category of bourgeois critic attacked by the mythology: those who did not understand a difficult philosophical question would admit defeat, thereby ignoring and reducing its importance. Then, two months later, Barthes had questioned Coiplet's judicial wisdom in 'Dominici or the Triumph of Literature', provocatively suggesting that *Le Monde*'s satisfaction with the guilty verdict had been written 'in the style of Mr Coiplet'.[39] But, whereas Coiplet's review made no reference to these earlier criticisms by Barthes, Emile Henriot did indeed notice Barthes's personalised attacks in 'Literature according to Minou Drouet' and responded accordingly.[40]

Firmer criticism came from the traditional right. In *La France catholique*, Jean-Pierre Morillon felt disturbed not by the satire on the Abbé Pierre, but by the threat to the family which, he thought, the book represented. Extolling the virtues of family life, Morillon asked indignantly whether any 'great marriage' had ever tried to stop a strike: a shop assistant might have a 'tender heart' for love and marriage, but she was still in a trade union; and he was incredulous that a sophisticated intellectual could put forward an explanation of social decay which ignored the breakdown of family values. For intellectuals such as Barthes, he said parodying Voltaire's famous dictum, 'if the bourgeoisie did not exist, one would have to invent it'.[41] For the readers of *Rivarol* Pierre-Antoine Cousteau – the elder brother of Jacques Cousteau, recently reprieved and released from prison for collaboration with the Nazis – felt that he had to translate Barthes's complicated prose into 'vulgar French'. He 'explained' to the readership of *Rivarol* what Barthes was saying: 'History with a capital H shows that the author is a Communist', for it represented 'a negation of the past which postulated [. . .] the inevitable arrival of a Marxist society'. Reminding Barthes of the imperialist nature of the 'Stalinist myth', Cousteau concluded that the book only served to confirm, in his view, the accuracy of the division between left and right: 'the right is acceptance of the real (no matter how ugly), and the left a belief in cloud-cuckoo-land'.[42] Less vitriolic, but more contemptuous, Pol Vandromme's review in *L'Echo du centre* was a good example of anti-intellectualism. Quoting Barthes's view of the 'ex-nomination' operated by myth, Vandromme mused ironically: 'Mr Barthes ought to be invited to the next debate in *L'Express* with Mrs Audry and Mr Morin, called "Does history turn in the direction of a washing-machine?" '.[43] If many of these reviews provided a diverse amount of material for Barthesian-style mythological studies, it was clearly the right wing which was most convinced of Barthes's left-wing explanation. However, Cousteau's belief in a clear division between left and right was not sustained by reviews in other sections of the press.

There was an irony in the view of Barthes's suitability to *L'Express*. Thomas Lenoir's review in that periodical was actually very hostile. Citing the example of the 'Blue Guide' mythology (which had mentioned *L'Express*), Lenoir rejected Barthes's class-based analysis and desire for omniscience in a travel guide. Furthermore, in attacking certain publications for the promotion of Minou Drouet's poetry, Barthes had forgotten, wrote Lenoir, that it was *LLN*, the original publisher of the 'monthly mythologies', which had first given space to Drouet's poems.[44] The ambiguity in the attitude of *L'Express* to *Mythologies* was underlined by the fact that Barthes's book was put on its summer 1957 booklist.[45]

L'Express was not alone in blurring Cousteau's distinction between left and right. Though treating the overall message of the book with a certain sympathy, Gabriel Venaissin, who had reviewed Cayrol's 'zero degree' of writing in 1954, writing in the radical Catholic journal *Témoignage chrétien*, was now sceptical about the accuracy of Barthes's descriptions: 'Roland Barthes is one of those who cannot handle the world's disorder: so he brings in order where there is not any'. This must be compared with the anonymous reviewer in the Protestant journal *Christianisme social*, which unequivocally commended Barthes's 'perspicaciousness': *Mythologies* had forged an accurate description of the relationship between bourgeois and petty-bourgeois classes, and the reviewer applied Barthes's 'vaccination' theory to French army atrocities in the Algerian war and to the media presentation of these allegations.[46]

A common criticism of *Mythologies*, and one which blurred distinctions further between left and right, concerned the book's attitude towards myths in general. Labour movement activist Georges Lefranc, in the syndicalist broadsheet *La République libre*, considered that myths could be useful in political battles. Barthes, he said, had clearly not 'read Georges Sorel nor been active in a popular movement' where myths were essential for the 'masses'.[47] A similar sentiment was repeated in Jean-Baptiste Morvan's review in the right-wing *La Nation française*; were the myths that *Mythologies* attacked not in fact 'a way of bringing a bit of colour and music into one's personal life?'. The difference was that Morvan used this to assert his right-wing standpoint: the 'psychological poverty' of 'social liberation' would, he thought, only lead to 'a revolutionary monomania of a classless society'.[48] The political nature of *Mythologies* caused other confusions. In a second review in *La Nation française*, Michel Vivier considered that Barthes's attacks on the church, the press and colonialism had placed Christian democrats, the readers of *L'Express*, and even certain socialists who were defending the colonial system, in the same right-wing camp. Where amongst this 'huge right wing' was the left, Vivier wondered, if most of the 'proletariat' read *France-Soir* and believed in Stalin and Abbé Pierre? Barthes's idea of the left was, he thought, the restricted number of intellectuals who read '*L'Observateur*, *Les Temps modernes* and *Les Lettres nouvelles*'.[49]

It was clear that the book had engendered a large debate in all sections of the press. Even regional newspapers and journals took the time to assess *Mythologies*. This success was reflected in the significant decrease in Barthes's journalism after its publication. Between 1957 and his appointment to the EPHE in 1960, he published fewer than half as many articles as in 1953–6. What was also striking about these articles was the diversity of the publications in which they appeared: whereas 130 articles had appeared in fourteen publications between 1953 and 1956, fifty now appeared in twenty-one. This variety suggested that Barthes's reputation was such that he could afford, in financial and intellectual terms, to write much less journalism for a wider readership. This relative fame seemed, however, to come at a price.

In his review of *Mythologies*, Bernard Voyenne noted the difference of tone between the book and the 'monthly mythologies' as they had appeared in *LLN*: 'What pleases in a periodical suffers badly in a book.' The originals, he said, 'had begun with a fanfare, but ended up rather dull and humdrum': Barthes's 'causticity' in the original 'monthly mythologies' had by 1957, said Voyenne, turned 'to bitterness'. We have looked at the political significance for Barthes, as well as for *LLN*, of the 'monthly mythologies'. The reaction to them (restricted to the pages of the *NNRF*) might have been more localised than the generalised attention given to *Mythologies* in 1957, but there was clearly a more intense political impact: no review of the book in 1957 inspired the intensity and length of Paulhan's exchange with Barthes in 1955. When seen in the context of *LLN*, the original mythological studies had been more political and polemical than the book versions, for they had been an immediate reaction to political and cultural events of the moment. The editing and subsequent abstraction of the original mythological studies did not mean that *Mythologies* lost its final charge; on the contrary, as the study of contemporary press reviews in this chapter has shown, Barthes's most famous book (of the 1950s, if not of his whole career) raised a number of polemics. However in all of the reviews of *Mythologies* that I have managed to find, it was 'Myth Today' which raised the most debate in 1957. This meant, automatically, that the critical nature of the original studies was overshadowed by this final section added afterwards, and that a number of important points about Barthes's early career have been obscured.[50]

First, the original 'monthly mythologies' were aimed at a specific audience. Not only was this evident in the jargon – for example, the 'dialectic of love' had meant little to those intellectuals, such as Paulhan, not initiated into Hegelian Marxist theory – it also suggested that Barthes was making specifically political assumptions about his readership. The 'monthly mythologies', published in the pages of a (relatively) small-circulation, left-wing literary journal, needed to take the readership's left-wing beliefs for granted. To understand the analysis of a myth's operations one had to accept, to some extent, that 'myth' existed. In this sense, though not a mobilising, persuasive discourse, Barthes's dialectical critical praxis had been aimed necessarily at a like-minded reader of *LLN*: in order to understand Barthes's dilemma, the reader had, at least, to agree with the political import of a critique of myth. If the readership was not preoccupied by the possible damage and ideological control that myths caused, as well as by the difficulty of analysing the ideology of the masses excluded from direct articulation of experience and thought, then a dialectical relationship with those myths was irrelevant. The impression that *Mythologies* displays 'tactics' but no 'strategy' represents a significant development from 1954.[51]

If, in 1954, Barthes's dilemma about myth was resolved by his dialectical attitude to myth, 'Myth Today' testified to a shift of emphasis. 'Phenomenon or Myth?' underlined a sensitivity to human alienation. The alienation that myth operated was, perhaps, the central *political* theme of the original studies in *LLN*; hating 'this alienation', but seeing its expression in myth as the only place to 'find [his] contemporaries', gave the studies a politically clear (if a strategically complex) aspect, which was omitted from *Mythologies*. Indeed, 'Myth Today' posed an entirely different tactical dilemma: Barthes's view that the mythologist could not both demystify and appreciate the goodness of wine at the same time suggested the abandonment of his dialectical strategy to solve the dilemma.

The main point about the addition of 'Myth Today' for an understanding of *Mythologies*'s success and importance for Barthes was that it attempted to expound (at least the beginnings of) a scientific theory of myth, which, by definition, had to suspend, if not ignore, a dialectical act of demystification. 'Myth Today' stressed the need to theorise a sociology of signs, found a new science, which abstracted the historical moment of the myth's transmission and consumption. Its remit was to point out the double-bind of the demystifier *only within* this science of signs. The whole thrust of 'Phenomenon or Myth?' had been the contemporaneous intervention of the mythologist in order to denounce an imposture *at that time*. As Barthes put it in 1954: 'All that counts is the general historical reality in which the myth appears; it is in the name of this History that we must judge this myth'; and it was this act of 'condemnation' which linked the intellectual 'most generously' to society. In other words, the act of demystification for Barthes was historically specific; the attitude the mythologist took defined his or her relationship to the society of that time. The book, by contrast, catering for a wider range of readership, perhaps including the more academically minded, needed a more timeless and theoretical, and less politicised, account.

This is not to say that *Mythologies* hides Barthes's left-wing analysis. But it appears that, paying close attention to Paulhan's criticisms of jargon and lack of clarity in his 'monthly mythologies', Barthes tried to shift the emphasis of these studies, when collected into book form, in order to give it a wider appeal. One result of this was that reviews of Barthes's book at the time were on occasions difficult to differentiate politically, and implied that *Mythologies* itself had blurred political distinctions; the contradictory assessments suggest that the highly political nature of the studies was clouded by the ambiguity caused by the attempt to marry two different projects. Barthes's theoretical galaxy of influences, dissolving epistemological barriers between literature and the real, myth and history, sociology and semiology, combined Brecht, Marx and Michelet, and finally Saussure and Hjelmslev. The fallout was that, whereas 'Phenomenon or Myth?' advocated the active, politicised demystification of bourgeois culture, 'Myth Today' was a descriptive, and, at best defensive, prognosis of action before the mystifications of culture. It took no longer an overtly political stance, but instead a more jaundiced, if not pessimistic and negative, view of mass culture. As Yves Velan's review put it, 'Barthes wants to do something, but his sympathy has been [. . .] transformed into sarcasm': the book could be no more than a 'committed poetry'. The book version of the 'monthly mythologies', with Barthes's editing and the appendage of a theoretical explanation of myth and the demystifier's relationship to it, had changed a dialectical praxis into a sarcastic negativity, by abstracting the playful critiques of a journalist into the timeless science of myth of a theorist.

It is here that Barthes's knowledge of Michelet played its part. First, Barthes began to consider not so much the exclusion of the masses from expression as his *own* exclusion from them as intellectual, in the same way as Michelet had done after 1851. The attitude of 'Myth Today' represents an important step in his career towards a consideration of the self within social and critical theory. Second, he began to see myth as the only solution to myth, building on his tentative praise in 1955 of Michelet's mythical account of the child. Finally, and perhaps most importantly, the 'two-term dialectic' in Michelet's analogic history, criticised by Barthes in 1951, formed the basis of his admission that the resolution by the mythologist of 'the contradiction of the alienated real' could be operated only by an 'amputation' not a 'synthesis' (OCi 718/M 158). It would be perhaps hasty to suggest that Barthes's sarcasm was analogous to the irony that Hayden White has found in (post-1848) Micheletian writings, but there is a definite sense in which Barthes was replicating this in his attitude to mass culture after 1956.[52]

The collection into book form, the editing and addition of a final theoretical essay, were indicative of the shift in his perception of his career, to the extent that his first article in *Annales* was signed 'Roland Barthes (CNRS) [Centre National de la Recherche Scientifique]'. The second half of the 1950s marked the end of a crucial and highly eventful phase in Barthes's career. He did not simply stop being a 'journalist'; he left the popular theatre, almost never (quite literally) to return. His belief in 1953 that theatre (first Vilar's and then Brecht's) could be a 'spark' for the masses and a powerful counter to bourgeois ideology (OCi 222) was replaced after 1956 by a belief in the victory of myth. There was an irony here: *Mythologies* is famous for its unrelenting critique of bourgeois ideology's static, tautological and essentialist view of the world. There is nothing more 'immobile', anti-historical or essentialist than to believe that the masses have actually swallowed all the myths of bourgeois society.

PART TWO

ACADEMIC

IN HIS ACCOUNT OF the avant-garde in France, René Lourau considers the 'self-sabotage' in 1962 of the journal *Arguments* as indicative of the 'rapid institutionalisation' in the early 1960s of left-wing thinkers.[1] To the list of those from *Arguments* taking up posts in research and teaching institutions – Morin, Duvignaud, Pierre Fougeyrollas – he could easily have added Barthes. For Barthes's work in the first half of the period 1957–67 seemed to promote an academic ethos over journalistic concerns.

After 1960, Barthes was now publishing regularly in *Annales*, based in the sixth section of the EPHE, where he worked. Helping to set up *Communications*, he also wrote in the *Revue française de sociologie* and the *Revue internationale de filmologie*. Indeed, the most sustained political journalism in this period, a new series of 'mythologies' in *LLN* in 1959 (OCi 784–92, 802–15, 828–9), made little of the impact of five years before; and though highly perceptive and ironic, they ended rather abruptly after only a few months.

This shift was evident in the difference between *Mythologies* and *The Fashion System*. Whereas the former had been predominantly a journalistic essayism, which 'Myth Today' theorised afterwards, the latter reversed this schema. Deploying a linguistic theoretics in Section One, 'The Vestimentary Code', which made up the bulk of the book (OCii 183–313/FS

59–216), the analysis was 'corrected' briefly by the essayism of the second section, 'The Rhetorical System' (317–54/225–73). Clearly, priorities had been inverted in the intervening six years: linguistics, system and theory came first in *The Fashion System*, with the more acerbic social comment relegated to second place. Though not a renunciation of the ideological critique in *Mythologies*, such a formalised and method-centred study was bound to result, as Barthes accepted in an interview in 1967, in a 'much less direct attack on the world' (OCii 472/GV 66).

Parallel to this academic turn in his publishing, however, was the creeping 'literarisation' of Barthesian thought and writing. Published just as he gained his permanent academic post in 1960, in a special number of *Arguments* on 'The Crisis of Intellectuals', Barthes's contribution, 'Authors and Writers' (OCi 1277–82/CE 143–50), promoted writing as an end in itself – a *non*-academic view if ever there was one. This non-teleological view of writing and thought seemed to be, paradoxically perhaps, a function of his work on fashion. This is not to say that his huge study of clothing systems did not inspire an academic rigour; on the contrary, it led to a spate of work in the early 1960s, on the visual arts in particular, which put his adoption of semiology into practice on the burgeoning mass culture. But, precisely as he began to see a linguistic study of fashion as an object of formal academic study in 1960, he was underlining the paradox of language as the 'institutionalisation of subjectivity' (OCi 1282/CE 150).

The dates are significant. *The Fashion System*, though not published until 1967, was finished just before the preface to the *Critical Essays* was written. The 'poverty' of forms estalished in the former no doubt influenced the view in 'Introduction to the Structural Analysis of Narratives' that the infinite number of narratives was balanced by a tiny number of structures (OCii 74–103/BR 251–95). But the ability of his study of fashion 'to make something out of nothing', as he put it in an interview in 1967 (OCii 472), also suggested the 'variety' of forms hinted at in the preface to the *Critical Essays* (OCi 1169–76/CE xi-xxi). Out of this contradiction, *Criticism and Truth* would go on to show that the resultant methodology did not entail the conclusion that there was necessarily a 'poverty' of literature and writing.

The move towards more academic inquiry began thus to establish a new set of poles in Barthes's work. Whereas the 'journalist' phase had counterbalanced financial expediency with intellectual responsibility, now academic requirements posed a new split in his work. It was this polarisation – academic and social scientific versus literary and aesthetic – which was to catapult him into the limelight. Though spending much of this period preparing his doctorate on fashion, Barthes became famous in the early 1960s for very different reasons. A collection of articles written between 1958 and 1960, *On Racine*, published in 1963, replicated his 1964 view of the Eiffel Tower (OCi 1370–400/ET 3–7): it attracted reactions and meanings like a lightning conductor. An important element in the argument over Racine and the 'new criticism' being developed was the antipathy to the 'new novel'.

Describing Barthes's promotion of new novelists as a '*coup d'état*', Pierre de Boisdeffre spent a chapter of his hostile book on the *nouveau roman* attacking Barthes for his role as Pierre Laval in Robbe-Grillet's 'Pétainist seizure of literary power'.[2] Of course, lumping Barthes in with the *nouveau roman* fitted neatly into the argument over *On Racine* in particular and the *nouvelle critique* in general. But it seems that Barthes's link with the work of Robbe-Grillet was more apparent than real. Naturally, there *were* a number of grounds for Boisdeffre's view. Barthes had been instrumental in publicising the new literary aesthetic of Jean Cayrol; his preface to Bruce Morrissette's study of Robbe-Grillet in 1963, coupled with its republication in the *Critical Essays* alongside the 1950s articles on Robbe-Grillet, suggested Barthes's adherence more strongly; and then, Robbe-Grillet's manifesto *Towards a New Novel* placed a warning by Barthes about tragedy as an epigraph to the infamous chapter 'Nature, Humanism and Tragedy', and the preface displayed a distinctly Barthesian influence.[3] However, Robbe-Grillet's view that a novel needed to be 'thought out' might have resembled Barthes's adherence to Brechtian theatre, and the plurality of 'interrogations' in *Writing Degree Zero*, but to consider Barthes as deputy in Pétain-style seizure of literary power did seem an erroneous overstatement. Indeed, there was also a chronological myth involved in coupling Barthes with the *nouveau roman*. By the time of the appearance of *Towards a New Novel* in 1963, Barthes had long since questioned the changes in direction by Robbe-Grillet, as his 1961 article in *Clarté* showed (OCi 934–5). Regretting how Robbe-Grillet's participation in Resnais's film *Last Year at Marienbad* had led to a return to a 'literature of adjectives' and an 'ideologically reactionary' narration, Barthes had already begun to back in its place, as we shall see in Chapter 4, the hyper-formalism adopted by *Tel Quel*. Barthes was still an important reference point for the 1960s debates around the politics of the 'new novel'. For example, that which opposed Beauvoir and Sartre to Jean Ricardou in 1965 was summed up by the latter's invocation of Barthes's distinction between 'Authors and Writers'.[4] But the perceived adherence of Barthes to a *nouveau roman* requires a comment similar to Picasso's apocryphal reply to the Nazis as to the creator of *Guernica*: it was not Barthes, but the literary institution which had created the myth.

The concentration on the *nouveau roman* has meant that the significance of fashion in Barthes's work has been, to some extent, ignored. Chapter 4 will suggest that, if the analysis of fashion represented a move towards semiology and structuralism, it was also an influence on the development of a new relationship between literature and science. The epistemological shift towards a literary view of science in Barthesian thought was dependent on the fact that, as Olivier Burgelin pointed out in 1974, *The Fashion System* had at its base a profound contradiction.[5]

If a minor generation of left-wing intellectuals, predominantly in the academy, moved from history to structure, the great debate of the 1960s between Marxism and structuralism had taken place much earlier for Barthes, in the late 1950s. And just as many others in the mid-sixties were coming to the conclusion that structuralism was a technocratic methodology, both post-Sartrian and post-existentialist, Barthes was reaffirming the importance of existentialist thought.[6] It was to be precisely this theoretical eclecticism in the 1960s which annoyed certain of his critics.

Georges Mounin, the eminent linguistic semiologist, was highly sceptical of his interdisciplinary approach. Barthes's analyses were not at all semiological but psycho-social.[7] Following André Green's view of *Mythologies*, we will consider briefly Barthes's sociological psychoanalysis.[8] Furthermore, for Mounin, Barthes's 'agility' and 'versatility' meant that when addressed as a researcher he replied as an essayist; and when as an essayist, complained Mounin, he became a researcher hiding in scientific and theoretical areas where few literary scholars dared to follow him. Similarly, the publisher of Picard's attack on Barthes, Jean-François Revel, suggested that Barthes's criticism needed to choose between *either* the 'exactness' of anthropology *or* the level of language, but he could not have it both ways: '[Barthes] has not got the right to reply: *I am a poet,* when his information is questioned, and *I am a researcher* when he is told *your poem does not move me.*'[9]

Such comments summed up well Barthes's ambivalence. Against the scientism expected of a sociologist working at the EPHE, he was 'balancing' an involved literary aestheticism. This was not simply a more experimental essayism – typified by the writers/authors distinction – but a constant undermining of the very scientism of semiology being posited. Just as a science of literature was being postulated by the *nouvelle critique,* Barthes moved, in his more adventurous writings, to fill in the distance that this new objective view of literature had tried to open out. Of course, the stark opposition between the *nouvelle critique* and 'university criticism' was crucial in his work, as the joust with Picard showed. But literature began, across the 1960s, to colonise all of Barthes's thought, as if by way of a foil to (dare I say, a relief from) a certain sterility of his more in-depth social science research.[10]

It is tempting to see this aestheticised essayism as a renunciation of political responsibility. But originating as it did in the 'Crisis of Intellectuals' debate in *Arguments,* it represented a non-Jdanovian, anti-propagandist form of *engagement.* The 'temporal freedom' of the artist, declared Barthes in November 1960 in reply to a questionnaire on 'left-wing criticism', had to be combined with 'political responsibility' (OCi 908). It was now as if this artistic formula had been applied to his own essayistic and critical practice.

3

Criticism and Mass Culture

Nothing is given. Everything is constructed.
Gaston Bachelard

AFTER THE EFFECTIVE COLLAPSE of the ATP popular theatre association in April 1956, Barthes returned to the CNRS. This time he was not a lowly *stagiaire* in linguistics, but, thanks to Georges Friedmann, a research *attaché* in the sociology section. The first fruit of this appointment came a year later with the impressive 'History and sociology of Clothes', his first article in *Annales,* which would lead to his seminal book-length study of fashion published ten years later, *The Fashion System.* In aesthetic terms, clothing fitted neatly with his work in the theatre, especially 'The Diseases of Costume', which had illustrated his Brechtian sensibility to clothes as meaning (OCi 1205–11/CE 41–50).[1] In epistemological terms, the study of clothes followed on from the work of Julien Greimas on fashion in the 1830s (and it was no coincidence that Barthes's first research project at the CNRS in 1952 had been on language in the 1830s).

It might be called a 'study of fashion', but what is clear is, that in the late 1950s, Barthes began to realise that this was at once too large and too small a subject. There is a real sense in which the shift of object from the first *Annales* article on (the history of) clothing forms – a social phenomenon affecting the entire population – to the contemporary fashion system paralleled his disengagement from popular culturalist activism in the theatre. After all, those 'clothes' exhibited in fashion magazines such as *Jardin des Modes* or *Vogue* were, like the recipes described in the 'mythology' 'Ornamental Cookery' (OCi 641–2/M 78–80), hardly within the financial grasp of the toiling masses. Barthes's decision, taken in 1959, to move from clothes history to fashion system, illustrated by his article in *La Revue française de sociologie* in April 1960 ' "Blue is in this Year" ' (OCi 856–68), was not coincidental to either his departure from the popular theatre or his entry into the EPHE.

Related to the shift of object of study was the application of the linguistic model to his methodology. Following his 1959 review article in *Critique*, 'Language and Clothes' (OCi 793–801), language now became the key element in his writings and research on fashion. And with the previous chapter in mind, we should not be surprised that epistemological adventurism should extend to literature and fashion. Indeed, underlining how Carlyle, Michelet and Balzac (amongst others) had given some of the best 'reflections' on clothes, this article, written the same year as his preface to Michelet's *The Witch*, displayed how literature and fashion could feed into one another. Similarly, fashion 'form' and linguistic methodology could inform, if only by default, the image-based aspect of his sociological inquiry. Following Edgar Morin's sociological thought, Barthes's analysis moved with the object of study, from clothes to fashion. This 'parametric' view was also to become a central aspect of his literary analysis (OCi 1372/CE 275).

This chapter will consider then the relationship between epistemological innovation and literary critical praxis. We will look at the effect of Barthes's adherence to Bachelard's 'new scientific spirit' on his attitude to a more orthodox 'formal' analysis by the Marxist theorist Lucien Goldmann. Was Goldmann's attempt to put what he called 'form' in relation to its history, by considering tragedy as a central feature of Racine's and Pascal's 'vision', the same as Barthes's view of 'form' in Racine? Barthes's acquaintance with a Nietzschean account of tragedy suggests that Goldmann's silence (blindness?) on Nietzsche in *The Hidden God* was to be an important divergence of analysis. But first, we must establish the rising importance of the literary critic, for it was this which pitted him against the academic orthodoxy.

The Rise of the Critic

> Even in its constructive and creative mode, the critical spirit corresponds to something which undoes itself rather than to something which makes itself.
>
> Albert Thibaudet

> Imagination imitates, it is the critical spirit which creates.
>
> Oscar Wilde

Once Barthes had left the theatre, his enthusiasm for Brecht's participatory and democratic theatre had to go somewhere. If the popular audience watching a Brecht play were empowered to 'judge' the decisions and action taken by the characters, then this 'power' of the spectator, when the possibilities for a politicised popular theatre (in Barthes's view at least) looked bleak in 1960, was channelled into literary criticism. Combining a sensitivity to dialectical and tactical positions with this belief in the power of the critical subject, the shift from stage to text that we observed in the previous chapter in his application of Brechtian categories to Camus's novel had important consequences.

The perfection of Brechtian theory suggested that the theatre required perhaps a less supple approach than literary and mythological criticism. It needed close attention to detail, categories and performance, in order to provide a total popular experience. But it also required a certain irreverence to classical drama texts. It was not simply that Barthes had recognised the importance of the critical response for a production to fail or succeed.[2] He had also come to realise that to combat the power of the 'bourgeois' critic, it was not enough to 'ignore' the likes of Jean-Jacques Gautier. One had to try to beat him at his own game. A prelude to this battle was to study the critical responses and to expose the premises, be they false or ideological. Hence the many mythological studies, numerous comments on critical reception, and often derogatory comments on the critics themselves contained in *Mythologies*. But, of course, by the end of the 1950s, Barthes was having to contend not only with the bourgeois critics, but also with theatre directors such as Jean Vilar, the great hope for popular theatre at one stage, who was now dodging his political responsibilities.

Replicating the director's relationship to a play, and in parallel to 'the rise of the director', of which Barthes's (early) praise of Vilar and then of Roger Planchon in particular had been a witness, we could speak of 'the rise of the critic'. Not only could the critic affect the reception of a production, in Barthes's politicised version he or she could 'produce' a new reading for a piece of literature. The (tacit) realisation of this 'power' by Barthes was to be a crucial political aspect of the burgeoning *nouvelle critique.*

The rise of the critic in the 1960s was first highlighted at the First International Conference on Literary Criticism, held in Paris in June 1962, which brought together literary critics from sixteen countries (mainly from Europe – East and West – and the Americas).[3] The representative from Britain was the Brecht specialist John Willett; from France there was Maurice Nadeau. It is worth setting out in some detail Nadeau's contribution to the conference, 'Beliefs and Methods in Contemporary Criticism', because it underlined the growing importance of literary criticism in general, and of Barthes's role in particular.[4]

Not only could the modern version of literary criticism help explain both old and new literary creation, suggested Nadeau, it could 'smash ("briser") the hold of the past and of tradition'. The two dominant types of traditional literary criticism – one impressionistic, the other academic – had not really engaged with literature. Either there was an absence of method, which tried to imply neutrality; or there was a very 'erudite' and historical form interested only in a work's 'biographical significance'. In opposition to these two traditional forms, Nadeau described the more recent forms of critical practice, all trying to establish a 'science of creation'. The oldest, Marxist literary criticism, had now abandoned a simplistic method which based its opinions on the author's political views and on the propagandist message in a work, in favour of historical, social and class-based analyses, especially in the work of Walter Benjamin, Georg Lukács, Henri Lefebvre and Lucien Goldmann. Nevertheless, Nadeau stressed, in trying to look for the 'rational' in literature, Marxist criticism tended to remain 'outside' of a work. In contrast, Freudian criticism tended to look for the irrational in a work – for example in Charles Mauron's work on Mallarmé and Jean Delay's interpretation of Gide. Finally, existential and phenomenological criticism – represented by Georges Poulet, Jean-Pierre Richard and Jean Starobinski – acted as a 'witness' to the lived feeling of existence evident in a work.

All three forms of modern criticism, in showing that a work was never 'gratuitous', demonstrated that there was a meaning which went beyond the work itself and that a work could be understood only in relation to the author's complexity. As 'criticisms of depths', they were less interested in the work than the author, the author less than the phenomenon of creation, creation less than the act by which creation took place. Indeed, a work was, on the one hand, often but a pretext in which the author of a work, reconstructed by way of psychology, sociology, philosophy or metaphysics, was given a particular image. This, once a new piece of evidence from an erudite academic was revealed, would see part of the interpretation collapse – hence the interest in well-known authors (Sade, Michelet, Mallarmé, Pascal, Rousseau). On the other hand, modern criticism made the work into a kind of gospel, in which no word or piece of punctuation was rejected as pure chance, play or irony, and in which the author was deemed to have meant exactly what was said. Concluding by giving examples and brief descriptions of a number of theorists, Nadeau ended with Barthes. Barthes's method, said Nadeau, was a synthesis of all the most recent trends described above. 'Marxist, Bachelardian, Sartrian', Barthes's critical practice was predominantly interested in language as a social instrument, in how language found 'certain structures' in the real and itself 'acted as if a structure of reality'.

The reference to Bachelard was an important point one. Praising the work of Jean-Pierre Richard in 1955, Barthes had attributed the notion of a writer's 'unconscious intentionality' to the Bachelardian theory (though Barthes had stressed that in concentrating more on the formal singularity of a writer than on a historicist view of content, Richard was moving beyond Bachelard's 'pre-scientific' category) (OCi 519–20). In

1959 Barthes had noted the importance of the 'imaginary' in writers' acts of constructing a poetic world (OCi 817); and Bachelard's presence had also been unmistakable in *Mythologies*, especially in the poetic analysis of food, even if a Bachelardian anthropologist had subsequently criticised Barthes's view of myth.[5] Bachelard's thought – characterised by an insistence on the essentially poetic nature of consciousness, a highly dialectical conception of science, and a belief in both the non-rational and the non-irrational nature of inquiry – was to be a major source of Barthes's epistemological adventurism in the 1960s.

Insisting on the 'open' concept of 'science' in Bachelard's work, Mary McAllester has shown the importance of 'fundamental incompleteness' for contemporary epistemology. Bachelard's 'approximate knowledge' seemed to be solving the problem of realism and rationality: reason and reality were interdependent, suggesting an effect of knowledge on the knowing subject.[6] For a critic concerned with both the dialectical and subjective acts of criticism, such a concept of science and poetry was fundamental. Thus, in the final essay of *On Racine*, the use of the Bachelardian view that poetic activity consists of 'deforming' images, when combined with an *Annaliste* critique of origins in history (OCi 1101/OR 169), was to be an important impetus not only towards psychoanalysis but also towards the 'Death of the Author'. It is worth stressing the negative dialectics in Bachelardian epistemology too. The 'philosophy of no' was not an obstinate refusal to listen but, on the contrary, an 'open philosophy' in which Bachelard sought to go beyond the reason/unreason dichotomy, typical of Freud, Husserl, Bergson, Descartes. We will see this at work in Barthes's seminal 1964 preface to the *Encyclopedia*. Bachelard's whole ethos – that thought should build on but supersede, extend but simultaneously work against, previous thought systems – was to become precisely Barthes's literary critical practice.

Rather than an investigation into *authors'* relationship to their literary product, Barthes began to insist upon the complexity of *readers'* relationship to it, be it in general from an objective twentieth-century point of view or from the particular subjective attitude of the critic. The ambiguous – or perhaps dialectical – shifting between objective and subjective perspectives of his critical practice was perhaps best illustrated by his attitude to critics working alongside him, such as Lucien Goldmann.

Barthes had praised Goldmann's *The Hidden God* in 1959 (OCi 817–8), and the similarity of Barthes's later ideas on 'intertextuality' to Goldmann's view, in the 1964 preface to *The Sociology of the Novel*, that literary creation was social not individual is unmistakable.[7] But Barthes's 1963 review of Goldmann's work was also important, because it set out the crucial differences that he had opened up in his understanding of 'form'.

In typically polite and deferential terms, reiterating the important break that all of Goldmann's work represented to him, Barthes now hinted at the limits to Goldmann's theories (OCi 1148–9). Already, in his first intervention in *TQ* in 1961, Barthes had called Goldmann's linking of the tragic form to a content a 'disguised determinism', a criticism which he repeated in *TQ* in 1964 (OCi 1285, 1369/CE 153, 271). Yet, in the latter, he considered that this 'disguised determinism' was justified in the case of Racine, since this classical dramatist did not appear 'at first' to be ideological in any way, in contrast to Michelet, for example, whose ideology was crystal clear (OCi 1371/CE 273–4). This 'stages' view of literary criticism helps us to understand one particular (apparent) confusion in his work.

Barthes's attitude to the British Hellenist and Communist Party fellow-traveller Georges Thomson, in relation to Lucien Goldmann, appeared contradictory. Praising Thomson's accounts of ancient Greek culture and its origins in the same breath as Bachofen and Engels on the one hand (OCi 1556/RF 87), Barthes was soon on the other hand critical of Thomson's 'sociological' insights in relation to poetry. The indecision was most glaring in *On Racine*. Thomson's idea was that the 'turnaround' ('revirement') in Greek culture which led to the rise of poetry had been caused by the 'passage' from a feudal to a mercantile system; an explanation relevant to the seventeenth-century tragedy of a Racine *only*, said Barthes, if used in an 'ideological explanation' such as Lucien Goldmann's (OCi 1017n1/OR 41n). But later in *On Racine* he considered Thomson's theories to be much less 'supple' than Goldmann's, with their 'brutally analogic relationship' between fifth-century BC overturn of ideas and the brisk move from rural to merchant economy and promotion of money (1100/169 n.1).[8]

We may wish then to explain this apparently contradictory attitude by way of Barthes's 'stages' approach to criticism. Wishing to avoiding repetition (as with Michelet), and wary of crude forms of determinism, the critic was a performer. The act of performing a criticism was a singular, unrepeatable one: Goldmann's work on Racine, in its ideological critique, had now opened up Racinian theatre to the possibility of a more formalist analysis. More dialectical than paradoxical then, one facet of Barthes's critical strategy was to start from a more radical and determinist view such as Goldmann's, to 'sit on the shoulders' of a historical materialist analysis. Thus, as Barthes put it at the end of *On Racine*, a work was both 'a sign of a history and a resistance to this history' (1090/155).

It was precisely in relation to these points about Goldmann that Robert Jones in 1968 distinguished Barthes's critical practice.[9] Not only had Barthes avoided the risk of determinism in his study of Racine, but also, like Sainte-Beuve, he had tried to 'get inside the skin' of Racine. Barthes had 'made Racine speak for himself, rather than Roland Barthes the modern critic doing it for him'.[10] Goldmann's work appeared 'pale' in comparison to Barthes's 'near total criticism'. For Jones, Barthes's study was a 'literary creation'; but he was not sure that this would work with Hugo, Balzac or Molière, suggesting that Barthes now ought to work instead on a more 'polyvalent and polymorphous', avant-garde writing. Ironically, as this book was published, Barthes was just beginning to apply his critical praxis to Balzac; but more importantly, Jones seemed to be taking Barthes's side in the wake of the heated debate over Racine and criticism in general that had erupted in the period 1963–6.

Picard versus Barthes

Much has been written on Barthes's joust with Sorbonne expert on Racine, Raymond Picard. In terms of the 'myth' of Barthes it was a crucial episode. If *Mythologies* had made him generally aware of his own mythology, the quarrel over *On Racine* showed he had begun to see himself reflected, often refracted, in the debate, as the self-awareness of the opening pages of *Criticism and Truth* displayed (OCii 17–29/CT 29–50). Importantly, it was Barthes's maverick account of Racinian theatre, rather than Goldmann's orthodox historical materialist analysis, which was singled out by the more traditional elements of the academy. Barthes underlined this point in *Criticism and Truth*: 'to be subversive, criticism does not need to judge, all it needs to do is talk about language'; and what the opponents of this did not like, he suggested, was the resultant 'redistribution of the role of author and commentator' (OCii 19/CT 33).

Barthes's attitude to Racine from the 1950s played an important role in his critical stance. An important point about *On Racine* was that it emerged from his popular theatre work. Marking his slow but steady departure from the popular theatre, the TNP production of Racine's *Phèdre* in 1958 had been little encouragement to a Barthes wanting a Brechtian politicised theatre. In a response to André Malraux's 'reform' of popular theatres a year later, which included a suggestion that more Racine be performed, Barthes sarcastically noted in a 1959 mythology, 'Tragedy and Nobility':

> All of our culture is saturated by Racine, performed everywhere from the TNP to companies touring the regions, analysed year after year in school, heaped with praise by the whole country from Thierry Maulnier to Vailland, from Kemp to the *Lettres françaises*. That's why we will be performing Racine just a little bit more. (OCi 814)

Published between two of the three constituent sections of *On Racine*, this rather bitter 'mythology' not only warned of a youth angered by such a diet (in an uncanny prediction of May 1968), but urged Malraux to have 'the courage to destroy' 'centuries of Racinian myth'. This was hardly the 'pleasure in the classics' ethos which Barthes had extolled in 1944: the irony of course was that, literature being what it is, subverting

Racine was the surest way of renewing interest in Racinian theatre.[11] This (apparent) rejection of Racinian theatre was an important element in Barthes's critical practice.

If Racine was 'dust in the theatre' (OCi 815), it could nevertheless still hold a certain polemic in allowing the critic to 'perform'. The critical power of the reader of theatre, as we noted above in relation to a Brecht play, could be equal to that of the director: the critic could 'correct' the more bourgeois and classical play by performing, re-presenting and (to continue the analogy with the theatre director) 'producing' it in a different way.[12] Of course, as with the theatre, a particular 'performance' was possible only once. So with the ideological imperative completed by Lucien Goldmann, Barthes could now take his sociological and 'performative' analysis to its formalist conclusion. Thus, Barthes in his aim to undermine the 'eternal truth' of Racinian theatre was no different in spirit to the director who played Racine in a certain way (OCi 986/OR ix). However, it was despite this theatrical ethos in Barthes's critical praxis that the argument over Racinian criticism developed. According to Bourdieu, there was a fundamentally academic tenor to the argument, as reviews of *On Racine* at the time suggested.[13] In *TQ* Jean-Louis Baudry praised above all the anthropological and social scientific aspect of Barthes's method.[14] Roland Albérès wondered why Barthes had to use the language of 'pedants' typical of a Molière play, rather than an 'honest language'.[15]

The other aspect of the quarrel which has been somewhat obscured was the amount of support given to Barthes. The view in *Criticism and Truth* that the attacks on him were 'collective' – echoed by Serge Doubrovsky[16] – appears to have been exaggerated (OCii 17/CT 30). In fact, there were a number of defences mounted, for example in *Le Monde*, the very place in which the argument had begun with Picard's 'review' of the *Critical Essays*.[17] Noting Guitton's comment that Picard's analyses of Racine would outlive his own, Barthes did not mention the other comments in the same article, made by a certain Henri Fluchère (OCii 18 n.3/CT n.5).[18] A professor at the University of Aix, Fluchère not only was *not* hostile to Barthes, but actually supported the renewal of criticism taking place. Barthes's views on the old form of literary criticism were far from 'contemptible', and, despite young people's fascination with new criticism, Fluchère predicted (with uncanny accuracy) that Barthes's style of criticism would itself one day become 'academic'. Similarly, the literary critic Manuel Diéguez – not noted for his affinity to Barthesian thought[19] – supported Barthes's efforts 'to show how a work questions the world rather than old criticism simply questioning a work'. Four days later, again in *Le Monde*, Lucien Goldmann now added his overall support – though, in his view (continuing the more conciliatory line that most 'defenders' of Barthes seemed to be taking), Lanson and Thibaudet had contributed important aspects to literary criticism, the problem being those who, following them, did not think that further reflection was needed.[20] The mitigated support for Barthes did not end there. The second round of debate a year later, in the wake of Picard's book-length attack, *Nouvelle critique ou nouvelle imposture?*, brought others out in Barthes's defence.[21]

Now the debate shifted grounds, from *Le Monde* to the *Nouvel-Observateur* and *Le Figaro littéraire*. In the latter, Guy Le Clec'h published interviews first with Picard, and, then, a week later, with Barthes.[22] Picard's comments made to Le Clec'h underlined the academic nature of the debate. Having stressed that Barthes too had used biographical accounts of Racine in noting his 'ingratitude', and having pointed to the literary inaccuracies of the consequences of Barthes's analyses of Racine, Picard gave an example of the methodological weaknesses that Barthes's study had inspired, reading from an undergraduate's essay on a Marivaux play. The analysis and logic were flawed; and though Barthes was perhaps not responsible, said Picard, the student's ideas were close to his. When asked if this was an exception, Picard regretted the manner in which his course on *Bajazet* had revealed that the students had all read Barthes with 'catastrophic results'. Bajazet had become an 'inconsistent being', which meant the tragic aspect disappeared: 'for two hours', Picard railed, 'I went back over things and sorted it out; following which the students were not at all happy with Barthes'. Finally, having rejected the 'game of chance' in which the *nouvelle critique* placed a work's meaning across the generations, Picard concluded that the new criticism did not appreciate the beauty of literature: 'it is like a man who is interested in women, but cannot appreciate them unless looking at them with an X-ray'.

Barthes's reply illustrated the manner in which the dialectical strategy of the 1950s was being continued into the next decade. The title given to Barthes's interview with Le Clec'h, 'Roland Barthes Considers Himself the True Guardian of National Values', completely misunderstood Barthes's comments on the 'ownership of Racine' (OCi 1563–5/GV 38–42). Though describing Racine, the most studied writer in school, as 'belonging to everyone', Barthes's comment that in Racine 'all the ideas of French national genius are reflected' was surely pure irony; for he followed this comment with: 'Racine represents a whole set of taboos which are excellent to destroy.' In response to Picard's charge that he too was using a 'biographical' form of criticism, Barthes now reiterated his critique of Joussain from 1950, in which he had rejected the denial of an individual's historical specificity. Picard's view that Racine's 'ingratitude' was well known, and that consequently Oreste in Racine's play *Andromaque* represented the playwright at 26 years of age, angered Barthes: 'what have', he thundered, 'all the people who are twenty-six years old actually got in common?' (1563/39). This type of biographical criticism which systematically linked an author's life to the work had, said Barthes, been rejected by psychologists. Furthermore, his own methodology, which showed that apparently different symbols could be linked by their common traits, both psychologically and psychoanalytically, was a distinctly twentieth-century one, which even the Vatican had acknowledged: he did not see why universities – adding fuel to the fire – should lag behind the church.

In response to Picard's charge that his making *Bajazet* 'inconsistent' undermined the tragedy of the play, Barthes brought out his Brechtian, anti-Aristotelian view that the inconsistent character of Bajazet was what held the tragedy together. Quoting Valéry at length, Barthes showed how university criticism, based on 'merit', tried to link a work to its author's intentions, whereas the *nouvelle critique*, a criticism of 'value', was more interested in how 'the work of the past linked with the reader of the present'. The confusion for Le Clec'h over Barthes's attitude towards literary nationalism, evident in the interview's title, clearly originated in the next comment. Insisting that it was he, not Picard, who had shown that Racine could still be read in the second half of the twentieth century, Barthes reiterated his earlier point about Racine being part of everyone, using an unfortunate turn of phrase which Le Clec'h made into the title of the interview: '*I* am the true guardian', he insisted against the author-based critical practice of a Picard, 'of national values.' Unless Barthes had very swiftly adopted a deeply nationalistic literary consciousness and forgotten his brutal critique of Racine in 1959, his comment was in fact a perfect example of the 'dialectic of love' strategy. His insistence that the *nouvelle critique* 'loved' its object of analysis, literature, was not only a response to Picard's comments on X-rays, but also a reminder of Barthes's dialectical strategy. He 'hated' Racine – a myth which served as an 'alienation' – but it was in Racinian theatre that he could find the people of his time. This attitude was summed up in the following comment in the interview: 'the *nouvelle critique* [. . .] reserves the right not only to pass over the object of its love but to *invest* it' (1564–5/41). We will come back to the question of whether there is any 'love' evident in *On Racine* in the next chapter.

After this interview, the debate intensified, with even *Rivarol* joining the fray.[23] Ex-colleague Jean Duvignaud signed a more than unfriendly account in the *Nouvel-Observateur*, under the ambiguous title of 'The Latest [Last?] Debate of the Avant-Garde'.[24] Barthes's own article in the same journal a week later, ' "If it Wasn't You . . ." ' (OCi 1537–8), was a rather damning criticism of Picard which made no mention of Duvignaud's comments. Misnaming (twice) Barthes's original study of Racine, and suggesting that it was one year (whereas it was at least two from Duvignaud's time of writing) since its publication, Duvignaud defended the *nouvelle critique*, but curiously not Barthes. Nevertheless, Barthes still had his supporters, of whom Bernard Pingaud was perhaps the most influential.

Pingaud's article in *Le Monde*, 'The *Nouvelle Critique* and its Defenders', replied in the 'affirmative' to Picard's question of whether Barthes's 'friends' were prepared to say that they stood by the analysis in *On Racine*. Disagreeing with Barthes's view that it was a question of 'new criticism' versus 'academic criticism', Pingaud wanted the debate to be taken outside of the purely institutional and academic terms in which Barthes had started the polemic. Pingaud meant to widen the challenge to encompass the 'common resistance' to an 'immanent' and worldly form of criticism, whose indifference was much more 'condescending' than the claims of new criticism.[25] Perhaps the most supportive and perceptive of articles was by Georges Raillard.[26] His account of the debate went to the heart of the polemic. He pointed out that university criticism could handle psychoanalytical and Marxist concepts in the new critical practice, but that it was the 'elsewhere', fixing the meaning of a work for all time, which Barthes rejected. But also, as Raillard pointed out, with Barthes's method 'we can establish a bridge between a dead past and our present concerns'.[27]

The publication of *Criticism and Truth* in March 1966 marked what Jean Bloch-Michel called 'round three' of the Picard/Barthes affair.[28] François Nourissier found the notoriety of the debate an 'absurdity', especially since Barthes's publisher, Seuil, had wrapped *Criticism and Truth* (as French publishers often do) in the words 'Should we burn Roland Barthes?'[29] But once again, Barthes was certainly not left on his own in the joust. Alongside works by Boris Vian, Beauvoir and Sartre, *Criticism and Truth* was one of the books that 'one should have read in 1966', according to *Options*; and for Pierre Daix, it was Barthes's 'best book'.[30] Though unimpressed by the *Critical Essays*, Yves Bertherat in his review thanked Picard for showing him why the *nouvelle critique* was important.[31] The last word in the debate went to Picard, who published his own view of *Criticism and Truth* in *Le Nouvel-Observateur*, 'A Comfortable Nihilism'. Reaffirming his belief in the 'solidity of language', Picard humorously called Barthes's method of joining science and creativity a 'science fiction'.[32] This sober and calming article, which considered Barthes's definition of criticism of literature as the 'death' both of the former and of the latter, was to fall on deaf ears: by the end of the month, after nearly three years of quarrel, Barthes had flown off to Japan.

It is difficult to assess the whole 'Picard' episode without reference to Barthes's career – some might say structurally. Clearly, there was an attack which singled Barthes out; but it seemed to suit him to generalise and overstate its power. As some of the reviews of *Mythologies* had suggested, and as his defence of Brecht and Sartre had displayed in the 1950s, Barthes tended to schematise in order to criticise. This is not at all to detract from the criticisms levelled at him, but to point out a strategy employed to deal with them. It suggested that the quarrel was not so much a politicisation as a polemicisation of literary criticism, in which there was no simple division between left and right. This blurring of the political implications of Barthes's work, evident already in the reactions to *Mythologies*, was perhaps a result of the eclectic procedures which characterised his work between 1957 and 1963. Barthes is often considered what François Dosse has called the 'mother figure' of structuralism.[33] But his entry into the formal structures of academic research was accompanied, if not dominated, by a hesitant and questioning reflection on the appropriate methodology.

Clothes/System, History/Function

If structuralism in the social sciences can be understood as a complex combination of Saussurian linguistics and functionalism, then Barthes's contribution to this mode of analysis was a highly ambiguous one. The 'dialectic of love' had set out an ambivalent attitude to social and cultural phenomena; similarly a dialogue took place in his sociological work, the *ir*resolution of which constituted itself an element of the methodology. This was evident in the battle over the usefulness of functionalism.

The linguistic and functionalist nature of structuralism has encouraged many to see it as guilty of 'evacuating' the human subject. In Henri Lefebvre's view, Barthes's structuralist analyses betrayed very little that was 'tragic' ('heurté') or 'full of passion' ('passionel').[34] Indeed, much of Barthes's work on clothes suggested that he had left behind the voluntarism of his earlier Marxian attachment to 'History' being made by popular actants. But before we look at his early analysis of clothing form, why choose clothes?

In voluntarist, and popular culturalist, terms, nothing is more mass and widespread than the clothes that we wear; nothing could be easier to innovate than the combinations of materials used to cover ourselves and project our 'identity' onto the world. However, and here was a crucial problem for Barthes, how was it that this most accessible form of self-expression (almost infinitely variable, especially since it was a projection of individual bodies) was, at the same time, the most structured, limited and formal of human social practices? Could we, following on from the 'degree zero' thesis, consider that 'History' was the determining factor in the forms that clothes took? In typical Barthesian style, this discussion – on the nature and extent of the determinant factors in the changes of fashion over history – was treated rather obliquely in the appendix to *The Fashion System* (OCii 373–7/FS 294–300). But in the 1957 article it had been the central debate.

An impressive study of the methods used so far to understand the history of clothes – hence the subtitle 'Some Methodological Observations' – 'History and Sociology of Clothes' was first and foremost indicative of Barthes's ability to conduct involved and detailed academic research. He began by describing how accounts of clothes in France had been virtually non-existent before the nineteenth century, and that those in evidence up until the 1860s had been essentially 'romantic', either supplying theatre designers and artists with a bit of 'local colour', or providing evidence of a particular spirit pertaining to a particular time or place (what he called '*Volks-*' or '*Zeitgeist*'). Real attempts to provide a scientific account of clothes did not begin properly, he suggested, until after 1860, when 'archivists' began to see what people wore as a kind of historical event, requiring a date and account of circumstances.

Barthes's main point was that this event-based view of clothes was still dominant in the 1950s, feeding the growing commercial myth of 'fashion'. This method had not benefited from the recent innovations in historical studies, such as the economic and social dimension of history, Lucien Febvre's definition of the links between clothes and 'human mentalities', and the Marxist insistence on the ideological nature of the past. In short, the 'institutional perspective' on clothes was missing in the nineteenth-century methodology of analysing clothing forms. This 'gap' was not surprising, said Barthes, since it was common to all 'historicist history' of this sort. Continuing the view that the contradiction of change and order was the major problem for 'modern historiography' (suggested in his critique of Caillois and Michelet in 1951), he now suggested that it was a much more general epistemological difficulty:

> The problem [. . .] is that posed by the analysis of any structure, as soon as this structure is placed in its history, but is not allowed to stop being a structure: a piece of clothing is indeed, at every moment of history, this balance of normative forms, but all of which are constantly changing. (OCi 741–2)

And, whereas Barthes had suggested in 1951 that Marx had solved the problem for historiography, his view here was that histories of clothes had solved the contradiction only 'by confusion'.

Barthes showed how the nineteenth-century histories of clothes had not even grasped the problem, by noting that they recorded, without knowing it, two (separable) levels of differences and changes. The first he called 'internal'. Changes in shape had been noted, but there was a general failure to define how a particular shape related to the values of any particular period. These he called 'the constraints', 'that which is ruled out or tolerated, considered an aberration or compatible, fantasies and exclusions'. In short, no one had defined the set of rules in any one 'clothes system' at any one time: all historians had managed was to describe simply what changed, with no clear distinction between a change in a piece's form and a change in its function. Barthes wanted to know when something really had changed, in its form *and* its function – when there 'really was some history' taking place.

The 'external level of change' had also been poorly treated in histories of clothes. Though this level linked clothes to history in general, which might be easier to trace, these histories thus far had again failed to spot the 'epistemological difficulty'. Rather than use the folklorists' geographical law, which stated that 'every clothes system is either regional or international, but never national', the historians had employed a national analysis. This was always based on an aristocratic leadership in fashion, which was never put in its political context (for example, European). Furthermore, said Barthes, they only ever discussed royal or aristocratic clothes. This meant not only that they ignored the 'ideological content' of these clothes, but also that clothes were not seen in their working, i.e. class, context: 'all the problem of the functionalisation of clothes was completely ignored'. Having set out these 'differential descriptions', Barthes concluded, in good *Annales* style, that a 'slightly wider view of history' could correct deficiencies (p. 743), by applying the notion of *longue durée* and insisting on the necessarily *im*precise nature of historical dating with regard to clothes and changes.

Another important mistake, suggested Barthes, had been to confuse the internal and external differences without looking at the methodology this implied: the changes in the signifier (one of Barthes's earliest uses of the word) were too often confused with those of the signified. The first problem was that these two histories were not the same. Clothing form had its own rhythm, and the changes in form had a 'relative independence' from the history in general which 'supports them': the finite 'archetypal forms' of clothing were dependent on a cyclical history, clearly not compatible with a linear one. Second, the numerous moments of speeding up and slowing down in history meant that the signifier and the signified could not be placed in a simple trajectory. However, considering clothes as an 'institution' and clothing as an individual concrete act allowed us to see the former's relation to age, sex, class and so on, whilst the latter remained a purely empirical phenomenon. The degree of untidiness or dirtiness was not a sociological fact, because it did not signify and so did not become part of the clothes system – 'unless', said Barthes, harking back to his appreciation of Brecht's sensitivity to costumes and theatre signs, 'we are watching a play'.

This was an interesting distinction. To suggest that dirtiness and untidiness were outside of sociology pointed to a rather restricted definition: surely (to take the most obvious example) this *was* a sign (unintentional or not) of poverty. Though not his first treatment of Saussure ('Myth Today' was largely written in summer 1956), the article pointed to an uneasiness with Saussurian linguistics. He warned against 'pushing blindly the analogy' which attempted to link the Saussurian distinction between 'grammar' ('langue') and 'utterance' ('parole') to account for forms of clothes: it was, he stressed, only the 'functional opposition' of the two levels which was of use. Early in the article he suggested in a footnote that the language used in the history of clothes was of little help – a change in function did not necessarily mean a change in name, and vice versa (OCi 742 n.2). He concluded by making his reservations on using language as an explanatory category explicit:

> We must at least propose two methodological precautions in this effort of final explanation, which is both structural and historical, by looking immediately at the experience of linguistics. First, we must make the notion of system more flexible, consider structures in terms of tendencies perhaps rather than in terms of a rigid equilibrium; clothes live in close symbiosis with their historical context, much more so than language; violent historical episodes (wars, exoduses, revolutions) can rapidly smash a system; but also, in contrast to language, the recasting of the system is much quicker. (p. 749)

Yet this mild scepticism towards the analogy of clothes with language was soon to disappear. The analogy with language was precisely what *The Fashion System* would use.

This study of the methodology of analysing clothes forms was important for his overall conception of sociology in 1957. The event-based history of clothes was not, he suggested, the only 'major' methodological deficiency. The psychological approach to clothes, typical of Anglo-Saxon thought, had also failed to 'unite at every moment the history and sociology of clothes'. Proposing protection, modesty and ornamentation as the three crucial reasons for which humans began to wear clothes, the psychological approach's view that the ornamentation motive was by far the most important was, for Barthes, pure 'illusion':

> [D]efining a social fact such as clothes as the sum of a certain number of instincts, which, identified on a strictly individual level, are then simply 'multiplied' to the group level is precisely the problem which sociology wants to get beyond. What should really interest the researcher, historian or sociologist, is not the shift from protection to ornamentation (an illusory shift), but the tendency of every bodily covering to insert itself into an organised, formal and normative system recognised by society. (OCi 744)

Barthes's example here was the manner in which Roman soldiers throwing wool cloth over themselves to keep warm had become part of a fashion system. Prefiguring the 'Death of the Author' thesis, which denied the relevance of authorial intention, he stressed the absence of aesthetic intention in clothes: 'the garment has become clothes without our being able to find in this shift any trace of an aesthetic aim'. This comment also had a resonance with his account of Michelet's writing of history.

The Roman soldiers acted in a particular way which had unforeseen and therefore unintentional consequences: their attempts to stay warm became part of a different social function. In the same way, Michelet's giving meaning retrospectively to the excluded masses, the 'social volume' of people acting in history, Barthes had suggested in 1950, had allowed these people to act upon history, despite having no knowledge of the significance of their acts. His work on clothes suggested not only a connection between Michelet's 'voice' for the forgotten masses of history and the literary critic speaking for the 'dissolved' and absent author, but also a modification of his voluntarist view of history.

Indeed, the rest of the article was a categorical denial of the influence of history on clothing forms, in a manner which appeared to be a development from the 'degree zero' view of history and literary form. '[V]iolent historical facts may disrupt the rhythms of fashion, bring in new systems and modify the regime of participation', declared Barthes, 'but in no way do they explain the new forms' (OCi 751). He now denied the *fundamentally* crucial nature of history that we saw in his earlier writings:

> The study of costume must retain continually the plurality of these [internal and external] determinisms. The central methodological warning is still never to postulate hastily a direct equivalence between the superstructure (clothes) and the infrastructure (history). Contemporary epistemology understands more and more the necessity of studying the historico-social totality as a collection of links and functions: we believe that for clothes (as for language), these stages and functions are of an axiological nature; they are the *values* which bear witness to the creative power of society over itself. (OCi 752)

Why, we may ask, would literature be different? Why was it that the period 1848–51 had been a crucial determinant in an explanation of the subsequent plurality of writings, but that a historical determinant had to be used extremely carefully with clothes?

Clearly, the specificity of innovation in clothes was very different from that of writing and innovating literary forms. Clearly also, as the Marxian terminology here implied, Barthes was rejecting a facile historical materialist analysis of forms in clothing. It was almost as if, in concentrating on forms that apparel took, he had found a space *outside* the direct determination of 'History'. This was not so much a utopian 'space' as described by Diana Knight,[35] but a case *in extremis* in which 'system' could be seen to be more important than historical determinant. Thus, by placing function over causality, the contradiction of change and structure could be obviated by a functional account of clothes within a system. This critique of historical determinism also seemed to have repercussions on his views of the relationship between the individual and the system.

Barthes's critique of a historical materialist account in history of clothing forms was linked to his final point, which reiterated the importance of a critique of histories of clothes hitherto. Since the 'science' of clothes history had been born around the same time as all other human sciences, the study of clothes necessarily threw up a crucial question for all 'sciences of culture': how to account, simultaneously, for both individual and system:

> [T]he history of clothes has a general epistemological value: it actually suggests to the researcher the essential problems in all cultural analysis, culture being both system and process, institution and individual act, a reserve of expression and a signifying order. [. . .] [It] bears witness in its own way to the contradiction in any science of culture: every cultural fact is both a product of history and a resistance to history. (OCi 752)

Was this conflict in the analysis of culture making a similar point to the contradiction of structure and change he had discovered earlier? For, here, Barthes did seem to be linking these two contradictions – change/order, individual/system – in the same way as he had linked and criticised Joussain and Caillois for their attempts to deny that humans made history. But he seemed to be saying now that it was the *denial of singularity* in a formalist use of analogy which prevented us from seeing how people signified resistance to a system. In other words, formalism was no longer considered a historiographical error. With this in mind, we can make some general points about Barthes's use of history in his analysis of clothes.

First, the oblique questioning of history as determinant of form was (paradoxically) dependent on a history of forms. Second, this inspired a formalist modification of his voluntarist historiography. Elizabeth Wilson has suggested that *The Fashion System* is not at all functionalist, but tied to a conspiracy-theory view of fashion.[36] For one thing, functionalism and conspiracy are not at all mutually exclusive. On the contrary, surely *Mythologies* showed that to impute social order without an agent can be paradoxically conspiratorial. Though the description of the myth of fashion is much longer and weightier than the ideological critique, to suggest that *The Fashion System* is not functional in its analysis implies a restricted sense of the term: the whole book is based on analysing the functioning of fashion, though without a rather crude imputation of blame, control and so on. Thus Wilson is right to see Barthes's analysis as in a 'vacuum', but not for the right reasons. Barthes retained the functionalism of his 1957 article, but remained on the internal level for the most part, over and above the external (historical) level, suggesting a connection between functionalism and a questioning of voluntarist historiography. Nowhere did Barthes deny categorically that people made history; but there is a link between functionalism, *longue durée* and an 'evacuation' of the subject from history.

I suggested in Part One that Barthes was influenced by the *Annales* in the post-war period. I noted the similarity of the defining feature of the *Annales* in the 1950s, the *longue durée* view of history, to Trotsky's account of the bourgeoisie's long accession to power which had informed the 'degree zero' thesis.[37] This long-term view of change was a crucial mode of his analysis of clothes and fashion forms. To consider history as made up of many rhythms over a long period (longer than any one individual's life, in any case) *and* to reject psychological factors seems to be formulaic in the extreme. This functionalism fitted with his analysis of Michelet's account of history: how was it possible that people make history (formally) without this being part of a longer and greater design? Michelet's great skill, in Barthes's argument after all, had been to resurrect forgotten actants, and then to give a meaning to their lives by showing the effect of their actions on and in future events. Thus, both Michelet's historiography and Barthes's proposed methodology for analysing clothes denied a certain mystery and contingent absurdity in the repercussions and repetition of historical phenomena. It was precisely this kind of 'hindsight' of functionalism which Yves Velan had rejected in his criticism of *Mythologies*.[38] Another importance of functionalism for Barthes was that it could be seen to solve the 'platypus' problem mentioned earlier. To explain a form by its functional relationship to a system seemed to allow the exception a place of sorts both within and against a 'historico-social totality'.

Two conclusions are possible from Barthes's 'parametric' shift with regard to fashion. The change in his object of study may have resulted from a realisation that the study of fashion (not to mention clothes in history) was so long and difficult to perform that he had to limit himself to its language. If so, then this shift tended to ignore, if not deny, the 'expressive reserve' which he had seen in clothes history in 1957, and presented fashion as something which we have to suffer as an impersonal whim of some fashion machine (a rather depressing determinist view of clothes). Or there may have been a tacit recognition that he had failed to solve the history/structure question in relation to clothes. Indeed, as I suggested earlier, his choice of object for study was an important one; for clothes are at two ends of a pole, both the easiest and one of the most fundamental acts of human existence. If we can see this shift of object as a triumph of structure over 'History', then it is no coincidence that Barthes began other studies of fundamental aspects of human existence around this time. Food, clothes and shelter were now set as topics in his seminars at the EPHE (OCi 1153). However, it was not as simple as this. Barthes's growing interest in the image, photographic and cinematic, showed how certain media could escape the 'poverty' of linguistic form.

Image, Form, Analogy

The promotion of language to the key level of analysis of the fashion system had other effects on his work. By 1963, Barthes was challenging the scientific basis of the tools being used. His comments on the structuralist activity taking place were important in relation to the history/structure debate:

> Structuralism does not remove history from the world: it tries to link to history not only contents (this has been done thousands of times) but also forms, not only the material [of history] but also the intelligible, not only the ideological, but also the aesthetic. And precisely because all thought on the historically intelligible is also participation in this intelligible, it is perhaps of little importance to structural man to be permanent: he knows that structuralism itself is also a certain *form* of the world, which will change with the world; just as he experiences its validity (but not its truth) in its ability to speak the world's ancient languages in a new way, so he knows that

> it needs only a new language to come from history for its job to have been finished. (OCi 1333/CE 219–20)

The provisional (and distinctly Popperian) nature of Barthes's view of structuralism here was a response to the Marxist critique that structural accounts denied, or at least relegated, 'History'. Barthes's response to this critique was simply to underline the necessarily historical nature of structuralism itself. Written in 1963, these comments suggest that, in locating Jacques Derrida as the first to question the scientism of structuralist analysis, François Dosse has overlooked Barthes's contribution.[39]

Indeed, this questioning of a functionalist-structuralist orthodoxy was being applied to his sociological research on the image (both moving and photographic) in the early 1960s. In a series of pieces for *Communications* on mass culture, reminiscent of his powerful 1953 study of the 'theft' of face and human alienation and reification, 'Features and Faces', he analysed images in the media. He combined the 'dialectic of love' strategy of 'refinding his contemporaries' with the analysis developed by Edgar and Violette Morin, into what he called the 'star-making' ('vedettisation') tendency of human consciousness.

This did not mean that his fashion methodology had made no impact. Important in this paradoxical and complex view of social psychology was his view that the 'vedettisation' came 'from nothing' (OCi 1132). It was precisely within this double paradox – first, people saw phenomena both passively *and* actively, both accepted *and* challenged them, and second, the phenomena themselves had no origin, and their promotion to stardom could not be explained – that fashion was seen to operate. The conclusion to his research on 'vedettisation' was in line with the conclusions of his study of fashion: analysing the press through which the stars were communicated by interviewing an audience told one nothing about their interest. But Barthes now seemed to reject a functionalist analysis in his sociological inquiry into the image, nuancing the arch-structuralist view that the burgeoning mass cinema culture was depriving people of their individuality.

His tentative research in 1963, 'Media Stars: Questioning the Audience?' (OCi 1111–35), tried to analyse (or at least find a methodology for analysis of) the manner in which people reacted to the proliferating, and increasingly domineering, phenomena in mass culture. Interestingly, most of his interviewees, he concluded, seemed to receive the 'vedettisation' of culture dialectically. There was both acceptance and challenge in the popular perception of Brigitte Bardot, royal families (both British and Monegasque), Soviet leader Khrushchev, and the very media through which these 'stars' were seen (OCi 1132). This dialectical response was paralleled by a realisation that people did not simply try to be 'other', as the 'Features and Faces' article had regretted, but that we simultaneously saw 'the other' and ourselves in the stars reifying our cultural experience. He called this paradoxical response the 'double other'. He made a similar point in relation to the mythology of the car. No longer representing the dream of humanity (as the Citroën DS had been seen to do in *Mythologies*), 1960s car culture was now a reflection of the freedom to be oneself, rather than someone else or 'elsewhere' (OCi 1141).

The resistance to a functionalist methodology returned in a review of the First International Conference on visual information held in Milan in July 1961, published in *Communications*, where Barthes regretted the manner in which interest at the conference had centred on the 'effects' of visual culture (OCi 953–5). Though of interest, the idea that 'the image can transform psychism' was perhaps, he suggested, a little out of date. More important than a picture's 'causality' was the image's ability to 'signify' this psychism: 'the image necessarily transports *something other* than itself, and this *something other* cannot be without a link to the society which produces and consumes it'. Research into the 'effects' of visual culture was 'disappointing' because it ignored the most recent studies of mass culture which showed that, rather than modifying, such information 'confirms above all the beliefs, dispositions, feelings and ideologies which are already given by the social, economic and cultural state of the public analysed'. Thus Barthes's subject-oriented view of visual culture wanted to question a purely functionalist view of media. In line with the 'dialectic of love' strategy, he wanted to see media images as indicative of a 'true history of the contemporary world' (pp. 954–5), what he called in relation to the study of motivations a 'psycho-sociology' analysing the 'total situation of the consumer' (p. 949). Comments such as these suggested that the developing structuralist-functionalist analysis was in constant conflict with a more Marxian awareness of psychic reification, a conflict which was illustrated in another article on photography.

In 1961, a year of intense work on photography it seems, Barthes published 'The Photographic Message' (OCi 938–48/RF 3–20) in *Communications*, a study of denotation and connotation that would have a bearing on the analysis of literary codes in *S/Z*. The paradoxical nature of the photograph in communication terms – it was merely an '*analogon*' of reality, yet it connoted constantly in the viewer's mind – constituted an important element in the 'consumerist' attitude to communication that he was advocating against the 'effects' approach. This held that the cultural code with which we looked at a photograph was more important than its denotative status. Thus, Barthes noted, there was a paradox at the heart of photography: photographs were taken in order to connote without their appearing to do so. The addition of text to photographs was just another element in this paradox.

Here, his study of fashion had clearly influenced his analysis. The view of the written connotation exterior to the photo (in both the writing accompanying it and the acculturated eye of the viewer) was a crucial element in his study of fashion; fashion was at once fully justified in its form, and yet (apparently) a form devoid of meaning, able 'to make something out of nothing'. But the final section of this article, 'Photographic Insignificance', was suggesting something far more important. The photograph could escape the structures of language, in a manner which prefigured the specificity of photography in his later work. The stills of Eisenstein, the theory of the 'punctum', would later replicate this more 'human' (albeit reified, lost) aspect of the 'communicating' phenomenon of the photograph. This 'reserve' from the highly determining powers of mass culture requires us to nuance our view of Barthesian structuralism.

Barthes's methodology in the study of clothes and then fashion clearly tended towards a functionalist evacuation of 'humanity'.

Functionalism's concentration on a phenomenon's effect or set of effects removes agency and also allows for an infinitely relativist form of interpretation. But the continued work on human alienation suggested that this was not his only contribution to the structuralism/ 'History' debate. The battle between these forms of analysis – functionalist on the one hand and human-dominated, in the form of alienation, on the other – seemed only to show to Barthes the impossibility of resolution. He had criticised a 'two-term' dialectical strategy in Michelet in 1951, saw it as inevitable at the end of 'Myth Today' in 1957, and now praised it in Edgar Morin's work in 1965 (OCi 1535–6). This irresolution suggested that a thorough formalism in social theory, encouraged by the study of fashion, was the only possible step to take. The Popperian and Einsteinian dimensions of the 'parametric' nature of analysis might have confirmed Henri Lefebvre's view of Barthes's 'dialectical thought of becoming'. But this dialectical relativism was mistaken by Lefebvre for a disinterested and inhuman form of criticism. His view that Barthes's style was 'cool' rather than hot misunderstood the wavering in Barthes's analyses. For, though anti-hysterical preoccupations dominated his ways of operating, there was much in Barthes's thought which was 'tragic', Gidian, if not conventionally 'passionate'. Previously rejected as alienating of human culture, form and analogy now became the arena in which Barthes's contradictory but distinctly human analyses would be played out.

4

Rhetoric, Theory, Surface

One suggestion . . . is that everything in the world exists in order to end up as a book.

Stéphane Mallarmé

There will be no need of science the day when essence and appearance become one.

Karl Marx

WITHIN THE RISE OF the critic, and the putative new discipline of 'criticology' emerging in the mid-1960s, Barthes was considered, not surprisingly, an important point of reference. Indeed, his name was invoked with stunning regularity at the 1966 Cerisy conference on literary criticism.[1] Naturally, this popularity and intellectual currency were tempered by antipathy in certain quarters. Giving a lecture at the Pesaro film festival in Italy in 1966, Barthes was theorising the cinema too much, in Michel Cournot's view. He, Christian Metz and Pier Paolo Pasolini were creating an 'obsession' with 'cinematographic language', what Cournot called 'OB', the 'Barthes Obsession'.[2] Nevertheless, the polemic unleashed by *On Racine* and the *Critical Essays*, as well as the work on narrative structures and the sociology of cinema images in *Communications*, meant that his opinion was sought regularly in the press after 1964 on diverse topics, from 'Artists and Politics' through James Bond to the anti-Semitic writer Céline.[3]

Barthes's response in 1965 to the question of the artist's relation to politics summed up the formal radicalism which was to characterise his writing for the next decade. He divided the possibilities for the writer into two – there was both a 'wide' and a 'narrow' door through to politics. He considered the first to be more conducive to conceptual and ideological choices (Marxist, Liberal and so on); but the second, though 'narrower', opened out onto a 'road going much further' than the first door:

> It is a question [. . .] of grasping the manner in which men speak about, act out and are alienated by, politics, a set of meanings which feeds a work. There isn't a day when, reading a newspaper, watching a TV programme, listening to a taxi driver, I don't want to transform what I read or hear into what I call mythological material, that is precisely into a discourse which is between criticism and the novel. (*Arts* 10 (1965), p. 10)

May 1968 did not profoundly engage him – politically, Barthes's intervention was insignificant compared to that of a Sartre, or even a Morin. None the less it would still be incorrect to deny the influence of this period of social and ideological turmoil. We will see this most clearly in Part Three, particularly in the hedonistic and erotic writing of the early 1970s. Though I do not intend to relate Barthes's thought to its history, in and immediately after the extraordinary events of 1968, there is quite clearly a shift of perception, worthy of Hébert's obscenities described at the beginning of *Writing Degree Zero.* One need only compare an interview in the Communist journal *Les Lettres françaises* in March 1967 with that a year later in July 1968 in the same journal. The change in language and perspective is colossal, from seeing the fundamental problem as the 'language of literary science' to asking how to perform a critique of an alienated 'capitalist culture' (compare OCii 453–61/GV 43–55 with OCii 523–7). We are talking, after all, about a pre-revolutionary situation. The students might have used barricades as 'signs' rather than as military tactics, but for the time the biggest general strike in human history (involving up to ten million workers) and the flight of de Gaulle to Germany to muster an army do not fall, *pace* Keith Reader, into the category of the 'symbolic'.[4]

Naturally, to diminish the significance of the 'symbolic' nature of the 'events' does not obviate the historiographical dilemmas of how to represent them. After all, the portrayal of history and the Revolution was central to Barthes's first piece on Michelet. And this relegation of the symbolic to the 'superstructural' level does not deny the influence of Barthes's ideas on the explosion. Indeed, as Patrick Combes has pointed out, the 'degree zero' thesis had a noticeable effect on revolutionary outfits such as the International Situationists.[5] In its 1963 bulletin, noting how language was at the centre of all challenges to alienation, the IS considered fundamental to avant-garde action the voluntarist/determinist dichotomy in *Writing Degree Zero,* which saw writing as a compromise between 'freedom and memory'. Combes also considers Barthes's review of Philippe Sollers's 1968 novel *Nombres* as one of a number of heralds of the coming social and political storm.

'The Refusal to Inherit', included as part of *Sollers Writer,* was originally a review published in the *Nouvel-Observateur* on 30 April 1968, literally days before the revolt broke out (OCiii 947–9/SW 69–74). The opening words – 'The idea of revolution is dead in the West' – were not a repeat of André Gorz's gross mis-recognition of the mood developing,[6] but heralded the 'literary contestation' which defined the 'passage between revolution and writing'. Barthes's belief that 'the subversion and ignition' of the 'plural' of 'quotes, numbers, masses, mutations, etc.' which began Sollers's novel could be revolutionary (949/74) proved uncannily correct in the following weeks.

Barthes's association with Sollers and *TQ* was important not just from the point of view of May 1968. It fixed an epistemological tendency which had developed out of the adventurism evident in the 1950s. The relationship began with the *Critical Essays,* one of the first books to be published in Seuil's 'Tel Quel' series, which supported the new avant-garde literary journal's rise to fame. The inclusion in the *Critical Essays* of two interviews which had appeared in *TQ* in 1961 and 1964 only increased this prominence. Totally away from academia in a sense, *TQ* seemed to become a way out of the more sober sociological studies that Barthes had been conducting for the EPHE. This was evident above all in the way that the breakdown of the opposition between literature and science, crucial to the theoretical fundamentalism typical of *TQ,* was replicated and developed in Barthes's work. In his account of May 1968, Patrick Combes juxtaposes two apparently very different attitudes towards revolt: creation and spontaneity (by José Pierre) on the one hand, and theory and anti-spontaneity on the other (*TQ*). Collapsing the oppositions of theory/creation and intellectualism/spontaneity, Barthes straddled these two tendencies of the period.[7]

As part of this 'modernisation' of the human sciences, and in parallel to his avant-garde literary activity, Barthes embarked on an impressive study – and eventually practice – of rhetoric. Emerging from his seminars in 1964 and 1965, 'The Old Rhetoric' (OCii 901–59/SC 11–94) was a thorough and academic piece of work which suggested, amongst other things, that the label of 'Hellenist' might also be added to Jonathan Culler's list of Barthes's attributes.[8] Published in *Communications* in 1970, this modestly subtitled 'aide-mémoire' was one of Barthes's last publications in the EPHE journal. Fittingly, its publication mirrored the (self-consciously) rhetorical writing practice which, as we shall see in Part Three, was set to dominate the last decade of Barthes's life. With its concentration on the figures and devices of rhetorical performance, the article also pointed, perhaps deliberately, to the techniques that Barthes himself used in his own essayistic strategies. For example, we should not be surprised to find the 'exordium' (the opening gambit of rhetorical discourse) described by Barthes (OCii 949–50/SC 82) as a common feature in his own writing and lecturing. This study also set out in detail the relevance of rhetoric, and of Aristotle in particular, to contemporary studies of mass culture.[9] Above all, it suggested a continuation of an epistemological adventurism. If all communication is language, and all language a function of rhetoric, then disciplines and the barriers between various *epistemes* can simply be melted away, but without losing the specificity of the language used. If it is possible to talk of 'surface' as 'depth' in Barthes's thought and writing, then rhetoric was the key element in this. It was almost as if a study of rhetoric could unite the avant-garde and the academic, with Barthes's assessment of Sollers's first experimental novel *Drame* serving as a good example.

Barthes's dualistic approach in the 1960s, combining both academic and avant-garde concerns, was evident in his changing use of psychoanalysis. Against those 'good' psychoanalysts who allowed May 1968 to be seen as a 'healthy' letting-off of steam, Maud Mannoni championed the anti-psychiatry tradition which saw psychic 'disorder' as evidence of creativity and even of revolutionary potential.[10] Far from solving the problems of psychic disorder, Barthes's understanding and use of psychoanalysis, in this tradition, were to harness theories of the unconscious to propel acts of creation and creativity. Elizabeth Roudinesco has insisted that Barthes, though using psychoanalytical discourse like another language, played an important role in the 'great universalist implantation' of psychoanalysis not only into literary criticism but also throughout French thought. Replaying the surrealist critique of the dominant Cartesian tradition in French thought which divided the head and the heart, Barthes in his argument with Picard had insisted on the existence in Racinian theatre of both rationality *and* barbarity.[11] Psychoanalysis, like historical materialism, became a language through which this collapse could be articulated. *On Racine* was Barthes's first sustained use of psychoanalysis; and according to Roudinesco that work's perspective, though using Freudian terminology, was 'as far removed from psychobiography as it was from psychocriticism'.[12] However, as we shall see, the psychoanalytical 'grid' as an explanatory category might ignore the author, but it tended to close down the literary and poetic heart to Racinian theatre. Far from showing any of the 'love' that Barthes went on to claim for his study of Racine in 1965, it could even ignore that heart.

Psychoanalysis: From Naturalisation to Formalisation

> The world of psychoanalysis, though defined by the bright light of explanation, remains a world of the Obscure.
>
> Roland Barthes

Clearly, there is much in *On Racine* which went hand in hand with the *Critical Essays.* However, we must not allow this to cloud our view of what Barthes was doing in his study of Racinian theatre. *On Racine* was a practical attempt to bring the most recent and exciting developments of the social sciences into the literary field.

In complete contrast to the ethos of the preface to the *Critical Essays,* which stipulated that a literary critic should superimpose a 'supplementary mask' on the literary object of study (OCi 1176/CE xxi), Barthes's application of psychoanalytical symbolism had certainly not attempted such a superimposition on Racine's dramatic poetry. Thus, the gap between *On Racine* and the *Critical Essays* represented a shift of perspective in Barthesian literary criticism. This point was made persuasively by Dominique Noguez in 1966, arguing that, between the two books, Barthes had moved from a critique of 'content' to a critique of forms. Speaking at the same conference as Noguez, Raymond Jean pointed out that Barthes's critical praxis was now one not of revealing or discovering, but of *recovering* a set of possibilities which revealed an erotic perspective, which both violated *and* loved the text in question.[13] This concept of 'recovering' ('recouvrir') – a pun on 'finding again' and 'running across once more' – is important in assessing Barthes's study of Racine. It would be difficult to see how *On Racine* was in fact 'recovering' Racinian theatre, let alone displaying a 'dialectic of love'. This is most evident in the first and longest part, 'Racinian Man'.

Ignoring the specifically theatrical aspect of Racine's theatre, particularly in the performative criticism that Barthes was operating, 'Racinian Man' also deliberately avoided talking about the poetic and literary 'qualities' of the seventeenth-century dramatist. If anything, the involved analysis of the second half of this first part, 'The Works', 'explained' meticulously the textual logic of the characters in a manner which tended to evacuate all mystery: form was sacrificed to interpretation. It used Freudian and psychoanalytical terminology – eros, enclosure, parental conflict – in a structural (i.e. non-biographical) fashion. The 'resistance' to history that Barthes saw in cultural phenomena – even suggested in 'History or Literature?' at the end of *On Racine* (OCi 1090/OR 155) – is difficult to find in his close study of the structure of Racine's plays. Thus, the attempt to counter bourgeois psychologism in readings of Racine and the belief that one had to 'distance' Racinian theatre might help to make the latter relevant to the twentieth century, but said little about the relationship between writer and form. One need only compare Barthes's writing on another seventeenth-century writer, La Rochefoucauld, published as a preface in 1961 (OCii 1335–47/NCE 3–22), to see what a 'recovering' of a classical author might produce.

Far from being a concerted effort to apply modern human sciences to the writer of maxims, Barthes's preface wrote *with* La Rochefoucauld. Extolling the 'discontinuous' 'modernity' of the form of La Rochefoucauld's maxims, his critical practice here was to *recover* this 'style' in his own text. '[To] write well', he declared in a maxim form which imitated neatly the seventeenth-century writer under analysis, 'is to play with words, because to play with words is necessarily to approach the design of opposition which is the fundamental basis for a birth of meaning' (OCii 1341/NCE 13). In comparison to this imitation-as-appreciation of La Rochefoucauld, written around the same time, what is the first section of *On Racine* but a *naturalisation* – albeit sophisticated and highly original – of Racinian texts?

Indeed, in contrast to the critical comments on *On Racine*, most of the reviews of the *Critical Essays* insisted on the now decidedly *literary* nature of Barthesian criticism. Otto Hahn underlined the mixture of science and poetry.[14] Mathieu Galey's article on Barthes and Butor put forward the view – humorously, with a picture of both writers balancing each other on a pair of scales – that Barthes was not a critic but a novelist, not in 'reprieve' as the preface had suggested, but as 'travesty'.[15] Jean-Pierre Faye's review in *Les Lettres françaises* suggested that Barthes's critical writing was 'fictional': the *Critical Essays* showed how the 'critique of fables' had become a 'fable of criticism'.[16] For Philippe Sénart, Barthes had managed to become the Jonas that Flaubert had wanted to be, having seen the 'belly of literature'; but Barthes's collection of essays also proved correct Flaubert's view that literary criticism was what you did if unable to create art.[17] Though a brilliant and well-argued view of the continuity of Barthesian thought in relation to the 'sign', Gérard Genette's influential 1965 review of the *Critical Essays* failed to mention the significance of *Criticism and Truth* in the development of Barthes's formalist criticism.[18] If interpretation and naturalisation were the thrust of *On Racine*, how did he change to a criticism of forms?

The formal radicalism which the preface to the *Critical Essays* seemed to initiate was then confirmed by *Criticism and Truth*: a change had indeed taken place between *On Racine* and the *Critical Essays*. Barthes's 'parametric' conception of literary criticism may have suggested that the state of classical French studies at that time required him to apply a rigidly structural and naturalising methodology to Racinian theatre, but this did not explain his 'recovery' of La Rochefoucauld, another classical author. Writing the preface to the *Critical Essays* in December 1963, just as his reply to the *TQ* questionnaire on 'Literature and Signification' was being completed, Barthes's choice of articles to include in the *Critical Essays* indicated perhaps less his work over the ten-year period covered than what he had been working on in 1963. The shift evident in the preface to the *Critical Essays* might be better explained by the growing interest at this same time in psychoanalysis.

Though an *Arguments* special number on 'L'Homme-problème' in 1960 had heralded the burgeoning of psychoanalysis of the early 1960s, the beginning of Barthes's ambivalent interest in psychoanalysis is difficult to date with accuracy. An implacable critic of the romantic notion of psychology in the 1950s, be it in drama or the novel, Barthes had appeared sceptical in his writing before 1960. 'Myth Today' had underlined Freud's interest in the 'signification' of the unconscious; but, as Barthes had pointed out in 1959, literary criticism used as a window onto a writer's unconscious was – with rare exceptions, such as Freud's *Gradiva* – simplistic (OCi 817). True, Barthes's 1953 review of Jean Paris's proto-structuralist analysis of *Hamlet* considered psychoanalysis 'a general method of elucidation, and explanation', rather than simply a Freudian methodology (OCi 234). But between 1960 and *Elements of Semiology* in 1965, which made a number of important references to Laplanche and Leclaire's Lacanian article 'The Unconscious', published in *Les Temps modernes* in 1961 (OCi 1492, 1507, 1515/ ESem 114, 134 n.78, 147 n.99), he had clearly changed his mind.

Discussing the *Critical Essays* in an interview in 1964, Barthes now acknowledged the influence of Jacques Lacan – though 'with many, many nuances' – on the later essays in the collection (OCi 1453). Lacan's structural reinterpretation of Freudian methodology was indebted to both the linguist Roman Jakobson and the anthropology of

Claude Lévi-Strauss. It insisted (amongst other things) that a symbol was more real than what it symbolised, that, far from the symbol being explained by its unconscious and hidden 'true' meaning, the symbol itself explained, even influenced, what Freud had called its 'latent' content. In semiological terms, the signifier was not simply an access to the signified, it was the founding principle of the subject's unconscious. In linguistic and structural terms, the code preceded the message.

After inviting André Green to speak on Jacques Lacan at his seminar in 1962, Barthes's first reference to Lacan's work appeared in an interview in *Cahiers du cinéma* in September 1963. Though 'On the Cinema' (OCi 1154–62/GV 11–24) was clearly related to the cinema, Barthes took the opportunity to mark an important shift in direction. Praising Buñuel's film *The Exterminating Angel*, he set out how the film fulfilled the Brechtian theatre technique of 'suspended meaning', a 'very particular responsibility of forms' which no other playwright had achieved. Without falling into the trap of becoming 'nonsense', which was itself closed, the film's meaning was repeatedly suspended; but rather than being an absurdist film, it showed meanings without imposing '*one* meaning'. This '*dispatching*' of meaning was similar, suggested Barthes in his first overt reference to the psychoanalyst, to Lacan's notion of '*signifiance*'. Buñuel's film showed how meanings were constructed without imposing any one in particular (OCi 1161/GV 21). Furthermore, Barthes had noted earlier in the interview how the film's 'psychology of denial' showed that there could be a 'valid link' between a form and a content even if they seemed to be ' ''natural' opposites'. This was also significant for the 'formalist' critical practice developing.

Barthes now wondered whether the reactionary nature of a particular form of cinema and of literature was more to do with technique than content. Importantly, he suggested that a truly left-wing literature and left-wing film were in themselves not possible, because only 'the responsibility of forms', with a catalogue of suspended meanings, could provoke answers without actually giving them, could be 'problematic' (1160/19–20). And just as he questioned all notions of political commitment anywhere but in form and technique – even Brechtian theatre 'ultimately' only suspended meaning – he admitted a complete change of perspective on psychology. Regretting the manner in which Marxism ignored 'private' life, he suggested that the 'rotation of needs and forms', typical of 'structuralist law', meant that 'psychological' concerns were coming back into fashion: '[T]he grand anti-psychological declarations of these last ten years (declarations to which, it has to be said, I myself contributed) ought to be reversed and become old-fashioned' (1162/24). Furthermore, rejecting the *nouveau roman*'s critique of 'story-line' and the 'degree zero' critique of the past historic, the story verb-tense *par excellence*, he said: 'what we want now [. . .] are films with a story, "psychological" films'. Prefiguring the *Communications* 1966 special number on the structural analysis of narrative, he suggested that the job of 'the critic, the analyst' was then to point out how the story-line was 'catalysed'.

Thus, as in the preface to the *Critical Essays*, Barthes now saw the work of the artist as directly linked to that of the analysing critic. Of course, this conjunction of analyst and critic formalised what had taken place since his arrival in the academy, but it also stood in direct conflict to the opening remarks of the interview. There, pointing to not only the later 'subjective' phase of his career but also the sustained consideration of the 'I' in this preface, he described how going to the cinema was a purely personal and 'projective', not analytical, act of consumption (OCi 1155/GV 11–12). This (reticent) adoption of Lacanian psychoanalytical theory was to be of the utmost importance for the next decade.

As his reply to a questionnaire in *TQ* suggested, Barthes's interest in Lacan was related, in part, to his aim of going beyond the traditional academy's use of Mauron's 'old psychology'. (Compare his 'building' on Goldmann's work, noted in Chapter 3.) But there was perhaps a more fundamental reason. In filling any deficiency that Marxism might have in talking about the subject, and in particular the alienation of the subject, Lacanian psychoanalysis could point to the gap between the self and our attempts to 'coincide' with ourselves. If, as Lacan had proclaimed, the unconscious was structured like a language, then the critic and theorist were unable to demystify literary language: the only option was to meet it head on, to 'recover' it.

From now on, Barthes did not try to smother, avoid or ignore this cleavage. On the contrary, the deeply disturbing psychoanalytical split was to become the place in which he would precisely see the (utopian) space of text. Under the influence of *TQ* Barthes's use of psychoanalysis became one of textual play, exploiting the opportunity to make the intransitive and creative exploration of writing dynamic. One writes then in order to fill in a gap, if not to celebrate the 'fissure' in the subject's mind; one creates in order to expend psychic energy, if not (temporarily) to disalienate oneself. Thus, the growing literarisation of Barthes's critical theory and praxis was more a reaction to than a continuation of the 'scientific delirium' which characterised the attempt to account for the logic of Racine's plays. Not surprisingly then, his association with *TQ* began just as Lacan became friends with Sollers. This collaboration with what Patrick ffrench has called possibly the most important literary journal since the war[19] was to take Barthes through the tumultuous events of late 1960s' France.

'Write Everywhere!': May 1968, Tel Quel

> We do not want a world where the guarantee of not dying of hunger is exchanged with the risk of dying of boredom.
>
> Raoul Vaneigem

Barthes's involvement with *TQ* should have been little surprise. Not only was the journal published by Seuil, but it had been inspired and impelled, as Philippe Forest has pointed out, by Barthes's one-time friend and literary mentor Jean Cayrol.[20] However, Barthes's relationship was not a straightforward one. This experienced journalist was *outside* of the editorial team, and it is important to note that he wrote less than a dozen articles in *TQ*, nearly all of which were excerpts from future books, in nearly twenty years. Though not negligible, his presence was – particularly when compared to his earlier, frantic journalistic activity – rather marginal and peripheral. Indeed, at the height of *TQ*'s fame and influence in 1970, Barthes described himself as a 'fellow-traveller', rather than a member, of the *TQ* group (OCii 994). Partly as a reflection of his own fame in the wake of *Mythologies* and the Picard affair, Barthes's role in the journal appears to be that of grandee and 'maître' rather than activist. Perhaps Patrick ffrench's description of Barthes as part of an 'intersection' is more appropriate,[21] since the metaphor does not preclude divergence. It is clear that, though *TQ* was crucial for Barthes in this period – above all for the 'Tel Quel' series at Seuil, in which nearly all of his books were published – journal and author had a number of important differences. This was particularly so in the question of 'taste'. In line with his dialectical view of the 'classics', Barthes perceived, at the height of his association with the journal in 1971, that 'certain members' of the *TQ* team went much further than he did in 'burning literature' (OCii 1279–80/GV 112).

Indeed, according to Forest, Gérard Genette's role in influencing the journal towards a Barthesian stance has been overlooked. First, both the book on Racine and the *Critical Essays* were Genette's idea, and it was he, not Barthes, who is credited with the earliest attempt (in 1963) to suggest in *TQ* that criticism and literature were integral to one another.[22] Thus, following Genette's impulsion, 1963 can be considered a turning point in *TQ*'s history. After Ponge's opening in a series of lectures set up under the journal's aegis in 1964, called GET (the 'Group of Theoretical Studies'), Barthes, Umberto Eco and Eduardo Sanguineti all came to speak.

Politely declining an offer of a place to publish an article on fashion just as the journal was being set up in 1959, Barthes had been highly sceptical of the 'Declaration' in *TQ* 1, written by 'literati', that language was able to show the world as it was, *tel quel*. Jean-Edern Hallier's attempt to address a first questionnaire to Barthes on whether he thought he had a 'writer's gift' was met with a firm refusal: Barthes thought that the question should be addressed not to him but to General de Gaulle, whose memoirs he had just reviewed sarcastically.[23] It was not until after *On Racine* and a second reply to a questionnaire in 1964 that Barthes met Sollers and the beginning of a close rapport with the journal can be located.[24]

Essentially *TQ* was a literary journal; and it is no coincidence that Barthes's first literary piece – on Japan in 1968 – appeared here (we will come back to the 'literary' status of the very first piece, on Sade in 1967, in the next chapter). Nevertheless, the journal's birth in 1960 was, in some sense, a reaction against the intellectual commitment and hegemony of Sartre's *Les Temps modernes.* The position which *TQ* took in the first number's editorial, driving a course between the content-based political commitment of *Les Temps modernes* and the gratuitous experimentation of the right-wing 'Hussards' literary tradition, looked very similar to Maurice Nadeau's in the launch of *LLN* seven years earlier (see Chapter 1). Comparisons with the pre-war heyday of the *Nouvelle revue française* under Gide and Copeau, and before its ignominy during the Occupation, have even been made. But above all, influenced by the poet Francis Ponge, *TQ* wanted to explore the poetic and literary excitement of writing and language.

As Leslie Hill has underlined, the importance of Barthes's *Writing Degree Zero* to the *TQ* ethos is difficult to ignore.[25] The narrow line between determinism and freedom, utopianism and liberation, which Barthes's analysis of writing had appeared to open up was confirmed in his reply in 1961 to the *TQ* questionnaire, republished in the *Critical Essays* (OCi 1283–91/CE 151–61). Here the 'responsibility of forms' which Barthes had championed with Brecht now became a radical literary modernity. Not only was literature a question about the world, but also, Barthes suggested, the 'as it is' of the journal's title could be a manner of looking at important events. The poetry of Ponge and the latest speech of Castro, that is, both literary and political – in short, everything – could be looked at in its form:

> The (narrow) road for a review such as yours would be to see the world as it is constructed through a literary consciousness, to consider periodically contemporary events as the material for a secret work, to place yourselves in this very fragile and obscure moment where the relation of a real event is going to be understood in its literary meaning. (OCi 1288/CE 157)

This Nietzschean attempt to make the world literary, evident in Barthes's celebration of Michelet's history of the witch, was typical of

Barthes's sociological eye, as he transposed the 'poetic' method from historical to contemporary accounts. If, in an alienated society, literature is also alienated, then the best way to look at that society is by using its reified image. Literature, particularly that which placed a premium on the surface reflection of the 'real' and posed this 'real' to the reader in the form of a question, was the best means of analysis. Since all in the alienated world is language, 'the work which is the most "realist" [. . .] will be that which explores in the deepest way possible the *unreal reality* of language', he suggested (OCii 1290/CE 160).

If this first interview in *TQ* showed a distanced Barthes making suggestions to the journal, then the 1964 questionnaire reveals his coincidence with the direction *TQ* was taking. Stressing the political and social radicalisation of the questions 'What is literature?' and 'What role does the literary play?', Barthes now appreciated the attempts (in good dialectical fashion) to understand, relate to and transform language, literature's material, rather than destroy it in a surrealist fashion:

> If we look at a younger generation, that of the *nouveau roman* or *Tel Quel* for example, we see that the old subversions of language seem to be digested or out of date; neither Cayrol, nor Robbe-Grillet, Simon, Butor, Sollers is interested in destroying the key constraints of the verbal system (there is rather regeneration of a certain rhetoric, poetry or 'blankness' of writing); their work is interested in the meanings of the literary system, not the linguistic system. [. . .] Surrealism certainly provoked a crisis of *denotation* [. . .]: but what is problematic today is not denotation, but connotation. (OCi 1373/CE 276)

This support for *TQ* still had its tensions. Forest has set out the two directions which the journal took on objective and subjective criteria in the novel, and suggests that, early in the 1960s, Barthes initially moved not with Sollers towards a more dreamy and imaginary optic, but with the Thibaudeau/Ricardou axis towards an objective and non-psychological writing. In a letter to fellow popular theatre enthusiast Jean

Thibaudeau (dated April 1960), Barthes welcomed Thibaudeau's first novel, *Une Cérémonie royale*, because it went beyond Robbe-Grillet by undermining 'psychological intentionality' and removing all 'depth'.[26] And though he had privately commended Sollers's second novel *Le Parc* for its 'swing' (in a letter to the novelist in 1960),[27] it was not until Sollers's 1965 novel *Drame* that Barthes publicly praised the novel-writing of the driving force behind *TQ*.

A further important aspect of Barthes's interest in *TQ* was the question of the relationship between science and art. If a tough Marxist theoretical scientism was the journal's hallmark in and after May 1968, its origins can be glimpsed in Barthes's 1964 reply. 'Already', he opined, 'the frontiers are collapsing, if not between the artist and the scientist, at least between the intellectual and the artist'. Reminiscent, in form, of the Renaissance, the tendency for 'science and art to recognise together a new relativism of the object and of analysis' was what Barthes called 'reflexivity' (OCi 1374–5/CE 277–8). This 'reflexivity' was to be central to his enthusiasm for Sollers's writing.

Outside of the editorial committee of *TQ*, Barthes became close friends with Sollers.[28] Barthes was impressed by Sollers's work on Poussin and Dante, on Mallarmé and Sade.[29] Their friendship was such that, despite not having a text to his name in *TQ* before winter 1967 (except for the two questionnaires), and not having intervened in the polemic between Dominique de Roux and *TQ* over Céline and another fascist writer, Rebatet – the 'biggest polemic since the joust with Picard a year before' – Barthes was very quickly lumped in with Sollers.[30]

An important element in his perceived close association with *TQ* was Barthes's enthusiastic review of Sollers's new novel *Drame* in *Critique* in 1965. This clearly showed Sollers to be the true inheritor of Robbe-Grillet's original importance for Barthes, in avoiding 'characters' above all. Barthes was now using the 'recovering' strategy to the full. Demonstrating how Sollers's novel was remarkable and also making it 'readable' ('lisible'), Barthes's review had shown to Raymond Jean, a recent convert to the 'recovering' strategy, that the '*truth* of a work was as if inseparable from the critical commentary'.[31]

Barthes's review of *Drame* also seemed to be continuing his application of a Brechtian participatory theatre to his critical praxis on the novel. In saying that the novel 'could be read only by the writer', he was asserting not some elitist, exclusive readership, but, on the contrary, that we had to put ourselves into the shoes of a writer, if not become writers. As we shall see in the final section of this chapter, this was an early sign of a 'democratic' view of writing. *Drame* seemed to join – hence the title, said Barthes – the theatre with the novel, but also the past with the present, ancient Greece with modernity. The nature of all artists' relationship to their raw material was always a 'struggle'; and this 'first and final meaning' of a work, hidden in contemporary society, had been revealed by Sollers. Here was the 'solution' to the enigmatic contradiction in the first paragraph of Barthes's review, which saw *Drame* as a beautiful poem being stymied by the author's refusal to let it be a poem: 'we have to consider it a poem', but '*Drame* is chosen against the poem' (OCi 932/SW 40):

> This struggle reproduced in mirror image ['*en abyme*'] all the struggles of the world; and this symbolic function of the artist is very old, less clear in contemporary than past works, in which the bard, the poet, had the job of representing to the world, not only its dramas, but also *his* own drama, the event of his speaking: the constraints of poetry, which were so prevalent in popular genres and the mastering of which always inspired an unmistakable collective admiration, were nothing but the homological image of a certain relationship with the world: there is only ever one side to the struggle, one victory. (OCiii 944–5/SW 66–7)

Sollers's novel was making other connections with Barthes's views of modernity. In a way reminiscent of his epistemological and generic adventurism (especially on Michelet's witch), and prefiguring his own *vita nova*, Barthes quoted Délécluze's astonishment in 1841 at seeing Dante's *Vita Nova* as a curious mixture of forms: 'memoirs, novel, poem' (OCiii 932/SW 41). The date of the astonishment doubtless interested a Barthes fascinated, as we saw, by a Michelet who in the 1840s stood on the cusp of modernity. Sollers's novel also linked social phenomena which were taboo in mass culture: 'Making language a *subject*, and this via language itself, still constitutes a very strict taboo (in relation to which the writer might be the sorcerer): society seems to limit equally talk of sex and talk about talking' (OCiii 944/SW 66). We will see a little later the importance of the perceived relation between sex and language in Sollers's novel.

This alliance with Sollers served Barthes well in his defence against Picard, since Sollers supported Barthes in *TQ*.[32] It also allowed *Criticism and Truth*, published in the 'Tel Quel' series, to postulate some serious points about the writer, novelist or critic, theoretician or practitioner, confronted with the alienation of language. However, this alliance with the avant-garde *par excellence* in the mid-1960s also suggested that Barthes's views on the avant-garde from the 1950s had been radically overhauled. The novels of a Robbe-Grillet might have been a stage towards 'distancing' the novel and the reader in the mid-1950s, but a decade after his swingeing critique of the avant-garde in the theatre (ironically, this is at the centre of his *Critical Essays* – the very text which now seemed to be placing him in the avant-garde camp), Barthes was clearly still not willing to apply the same category of swingeing critique to the avant-garde novel. If anything, he had brought the novel and the theatre together here in Sollers's writing, at the same time as closing the door finally on theatre proper in his 'Witness on Theatre', published two months before (OCi 1530–2).

Politically too, his sensibilities had shifted, as he appeared to endorse *TQ*'s new interest in the French Communist Party. The journal's 'alliance' with the party,[33] which began in 1967 and lasted until 1971, was to play an important part in the split in the group at the end of the 1960s, provoking the departure of Jean-Pierre Faye and a dispute between his new journal *Change* and *TQ* on who held the true mantle of revolutionary avant-gardism. Barthes's comments at the beginning of his 'revolutionary' review of *Nombres* on the eve of May 1968 seemed to endorse the 'turn' towards the Communist Party. Barthes pointed out how Sollers's 'refusal to inherit' marked a 'certain rupture' with those 'political fathers' who, for the last twenty years, had been 'preoccupied' by the 'anti-Stalinist battle'. He argued that if the Communists had ignored the 'responsibility of forms' – evident in the doctrine of socialist realism and the official party line on Brecht – they were not alone: the anti-Communist left-wing intelligentsia was just as guilty of not considering 'form'. So, providing this was rectified, why should there not be, asked Barthes rhetorically, a 'Communist at *Tel Quel* overcoming the divisions between Communists and the anti-Communist Left' (OCiii 947/SW 70)? Then, in the heat of the argument between *TQ* and *Change* in 1970, Barthes wrote a letter to the former *TQ*, which, alongside letters from François Wahl and Jean Cayrol, defended the journal against Faye's criticisms.[34]

Throughout the battles of 1968, Barthes showed himself a loyal and articulate *Tel Quel*ian, arguing that theory was crucial to social change, fully in line with what Patrick ffrench has called the 'time of theory' in *TQ*'s history. This theoreticism was particularly evident in his interview with Pierre Daix in the Communist Party's weekly *Les Lettres françaises* in July 1968. Here Barthes applauded the attempts by students in revolt to attack educational manuals for their bourgeois ideology; but, he warned, there was a body of work – Marx, Freud, Nietzsche – which had already initiated the 'cracking of ideological envelopes' (OCii 525–6). Barthes's sentiment that 'there was no need to start this theoretical task from scratch' (by the end of the interview, he took a rather jaundiced view of a crude student Marxism, which, in its baser forms, looked like 'Poujadist anti-intellectualism') seemed to endorse the comments on May 1968 of the opening pages of *TQ* 34, 'The Revolution Here Now'.[35]

This editorial makes for stunning reading today, particularly in the light of those postmodernists who champion Sollers, Kristeva et al., or precisely because of its 'hard' Leninist line on the need for Marxist theory. Despite its title, it was a critique of an anarchist and Trotskyist spontaneism, and a call for a deep theoretical politicisation of the mass of students and workers in struggle. It also denounced the 'recuperation' by 'so-called left-wing newspapers' which, with a spontaneism inspired by petty-bourgeois and ultra-left politics, aimed at demobilising the proletariat. On receiving this number, Barthes apparently wrote to Sollers to offer his 'full agreement' with its political texts.[36] Indeed, there is thus little doubt that Barthes's seminal article on May 1968, 'Writing the Event', published in *Communications* in November 1968 (OCii 496–500/RL 149–54), owed much of its political critique to this editorial.

Barthes praised the ' "wild" language' of the graffiti, which, 'very close to *écriture*', had begun to flourish collectively on walls around Paris. The movement, he said, following *TQ*'s warnings about 'recuperation', had soon been undermined by the calls for an interdisciplinary approach. In a way reminiscent for Barthes of American university technocratic rhetoric and indicative of a lack of theory, 'the "wild" language', he opined, 'was fairly quickly eliminated, embalmed in the inoffensive folds of (surrealist) literature and the illusions of "spontaneity" '(OCii 498/RL 151). Though his addition of Nietzsche and Freud to Marx as the 'theoretical' line-up that the students ought to be looking at seemed soft in comparison to the 'hard' Leninism of the *TQ* editorial, it prefigured a 'softening' of *Tel Quel*ian theory. After the revolutionary failure of May 1968 and throughout the 1970s, this pervaded the journal, with a more nihilistic and psychoanalytical, less Marxist discourse.

Barthes's view in 1968 was that it was now necessary to read the event as text, written literally and metaphorically. The *real* revolution had to involve a break with the symbolic order, which the 'marginal fragments of *écriture*', represented by the explosion of graffiti because not printed, could not effect. As *S/Z* was to point out in Balzac's short story, the events of May 1968 had in them a '*mise en abyme*': the very rupture which the events symbolised but did not accomplish. Like the 'void' established by *S/Z*, the events showed how a *true* rupture could now be completed:

> For interpretation we must gradually substitute a new discourse whose aim is not to reveal a unique and 'true' structure but to establish a play of multiple structures, itself built on the *written*, i.e. removed from the truth of speech; to be more precise, it is the relations linking these concomitant structures and operating

> under rules that are still unknown to us which must become the object of a new theory. (OCii 500/RL 154)

The play of meanings in history which he had analysed in Michelet's historiography fifteen years before was an obvious influence here. It is no coincidence either that in the months preceding this period of social turbulence, Barthes had returned explicitly to the notion of history and historiography. This analysis of the rhetoric of history was an important element in his changing view of the relationship between science and literature.

Discourse and the 'Corrosion' of Science

> It is not unlikely that literature will forever give far deeper insight into what is sometimes called 'the full human person' than any modes of scientific inquiry may hope to do.
>
> Noam Chomsky

> If the big structures of economic alienation have been just about brought to light, the structures of the alienation of knowledge have not.
>
> Roland Barthes

I have treated briefly the Bachelardian and Popperian limits that Barthes placed on the scientistic excesses of structuralism. To complete this analysis, I must take stock of the radical manner in which the scientific first was corroded and then replaced by the literary in Barthes's thought. This theme ran through the analysis of Cayrol's novelistic 'sociology' and the anti-anthropomorphism of the *nouveau roman,* and finished with Michelet's 'poetic' history of the witch during the 1950s. In the 1960s and early 1970s, it was to become integral to his conception of '*écriture*'. Indeed, an important element in Barthes's move towards a 'novelistic' practice of writing was the corrosion of science by *écriture* which the work on rhetoric had begun.

His fascination with rhetoric stretched beyond new literary forms and educational training in language, and to the area of history. The idea that 'post-structuralism' began in 1966–7, as some critics have suggested,[37] appears to be based, in part, on a consideration of the 'Discourse of History' which Barthes published in 1967. However, any view of a rupture *tout court* in Barthes's thought is spurious, for, as we have seen in the earliest, Marxian writing on Michelet, he had already initiated a study of historical discourse. Nevertheless, we cannot discount the quite serious development in his thought which, in fifteen years, moved from a critique of historical formalism in Caillois and Joussain to a consideration of the form of history's narration. However, the view that the analysis of the 'discourse' of history denied the existence of history as anything but a 'text' – thereby leaving Barthesian thought open to the charge of a denial of history, which, in relation to an issue such as the Holocaust, is a serious charge – needs brief consideration, especially given his friendship with (at least) two victims of the Nazi concentration camps.

Indeed, in an interview with Stephen Heath in 1971, Barthes explained what he meant by looking at a 'discourse of history'. The idea was not to 'ransack' history (for which structuralism had been criticised), but to 'make the walls fall', to transform historical discourse into something else. Leaving the question of a resolution of the history/structure contradiction to one side, it is clear that there was no intention by Barthes to undermine history *tel quel*. Having realised that it was a mistake perhaps to make the history of *écriture* follow that of literature (as the 'degree zero' thesis had tended to do), Barthes wanted now to develop a new writing of history which was able to take *écriture* into consideration: 'Are we now in a position to conceive a historical discourse – I am not saying a concept of history but a historical discourse – which would not naively suggest itself as such?' (OCii 1299/GV 140). Far from challenging history as such, he wanted to found a 'history' relevant to *écriture*. It seems he was not simplistic enough to believe that all is 'text', as some have suggested. At the end of the same interview, he said: 'The teaching problem of today is to upset the notion of literary text and to manage to make adolescents understand that there is text everywhere, but also that not everything is text'

(OCii 1305–6/GV 149). Such a concept of history was indebted to a view of history as monument, which the writing of Sollers had instigated. Barthes's 1968 'commentary' on his own review of Sollers's *Drame* underlined this concept.

Barthes added a set of explanations in the infamous *Théorie d'Ensemble*, the apogee of *Tel Quel*ian theory published just before May 1968, to his original review of *Drame*. This suggested a complex reason for his use of 'anthropological' in the original article: 'History', he noted, was 'less and less conceived as a monolithic system of determinations', rather 'a play of structures'; it was 'itself an *écriture*'; and in order to 'shake' the symbolic system, all writing, including historical, needed to be changed. Thus, Sollers's *Drame* was one of the first efforts to show History in a different way, 'a practice founded on theory' (OCiii 933 n. [1]/SW 43 n. [1]). Thus Barthes's work on the discourse of history was part of a wider critique, by the 'literary'. Distinctly following Bachelard in ethos and Michelet in practice, the combination of the scientific with the poetic could challenge the positivistic and oppressive claims of scientism, which tended to deny the subjective but also mythical dimension of human research and knowledge. An essayistic performance could be one step in this direction, as Barthes's 1964 preface 'The Plates of the *Encyclopedia*' (OCii 1348–58/BR 218–35) brilliantly showed.

Originally called 'Image, Reason and Unreason', in good Bachelardian fashion, this proto-scientific preface treated Diderot's and d'Alembert's arch-Enlightenment text of the eighteenth century precisely as a literary text. Suggesting that we can no longer look at the *Encyclopedia* with 'pure ends of gaining knowledge', he proceeded to perform a literary analysis of the book's structure, form and significance.

Barthes wanted to underline the 'subversion' of the *Encyclopedia*, not only on the level of ideology – the great work of human Enlightenment was in fact highly poetic – but on that of human rationality. The manner in which the calm, relaxed and placid world of the 'vignette' was 'shaken' by the '*violence*' of the analytical pictures suggested a 'poetic troubling', a battle between reason and unreason. The shifting between a general overall view and a close focus on particular elements did not show us (as we might expect) a more detailed and reasonable world, but tended, said Barthes, to explode our understanding of objects. Providing images of particular components next to their 'whole' function only showed us the ridiculous number of objects existing at a lower micro-level. Like a dictionary (a favourite image of Barthes's), where a word is explained only by other words, the detailed examinations were nothing but an invitation for *more* analyses. Paradoxically then, the breaking up of the world into humanly analysable constituent parts, a key element in the human appropriation of the world, only generated more objects to analyse. But far from this infinite proliferation frightening us as part of the absurd (as in an Ionesco play, for example), this infinity was a way of hiding the absurd: 'the fracture of the world is impossible: all that is required is a glance – our glance – for the world to be eternally full' (OCii 1358/BR 235). Here was the importance of a literary sensibility within science.

Long before literature's treatment of the object as inaugurated by Balzac's novels, the *Encyclopedia* had already been 'poetic' in its treatment of objects, Barthes suggested. The illustrations in it were put together ('the syntagmatic level') in such a way that it displayed the 'novelistic truth' of all human action (1348/218). Though this was a 'knowledge of appropriation' (not unlike Barthes's view of Dutch seventeenth-century painting), the pictures in the *Encyclopedia* showed the 'infinite vibrations of meaning' of those objects appropriated by humans; and its different levels of analysis produced a variety of focuses which allowed us to see things in a different light. Thus the *Encyclopedia* was both didactic and poetic, said Barthes, implicitly referring to Brechtian theatre: the book was a 'spectacle' but not, a crucial point for us here, an 'art form'. Barthes's distinctly literary analysis of the *Encyclopedia* marked another step away from the opposition of science and literature. The *Encyclopedia* was both rational *and* irrational; and if history had been deemed an '*écriture*', the notion of science itself was now ready for the literary treatment.

This 'corrosion' did not simply point to an intersection of the literary and the scientific in Barthes's work in the mid-1960s. A 1967 interview had actually considered *The Fashion System* a 'scientific poem' (OCii 470–3/GV 63–7). Indeed, Lucette Finas in *La Quinzaine littéraire* had hailed the study of fashion as an 'essential book, as method, poem and dream'.[38] Tzvetan Todorov, a literary theorist and colleague at the EPHE, wrote a piece for *Annales* underlining how 'social life' for Barthes was 'but one type of literature'.[39] Gennie Luccioni in *Esprit* saw the book's skill, method, humour and modesty as indicative of Barthes's status as writer, and his research as a 'work'.[40] The 'corrosion' of science by the literary had distinctly political ramifications. Barthes's friendship with Julia Kristeva, now married to Sollers, was of great importance here.

By far the more theoretically skilled of the couple, Kristeva's seminar on Bakhtin had created an impression on Barthes;[41] and her review article in *Critique* on *The Fashion System* was a brilliant attempt to adapt Barthes's 'literary' account of the 'poor' system of fashion to her radical theoretical purposes.[42] If the piece is a masterly attempt to repeat (recover?) Barthes's own effort of making 'something out of nothing', then it posed a further critique of the semiological method over and above the Popperian one outlined in Chapter 3. Using Marx's view that clothes only had value as clothes and Barthes's comment that 'it is meaning which sells' as the epigraphs to her article, Kristeva was implying that *The Fashion System* represented a complementing, if not a completing, of Marx's original analysis. She noted the 'annoyance' with which Barthes's study had been received in the press (she did not say where), and suggested Barthes's 'crime' was to have undermined the 'reassurance' of semiology by 'exposing' the very signs which show that society was full of signs. Quoting Marx and Engels's view that in real exchange 'abstraction has itself to be reified, symbolised, realised by using a certain sign', she believed that *The Fashion System* was trying to draw out the commodity fetishism in which Barthes was placing the science of signs, based as it was on the denial (alienation) of a product's laborious – as opposed to commercial – origins. In other words, Kristeva thought that Barthes's study of fashion was displaying the way semiology had been caught out mythologising, because it found itself compromised by the arch-commercial and anti-historical materialist object, fashion. The alienation of work that fashion operated was a simulacrum of alienated production; and the 'forgetting' of work meant that we were back with commerce as the origin of how we perceived the world.

Thus in *The Fashion System* Barthes seemed to have come full circle (Kristeva called it a 'tautology'). The exchange society, reified by science, met its own reification as an object of fashion. Her conclusion was that semiology, having laid bare the 'apparatus of meaning' and its corruption, must now reorganise the surface of language into a textual space called 'disjunctive-alternating'. Using this and 'hypersemiotics' from outside Europe (India, China), it must 'pervert' the discourse of the science of exchange: the sign was to be seen as made up no longer of 'depth' but of surfaces in a chain.

If semiology had shown that fashion was simply a poorer version of the literary and semiology itself was now caught out mythologising, what was the solution to this interrogative syllogism? Precisely as Kristeva pointed to the contradiction of a semiological analysis of fashion, Barthes began to posit the surface of phenomena and the 'freedom of the signifier' in literature as a way out of the alienated and reified dead-end of semiology. His review in May 1967 of the second novel by Cuban writer and *Tel Quel*ian Severo Sarduy, *Ecrit en dansant*, in Nadeau's new journal *La Quinzaine littéraire*, was the opportunity for Barthes to show literature could escape the 'poverty of fashion'. Sarduy's novel demonstrated that there is 'nothing *behind* language'. 'Hedonist, therefore revolutionary', the novel's 'baroque' language challenged the classical Jesuit view of rhetoric, which, for centuries, had related 'good writing' to the ability to be transparent and communicate a work's 'content'. It suggested that, even in translation, '*écriture* can do anything with a language', and could 'above all, give it its freedom': 'By showing the ubiquity of the signifier, present at all levels of the text, and not, as is usually thought, on its surface, this baroque modifies the very identity of what we call a narrative, without the pleasure of the tale being ever lost' (OCii 409). In a review of Eduardo Sanguineti's work the same month, Barthes celebrated the 'critical baroque', a 'carnivalesque writing' *à la* Bakhtin (his first reference to the Russian theorist) (OCii 410). 'From Science to Literature', published first in the *Times Literary Supplement* in September 1967 as 'Science versus Literature' (OCii 428–33/RL 3–10), continued the 'baroque' theme: 'only the baroque, a literary experience barely tolerated by French society, has dared to explore in some way what one might call the Eros of language'. This view of language and writing was to become a solution to Kristeva's puzzle.

Since structuralism had been caught out wanting to be a metalanguage of culture, Barthes's conclusion was a radical one with regard to literature:

> The role of literature is to *represent* actively to the scientific institution what it denies, namely the sovereignty of language. [. . .] The task which remains for structural discourse is to make itself entirely homogenous with its object: this task can be achieved only in two ways, each as radical as the other: either by an exhaustive formalisation, or by a complete *écriture.* (OCii 433/RL 10)

This article represented perhaps the height of Barthes's epistemological adventurism: if science was appropriate to literature in the form of the *nouvelle critique,* then the opposite was equally valid. Questioning the division of disciplines in the education system, Barthes reiterated a theme common to his work on Michelet:

> It is not a coincidence if, from the sixteenth century onwards, a concerted blossoming of empiricism, rationalism and religion (with the Reformation), i.e. of the scientific spirit (in the broadest sense), accompanied a step backwards in language's autonomy as it became relegated to the level of instrument and 'fine writing'; whereas in the Middle Ages human culture [. . .] had treated almost equally the secrets of communication and those of nature. (OCii 429/RL 4)

Extending the 'degree zero' view of language to show how the rise of science heralded, if not helped precipitate, the enslavement of language to human – bourgeois – control of the world, Barthes now wanted to turn the tables, and redress this imbalance. He did this first by setting out how structuralism, in mobilising science for its analyses of literature, needed to understand its own linguistic status:

> Structuralism will never be anything but one more 'science' [. . .] if it does not manage to place in the centre of its activities the very subversion of scientific language, to 'write itself': how could it not question the very language which allows it to analyse language? (431/7)

Undermining the positivist division of subject and object, he stressed that *écriture* was the only way to recognise that there was no 'neutral state of language'. Following Derrida's critique of Western science, which was gaining intellectual currency in and around *TQ* at this time, Barthes's view was that only *écriture* could 'unmask the theological image imposed by science'.

The only way to complete the overturning of science's appropriation of language was to assert the pleasure, and practise the 'baroque', of language, against the classical view of it and its scientific instrumental counterpart. Here was the politico-epistemological basis for his praise of the 'writerly' explosion of graffiti around May 1968. *Écriture* was no longer simply a description of a writer's relationship to the infinite possibilities and constraints of language and to the literary institution, but the surface critique of the deep structures of thought justifying and maintaining bourgeois control.

Armed now with this new concept of *écriture*, Barthes returned to the literary, whence he gained this new approach. Rather than simply 'recovering' a literary text, the job of the critic was to 'liberate the signifier' by showing how its codes worked. This went hand in hand with empowering the reader to perform acts of reading which, both singular (i.e. individual and unrepeatable) and simultaneously 'intertextual', recognised the limits and infinite possibilities of language.

Once the signifier was liberated, Barthes was now able to move towards the 'literary' without further impediment. The 'Death of the Author', written and first published in English in autumn 1967 (OCii 491–5/IMT 142–8), suggested the best way not only to revalorise the reader and keep the signifier free, but also to undermine the compromises of semiology by way of a 'surface' analysis of literature as a 'baroque' use of language. If literature was the only way to 'modernise' human sciences, then the literary was to be the ground henceforth on which Barthes would operate. Barthes 'the novelist' could take his place amidst the debris of epistemological and academic inquiry.

A number of critics have underlined the shift between *The Fashion System* and the 'Introduction to the Structural Analysis of Narrative' on the one hand, and *S/Z* on the other. In the former, the denotation level of analysis is abandoned for a connotation paradigm, as Régis Salado has recently suggested.[43] However, this shift had been evident in the work on photography in 1961, as we saw in the previous chapter. The concentration on the connoting codes of language in *S/Z*, by applying his early 1960s' work on photography to literature, was evidence perhaps more of Barthes's epistemological adventurism than of any radical rupture. The move was also to be mirrored in *Camera Lucida* a decade later, where the 'literary' became a way into the photograph. Thus, the notion of 'rupture' between 1965 and 1970 has perhaps been stressed too much. Surely, the opening words of *S/Z*, on no longer seeing 'the whole of a countryside in a bean', were a minor criticism of the pretensions of one small, tentative aspect of his previous work. The main significance of *S/Z* was that it was a systematic attempt to show how close literary commentary could itself be *almost* as creative as the text it purported to explain. In other words, what happens, as a critic in 1971 invited, if we decided to 'read this reading' of *Sarrasine*?[44]

Textuality and Style

> A work of art in which there are theories is like something with a price tag left on it.
>
> Marcel Proust

Though the fruit of Barthes's work in seminars at the EPHE, this study of a short story by Balzac represented a sceptical view of academic discourse, in the wake of May 1968. In a famous 1970 interview with Raymond Bellour, Barthes explained how he had been his happiest whilst writing and researching *S/Z*, how he saw the work as a move away from the strong feelings of boredom with, and dislike of, rhetorical, syllogistic ways of writing dissertations, to be replaced with 'discontinuous discourse'. Thus, the discourse of criticism, which had dominated his work throughout the 1960s, was to be supplanted by what he called a 'writing-reading' (OCii 1007/GV 73). This 'writing-reading' was, as we shall see, to encourage a return to 'style'. To finish this chapter, I must set out briefly how he applied his own 'creative' and 'poetic' baroque in *S/Z*.

The best example is perhaps that which occurs as the commentary begins to reach fever pitch in the passage on the painting of Endymion adorning the front cover of *S/Z* (fragments 29–31, OCii 601–5/SZ 69–75). Describing how Girodet's painting hid Endymion's sexual regions in the manner in which Balzac's narrator hides Zambinella's own castrated status, Barthes is commenting on seven lexical groups (106–12) in this fragment. Yet, in highly self-conscious fashion, he divided the final one (112) from the others preceding – not to mention the dependent clause which followed (113) – to great *literary* effect. This isolation of the moment when Zambinella points to the beauty of Adonis in the painting allows Barthes to make his point about the isometric nature of the textual layers. It also serves to heighten – that is, add to – the tension of Balzac's original story. Furthermore, not only does Barthes add to the tension and excitement of the lexis and episode in general, he also introduces a further layer of analysis. In reading his commentary, it is difficult *not* to see Zambinella's question to Sarrasine – ' "Does such a perfect being exist?', she asked me" – as isolated in such a way that it becomes a question not just for Barthes but for us (i.e. the readers of Barthes's own text). The rhythm of this episode – as read and rewritten by Barthes – is taken to another crescendo two fragments later.

Having 'calmed down' the reading and rewriting in the fragment which follows Zambinella's question to Sarrasine (30, which covers the lexical groups 113–18), Barthes interrupts the relative calm introduced in his commentary on codes in fragment 30, 'Beyond and Short' (OCii 602–3/SZ 71–3), only to return to a sense of panic. Fragment 31 prefaces the tension of the question and highlights the play of codes and levels in the story by finishing with the fear and indecision of lexis 119 and 120. Barthes's text then returns once more to the relative calm of fragments 32 and 33 (605–7/75–8) 'uninterrupted' by the Balzac text.

It is not easy to illustrate the point I have tried to make here without, above all, falling into a literary rewriting of *Barthes's* book. Nevertheless, if the reader takes the time to look at the structure, this passage of *Barthes's* book appears as a highly crafted and carefully divided and restructured piece of writing. It is reminiscent of the excitement of a Michelet, as described twenty years before *S/Z*, racing to catch up with the next piece of history to be recounted (see OCi 255/MI 19–20). Indeed, in reading this episode it seems that there is a tendency to take less and less notice of the small type under the Balzac text, which describes the code status of the heavy type. This is perhaps a function of the fact that I have read *S/Z* more than once and am not looking at the codes level in Barthes's text. Still, this re-reading allows us to see the craft – the 'style', the performance – with which Barthes has 'rewritten' Balzac. Indeed, this is just one (albeit perhaps the first) of a number of examples of a highly stylised cutting up of Balzac's story in *S/Z*.

The coincidences of Barthes's and Balzac's texts are unmistakable, for example in the final passage of *S/Z*. Barthes's comments on the closure/suspension paradox at the heart of Balzac's story can quite easily be read as a comment on Barthes's *own* text. Not only does the rhythm of the final pages of *S/Z* reinforce our earlier analysis, it points to the almost triumphant tone of Barthes's realisation that he can replay the paradox of closure/suspension in his own writing. Thus, by concentrating on the level of referent and on the level of '*mise en abyme*' too, Barthes mimics the self-referentiality of Balzac's text. One can read the whole passage by substituting Barthes's *S/Z* for Balzac's text.

It was precisely this literary 'rewriting' of Balzac that divided the critics in early 1970s' France. Jean-François Josselin underlined how Barthes and his students had '*produced*' a text of thirty pages which happened also to be a short story by Balzac, and how placing the commentary before the story was an invitation to the reader to read as if the author.[45] For Alain Bosquet, *S/Z* was criticism becoming 'a dream of poetry', 'escapism' ('fuite'). Barthes's method was a synthesis of contradictory critical practices.[46] Bosquet's 'deformation' of *S/Z* was an attempt to join the spirit of the study, in which readers were accomplices and witnesses, 'exonerated' from the sin of understanding only if they attempted to become part of the text. Philippe Sollers wrote the review in *La Quinzaine littéraire*, with no hint of the vitriol of the exchange between him and Pierre Bourgeade which followed six months later in Nadeau's weekly paper, over *TQ*'s stance on literature and politics.[47] Sollers pointed out that Balzac's short story was an episode in the 'crisis of representation' which preceded the *écriture* of modernity. To this 'bourgeois narrative' he counterposed the modern writing that abandoned the 'fully "pensive" ' in favour of an 'infinite excess', which aimed not at a lost object but at 'a dialectical and multiplied surplus, thereby opening up the text, and announcing the passage (still taking place), to a new mode of production'. For Gennie Luccioni, Barthes's semiotics was like a passage from philosophy to praxis, from the written novel to the act of writing, from consumption of a work to the operation which opens it, from analysis to entry into the game of production'.[48] Bernard Vannier's review looked like a polemic *à la* Picard, in which Vannier took sides against the new Picard of Balzac studies, Pierre Barbéris, who had seen Barthes's method as part of a new fad.[49] Vannier showed that Barthes, the ardent critic of traditional notions of the opposition of form and content, had applied his theory to his own practice. Thus, from the start, the 'essay' put itself in the 'narrative horizon': the idea that Z was at the heart of Balzac's came at the heart of Barthes's own text (see OCii 626/SZ 106–7), the 'starring' in *Sarrasine* had been replicated in his own. Barthes produced a web of voices in his own text and played with the illusion of a final truth. In short, Vannier concluded, *S/Z* was the 'simulacrum' of Balzac's text. Clearly, as these reviews showed, the debate had moved a long way from the time of Picard and Racine, especially in the spirited, sophisticated and self-assured nature of the defence of Barthes's work.

But the two reviews in *Le Monde* showed the debate clearly.[50] The novelist Raymond Jean supported Barthes's efforts to implement a medieval conception of written production, in which Barthes played all four roles of *auctor, compilator, scriptor* and *commentator*. Pierre Citron, by contrast, missed the 'active' and creative aspect praised by Jean, insisting on the fundamentally 'subjective' implications of the book. Barthes's psychoanalytical approach had missed the orientalism in Balzac's 'erotic' and bisexual short story, not to mention an opportunity to suggest Sarrasine as the double of Balzac. Wondering why Barthes had not looked at other Balzac short stories – such as 'Une Passion dans le désert' and 'La Fille aux yeux d'or' – Citron was contesting the 'death of the author approach'. Barthes's 'plural' reading would lead to twenty-five discrete readings, each employing a different set of codes, and here was the 'danger': if the text was 'made volatile' in this way there would be nothing left of Balzac's novel-writing ('romantisme'). But, if Citron was clearly prepared to give Barthes's reading a chance, the same cannot be said of Robert Kanters. Marginally more sympathetic to *Empire of Signs*, the review in the *Figaro littéraire* considered that *S/Z* displayed a 'hatred' of literature, of the cultural 'babble' of language, of anything which linked 'man to all men'. With pedantry more mind-blowing than any university criticism, Kanters said, Barthes used a jargon at which one had to laugh.[51]

If, as Kanters and Citron suggested, *S/Z* did not escape university jargon, then it did seem to herald a new form of literary history. If Balzac now became 'writable' ('scriptible'), did that mean that the 'world of difference' between Balzac and Flaubert, suggested by the 1848 theory in the 'degree zero' thesis, now ceased to have any significance? Doubtless, the 'Pleasure in the Classics' strategy was bound to come into conflict with a modernist perspective on literature. But what about the *longue durée* view of bourgeois ideology's false universality and linguistic exclusion? Part and parcel of the move towards becoming a 'novelist' was the tentative undermining of the historical schema of the 'degree zero' thesis. It is no coincidence that one of the earliest hints of this modified literary history appeared in a 1967 interview (OCii 456–7/ GV 48–9), precisely at the moment when Barthes published his first piece on Sade.

Indeed, the writings on Sade and Japan, and then on Loyola and Fourier, emerge from exactly the same period (1967–71) as *S/Z*. More so than any other text, however, *S/Z* marked clearly the cross-over into the 1970s, not only in temporal terms (which decade is 1970 in?) but also in writerly ones. *S/Z* is perhaps the classic of 1960s French avant-garde writing – if this is not a contradiction in terms (indeed, the classical/avant-garde distinction is shaken by the work). *S/Z* developed a 'theoretical mutation' which underlined Barthes's own mutation, that from academic to 'novelist'.

PART THREE

'NOVELIST'

Writing changes us. We do not write according to who we are; we are according to what we write.

Maurice Blanchot

I write to find out why I write.

Alain Robbe-Grillet

I do not consider myself a critic, but rather a novelist, a 'scripter'; but I am not writing novels, rather the 'novelistic'.

Roland Barthes

THERE IS NO EQUIVALENT for the 'romanesque' in English, except for the odd-sounding 'novelistic' or the highly specific 'literary theorist'. And there is no word in French to make the word 'romanesque' into a noun which describes he or she who writes the 'romanesque', in the same way as 'roman' (novel) goes to 'romancier' (novelist). In keeping with the Barthesian spirit, one might create the neologism in French 'romanesquier/ière', whereas in English one would perhaps have to make do with 'literary theorist'. Whatever, the link between the novel – 'le roman' – and romanticism – 'le romantisme' – will be, as we shall see, more than simply semantic in Barthes's 'late' work.

Noting the 'correspondence' between Baudelaire and Barthes in his final book, *Camera Lucida*, Nancy Shawcross suggests that 'Photography allows Barthes to assume the role of novelist'.[1] To consider Barthes a 'novelist' may be to ask the question not only of how, but also when. As we saw in Part Two, certain critics located the fictional turn as early as 1964 (with the *Critical Essays*). After this *Criticism and Truth*, in seeing 'old-style criticism' as the equivalent of a mass art form such as cinema or literature, proposed an avant-garde, creative criticism (OCii 20/CT 34). *S/Z*, *almost* as creative as the Balzac short story it set out to describe, was the most significant result of this creativity. At the same, the first piece on Japan appeared in *TQ* in 1968, and we might wish to consider *Empire of Signs*, with all the gloss and colour of an ethnographic novel, as a 'fictional' visit to Japan. However, it is ironic that the *Complete Works* have not placed another candidate for the title of Barthes's 'first' overtly literary work in its chronological place of creation.

Written in Rabat in 1969, but published only posthumously, *Incidents*, a parody of literary scribblings, diaries and jottings, might well be Barthes's own 'limit-work'. If the epigraph – 'In Morocco, very recently . . .' (OCiii 1255/I 23) resembled a wistful 'once upon a time', then the (very explicit) lewdness represented a Flaubertian pastiche, with the haïkuesque fragments suggesting an uneasy relationship to nineteenth-century 'orientalist' writing. Another candidate might be the set of articles written across a four-year period beginning in 1967, and published in 1971 as *Sade, Fourier, Loyola*, which revealed Barthes's own essayistic *combinatoire* in operation. In placing a Jesuit, a utopian and a pornographer under the same heading, he could not but point to his own writing's act of combining, as a more assured use of fragment and anecdote laid the basis for the brilliant, baroque final essay 'Sade II'. Thus, we will consider the shift to 'novelist' as taking place across a crucial period in France, 1967–71.

Interviewed in *TQ* 47 in 1971, Barthes set out how he wanted to undermine the old opposition of 'style' and *écriture* described in the 'degree zero' thesis, by way of an 'inversion': 'écriture in new theory would occupy [. . .] the place of what I used to call style' (OCii 1320). Though this autobiographical interview was the beginning of a highly ironic presentation of the self, this comment indicated changes taking place. Discussing the *Empire of Signs*, he recognised that wanting to 'write' had something old-fashioned, even 'stylistic' about it (OCii 1292/GV 130): to be 'in écriture' was, as he put it in *S/Z*, to write the 'novelistic without the novel' (OCii 558/SZ 5). One technique was to 'recover' a text, by using pastiche, citation, copy, repetition, rewriting. Thus, the inclusion of his 1961 preface on La Rochefoucauld in the *New Critical*

Essays, published in 1972 with a new edition of *Writing Degree Zero*, mirrored his view of writing *with* Artaud in 'Artaud: Ecriture/Figure', written in 1971 (OCii 1186–7).

The 'redistribution' of style and writing became a key element in Barthes's assumption of the 'novelistic'. Barthes's essayism now suggested a coincidence of an interest in music with this new 'novelistic' perspective. Following Sollers's view in his 1971 novel *Lois* that the novel should be read out loud and 'performed' by the author like a conductor (OCii 1438), *The Pleasure of the Text* linked 'writing at the top of one's voice' with the material and bodily act of creation (OCi 1528–9/PT 66). However, by the same token, look what happens when, in 1972, Barthes wrote up, with little care it seems, a seminar on Lucan's *Pharsalia*. The result, 'A Lesson in Sincerity', is disappointing in my view, both pedestrian in its delivery and stylistically drab (OCii 1424–32).

Precisely during this period Barthes began to publish in fine art books. His commentary on Erté's early twentieth-century woman-alphabet, published by Franco Maria Ricci in 1973, is, by all accounts, a beautiful book.[2] The notion and practice of *écriture* began to cover the act of writing, in its material, physical and anthropological significance. At the same time as beginning a regular pastime of calligraphy, Barthes wrote 'Variations on Ecriture'. Unpublished in his life-time, this study of the history of writing presents an (enormous) irony, in that the study was concerned precisely with the 'manuscript' in the etymological sense of the word (i.e. written by hand). That it remained in manuscript form until after his death – published only in 1995 in the second volume of the *Complete Works* (OCii 1535–74) – is perhaps a fitting tribute to the handwritten rather than the typed. A good example of the material and corporeal intersections that he saw in *écriture*, this piece also combined an academic rigour with a powerful writerly and essayistic sensibility, both a description *and* a performance of the importance of writing.

A crucial element of the 'novelistic' was an undermining of academic discourse: against the formal and logical sequences of the academic dissertation, Barthes celebrated the 'discontinuous'. But this was tempered by a reaction to the 'Maoisation' of left cultural thought, which, briefly dominating politics in the wake of May 1968, promoted a rather crass cultural populism. Against this class purism, Barthes promoted his own 'pleasure in the classics'. Here was the ambivalence in the anti-academic critique of 'dissertational knowledge' in *S/Z*, which Pierre Citron's review had pointed out: Barthes's own rich culture (Dante, Proust, Brecht, Furetière, Genet, Flaubert) was trying to find a 'middle way' between the two extremes of bourgeois academia and ultra-left *proletkultism*.

His post-1960s fame was such that the first entire book dedicated to Barthes appeared in 1971.[3] *Le Monde* published an extract from the forthcoming *Sade, Fourier, Loyola*; and his work on Sade was quoted in the 1973 preface to a new edition of Sade's *Justine*.[4] Louis-Jean Calvet's 1973 study underlined the political aspect of Barthesian writing, whilst insisting on the playful and humorous moments: at one point, following the autobiographical irony in *TQ* 47, Calvet joked about Barthes's 'image'.[5] Thus, following the special number of *L'Arc* in 1974, Stephen Heath's book *Vertige du déplacement* attempted to describe Barthes's eclectic mode of theoretical slipperiness. Following the publication of *Roland Barthes by Roland Barthes* in 1975, *Le Monde* produced a 'what they think of Barthes', and, the same month, the *Magazine littéraire* ran a special number.[6] Barthes now moved into other media, including numerous appearances on French radio and even a cameo role in a film. Dinner with President Valéry Giscard d'Estaing, an appearance on French television to discuss *A Lover's Discourse*, followed by a *Playboy* interview and even a play adaptation of his writing on love, demonstrated that the 1970s were to be Barthes's decade. Finally, the chair of semiology at the Collège de France – with illustrious predecessors such as Michelet and Valéry, and contemporaries such as Foucault and Lévi-Strauss – inspired the organisation of a Colloque de Cerisy on Barthes (normally reserved for dead writers) for his fans and friends, *Le Roland Barthes sans peine* for his detractors, and the *Comprendre Roland Barthes* for those completely lost by Barthesian theories.[7]

Despite his scepticism of 'academic discourse', Barthes's rise to fame in this period was thanks, in part, to the prestigious names alongside whom he worked. The 'marginal' sixth section of the EPHE had changed its name in 1974 to the Ecole de Hautes Etudes en Sciences

Sociales (EHESS), thereby stressing social sciences; and Barthes was considered one of the 'high priests of the French University', along with Foucault, Derrida, Lacan and Lyotard.[8] The new 'novelistic' role did not prevent him from being invited onto editorial boards of new academic journals (*Poétique* and *Semiotica*), nor stop him publishing in established and prestigious journals. It meant only that Barthes saw the freedom that he had missed as essayist to write more openly and experimentally. An excellent example of this was 'An Idea for Research' (OCii 1218–21), in which he was clearly toying with the idea of writing 'with' Proust. His work became a *mise en abyme* of its own conclusions and difficulties: just as *S/Z* showed Balzac's novels as 'empty', so his writing began ultimately to have itself as its only referent. But there was still no prize forthcoming. Was this because his work eschewed a more traditional compartmentalisation, typified, as Todorov suggested in 1979, by a 'following' but no Barthes 'school'?[9]

Indeed, Barthes's rise in the 1970s from prominence to near-stardom attracted criticism. A number of hostile critics predicted – unintentionally it seems – precisely his trajectory in this period. In 1970, Georges Mounin berated Barthesian semiology for its inconsistent use of sign. The resultant confusion of symbols and signs had led, said Mounin, to a 'rhetoric' in Barthes's work; and Barthes's assertion (*pace* Saussure) that linguistics was the founding aspect of semiological analysis, not the other way round, meant that Barthesian semiology was relevant really only to 'stylistics and literary exegesis', in which it was difficult to locate an author's intention. Finally, said Mounin, his 'frankly inadequate' and 'nearly always incorrect' use of semiological terms showed Barthes to be more stimulating than convincing.[10] Then in 1971, the French critic and theorist Michael Riffaterre, working in the United States, attacked the formalism of Barthes and *TQ*.[11]

Unlike the Russian Formalists operating at the time of the social, political and aesthetic upheaval of the October Revolution, who had been concerned almost exclusively with avant-garde artists such as the Futurists, Barthes and *TQ* seemed interested in a literature which was 'paradoxically as dated as the criticism which they rejected'. These French 'formalists' found in literature only the 'coherence of its internal workings'. In asserting that only the non-referentiality of language could be revolutionary (because it exposed the bourgeois ideology of traditional criticism as the product of its class origins at a certain stage of the bourgeois rise to domination), they were suggesting that literature had no truth to bring to bear on the world. Indeed, the arranging of structures of the critical apparatus until 'total pertinence' was found only succeeded in denying a 'resistance of the text'. Pointing to the Russian Formalist use of 'perceptibility', Riffaterre denied, implicitly, the relevance of a (Saussurian) interest in the 'paragrammatic' nature of language. Barthes's 1959 analysis of Tacitus's historical writings (see OCi 1247–9/CE 99–102) had 'functionally' transferred onto the text what Barthes had found in his own mind: lacking anything more than 'a few textual facts', Barthes was, suggested Riffaterre, subject to an 'obsession' with 'softness'. Inventing words to invent structures (the tenderness of wood in *Mythologies*), Barthes's phenomena were based on a false concept of 'latency', which, using a surface/depth structure, tried to 'transform a non-existence into a secret existence'. Abstraction and latency were not the same thing, suggested Riffaterre; a structure was invariable and abstracted, but not latent. However, its variants were perfectly tangible and stylistically coded; hence, Barthes and these 'French formalists' had ignored 'style'.

If 'style' and rhetoric were to become precisely the central feature of the last phase of Barthes's career, then the other accusation against his work in the 1960s seemed to be dealt with. One of the characteristics of anti-structuralist criticism was that it evacuated the human 'subject'. However, presenting Barthes in the interview in 1970, Raymond Bellour's perception of Barthes seemed to herald a return to the 'self' which would characterise Barthes's and much *Tel Quel*ian writing in the decade to follow (OCii 1004/GV 68–9).

Like a reply from across the Channel to John Berger's experimental novel *G.*, which had won the Booker Prize in 1972, Sollers's complex 1973 novel *H* – typical of the alphabetical dialectic of order/chance dominating thought at this time – teamed up with Kristeva's 'The Subject on Trial/In Process' tribute to Artaud, to mark a return to concerns with the 'self'. Philippe Lejeune's work on autobiography in this period is the general context in which it is difficult not to see the influence of *Roland Barthes* on Robbe-Grillet's memoirs *Le Miroir qui revient*, begun in 1976 and published in 1984, and in the same year on Annie Ernaux's effort to 'break down' literature and autobiography in *La Place.* As a *TQ* fellow-traveller, Barthes had interests that now dovetailed with the journal's growing concern with love, the singular and the personal, but also the visual arts. Though he was not a 'spiritual' writer, in the second half of the 1970s his interest in Zen and its concomitant 'silence' prefigured the *TQ* interest in theology.[12] Indeed, despite the tangential and intersecting nature of Barthes's relations with *TQ*, his death is cited as one reason for the dissolution of one of the most important literary journals in France since the war.

The end of *TQ* in 1983 marked the end of a theoretical adventure which had begun in the 1960s. After the explosion of May 1968 and its failure to shift social relations and the political landscape fundamentally, de Gaulle, though no doubt shaken, had managed to head off skilfully (and with Reformist complicity) this most serious of challenges to state power. And though, as many commentators seem to forget, the spirit of May continued well into the 1970s, a number of intellectuals and thinkers took up the implications of the theoretical adventures which had accompanied the struggles of the 1960s. If *Change* with Faye and Jean Paris suggested a hardening of Marxist theory, Jean-Marie Benoît could simultaneously proclaim the 'Death of Marx'. This had important consequences for the theoretical revolution which had taken place. Chapter 5 will suggest that it was precisely around (perhaps also because of) the debacle of May 1968 that Barthes turned towards a textual and utopian Japan. The *longue durée* view of capitalism had not so much disappeared as been displaced: Japan was valorised now for its *pre*-capitalist 'feudality'. Thus, Barthes was no overt radical. His descriptions of advertising and fashion in mass culture in the 1960s had led only to his being consulted on a new advertising strategy for the Renault company, and asked to write in *Marie-Claire* on the battle between two rival fashion designers (OCii 413–16). His radical acts of writing in the 1970s would show how he worked (more and more as time went by) on the *inside* of the economic and signifying 'system'.

5

Writing and 'Rêv-olution'

In the present state of society, happiness is only possible for artists and thieves.

Oscar Wilde

In 'How to Speak to Literature', published in the *TQ* special number on Barthes in autumn 1971, Julia Kristeva described the three ways Barthes's writing, in theory and practice, had obtained 'a new epistemological status'. First, the 'materiality' and practical acts in language which constituted writing necessarily came up against the most recent sciences of language (linguistics, logic, semiotics). Second, writing's 'immersion in history' meant that it looked at social and historical conditions. Finally, the 'sexual overdetermination' of writing oriented it towards psychoanalysis and – to complete the circle – towards corporeal, physical and substantial categories.[1] This neatly summed up the importance of Barthes not only to the *TQ* group but to writing in general. It is within this triple characterisation that we will examine the 'literarisation' in Barthes's work in the years following May 1968. Since Kristeva's formulation is circular, it matters little with which of the three we begin. It might be a good idea to start with the last, loop back to the first and on to the second; for the second is a convenient point from which to show how Barthesian theory moved into a new conception of, if it did not abandon, social and historical conditions.

Henry Rousso has described the post-1968 period as 'retro'.[2] With Fascism reviewed and recycled, particularly in the work of Patrick Modiano and Louis Malle, sexuality now became linked to political critique. In Britain in the 1970s, we had the sight of Nazi insignia mixed with the most blatant sexual metaphor of revolt in transvestism: there is nothing more 'retro' than punk rock. In a similar way, Barthes began to see the perverse as a source of social critique – he gave an impulse (and a preface) to this type of study in Gérard Miller's Reichian/Freudian account of Pétain (OCiii 277–9). Both pleasurable and scandalous, the erotic has seen a revival of interest today, with the pornographic writings of Sade, Bataille and Klossowski being revered as the latest avant-garde.

Philippe Roger has recently traced Barthes's reading and application of Sade, and Diana Knight has shown convincingly the erotic subtext of the passage of the *Empire of Signs* on the Japanese game-machine pachinko.[3] Mohand Boughali has looked in detail at Barthes's erotic relationship to language in general, covering Barthes's three books of the 1970s.[4] As early as 1962, in an interview concerning the *nouveau roman*, Barthes had noted the absence of the erotic in literature: if the reader and the novelist 'can also ask questions', he wondered, 'why has eroticism disappeared from literature?' (OCi 980/GV 10). He had also been an important supporter of Pierre Guyotat, whose erotically graphic novel *Eden, Eden, Eden*, prefaced by Barthes in 1970 (OCii 967/RL 236–7), had become the object of state repression and a vibrant defence campaign. In *TQ* in spring 1971, Barthes was one of the earliest signatories of a petition denouncing the Interior Ministry's near-banning of the novel.[5] This episode was an important one, as Jean-François Revel's review of the novel pointed out, for it pointed to the relationship between social upheaval and sexual revolution, in a way reminiscent of Sade's gesture towards the French Revolution and Lautréamont's to the Paris Commune. However, only Fourier had made the sex/revolution connection explicit, said Revel, agreeing with Barthes's view on the interdependence of sex, language and censorship.[6]

The relationship between textual and sexual categories had been an important element in Barthes's work in the late 1960s. Stating in an interview in 1967 how he had originally planned to analyse Kleist's *The Marquise of O* (a bizarre short story describing a Prussian noblewoman's embarrassment at not knowing who has made her pregnant), he had in mind a particular kind of narrative which lent itself to psychoanalysis and the unconscious (OCii 457). In choosing *Sarrasine* finally, it was clear that sex, gender and hidden identity would be at the heart of his analysis. However, whereas the 1967 interview stressed how he had been looking for a ' "double" work which put itself forward as so literal a narrative that it challenges the very model of the narrative; [. . .] an apparently naive but also awkward work' (OCii 457), he suggested in an interview in 1970 that he had chosen Balzac's story for its 'symbolic extravagance' (OCii 1005). It was between these two imperatives that we found the creative aspect of Barthes's literary analysis. *S/Z* showed how the scandalous revelation of the castrato's true sexual identity was reflected, even supported, by a different level of analysis of Balzac's short story. 'This fable', Barthes declared at the end of *S/Z*, 'teaches us that the narration (object) modifies the narration (act): the message is linked parametrically to its performance [. . .] what is narrated is the "narration" ' (OCii 698–9/SZ 213). This link between narration and the narrated was like the map of Tokyo in *Empire of Signs*: and the map was an emblem not only of Japan but of Barthes's book and writing in general, for it had no centre.

Therefore, of crucial importance to this move towards the 'novelistic' was the concentration on the *form* that thought, writing, and social discourse in general took: hence, a relentless search for the singular, the novel, the unrepeated. Barthes's critical strategy on Michelet and Goldmann had been to avoid repetition, and to build, dialectically, upon what work had already been done. In the wake of *S/Z*, he wanted to avoid the scientism of models in favour of writing, in (paradoxically) as 'rigorous' a fashion as possible (OCii 1012–13/GV 81–2). Thus, prefiguring a trend in *TQ* in the second half of the 1970s, he began to concentrate on the singular, exceptional nature of writing and experience. This was linked to the post-1968 cultural and political situation. Cynical now about the 'stereotyped' fashion in which students had tried to criticise the 'structuralist myth' (OCii 1199/RL 316), Barthes began to stress the worn-out and repetitive nature of political language.

The perspective of this penultimate chapter will be that after the re-establishment of civil order in the wake of May 1968, Barthes sought new ways of undermining the 'recuperation' that the institution inevitably operated, which, for him, meant that both language and writing had to be revolutionised. The realisation of the all-encompassing strength of bourgeois language encouraged him to see his only possible role as one of subverter, 'thief' and (re)writer.

'Less *directly* engaged in ideological critique' (my italics), Barthes was clearly entering a phase of Nietzschean nihilism, in which the fracturing of meaning was more effective than being compromised by it (OCii 1292/GV 130). However, the only way to do this was from *within* language. There needed to be a critique of the ideology of semiology (OCii 1278/GV 109–10), but this had to come from within semiology itself, a perspective entirely in keeping with *TQ* at this time.[7]

In the final chapter of his 1973 study, Louis-Jean Calvet had insisted on the fundamentally political import of Barthes's work. Showing how the critique of science and linguistics was central to a revolutionary perspective, Calvet now moved Barthesian theory away from the (dominant) Althusserianism of the time, which saw science as the destroyer of ideology. He put Barthes with Sartre, and (interestingly) with the guru of May 1968 and social liberation, Herbert Marcuse, whose *Towards Liberation* saw communication as a crucial place for resistance. Calvet's political analysis was based not on the most obvious texts (*Mythologies, Criticism and Truth*) but on the more recent ones (*Empire of Signs* and *The Pleasure of the Text*). Under the guise of hedonism, Barthes's study of pleasure saw, according to Calvet, 'class conflicts' taking place in their trace in language. This view of language was by no means rare for the time; Jean-Pierre Faye, Calvet underlined, had analysed these traces in detail in 1972, thereby uniting (perhaps unexpectedly) Barthes with the *bête noire* of *TQ*. Barthes's question in *The Pleasure of the Text* was not (*à la* Lenin) 'What is to be done?', suggested Calvet, but 'What is *not* to be done?'.[8]

But, as we shall see, Calvet's view of Barthes's political importance in 1973 needed to be nuanced: *The Pleasure of the Text* was to represent the beginning of a definitive end to overt, political subversion. But first we must look at the experience of post-1968 France; for here Barthes instigated his own personal way in which to deal with the vicissitudes of social and ideological alienation.

(Dis-?)Alienation in Post-1968 France

> If France had had a revolutionary party open to ideological struggle [. . .], no doubt RB would have had his place [. . .] and reinforced it with very specific qualities.
>
> Philippe Sollers

> We have to live in the unliveable.
>
> Roland Barthes

In his 1971 preface to the *Esprit* special number on 'Mythology' (OCii 1183–5/RL 65–8), alluding (perhaps inevitably) to *Mythologies*, Barthes underlined that something had changed; though not mentioning May 1968 explicitly, this was clearly at the back of his mind.[9] It was almost as if the recent dramatic events had confirmed what he had been saying since 1956. 'To talk about bourgeois culture is false', he started his ironically titled article '*Pax Culturalis*', also written in 1971 (OCii 1188–91/RL 100–5), 'all of our culture is bourgeois'; and not only is culture 'bourgeois', he went on, but the 'idea of *challenge* itself becomes a bourgeois idea' (1190/103). Though, in essence, no different to the conclusions of 'Myth Today' that there was no proletarian art or culture, only bourgeois cultural hegemony, there was a crucial difference, as he now spelled out. Confirming his prediction made in the foreword to *Mythologies* in 1957, he emphasised that the semiological critique of myth had itself become a myth: myth had freed itself from the analysis under which it had been held. The interesting point for us was the manner in which Barthes proposed to deal with this.

The only way to undermine myth was to 'steal it' back. 'If', he said reiterating his 1950 view of 'explanation' as the most revolutionary of acts, 'the alienation of society obliges always a demystification of languages', this meant the task had to be to prioritise the levels of reification taking place. The dominant 'idiolect' of social doxa – full of quotations, stereotypes, habits, clauses – could be exposed only by a further deployment of writing:

> [L]anguages [. . .] could be taken in the cross-fire of a 'trans-écriture', in which the 'text' (which is still called literary), as the antidote to myth, would occupy the pole, or rather the region which was both free and noble, decentred and open, light and aerated, where écriture is deployed against the idiolect: that is, at its limit and fighting it. (OCii 1185/RL 68)

Both within and against, this writing would change the object itself, thereby establishing a new science to pick up from where Marxian critique had ended.

Far from this being a 'rupture' in Barthes's own thought, such a strategy had been hinted in as early as 1955, in his 'Childhood' mythology's view that Michelet's 'myth' was useful in breaking down bourgeois conceptions of children (OCi 459). However, it was the decidedly literary, rather than social science, conception of myth that he was now advocating. A literary rhetoric could become part of a revolutionary challenge to bourgeois control of language.

In an interview in 1971, he pointed out that, up until the time of Flaubert, rhetoric had been on the education syllabus: 'the art of writing used to be taught', he complained (OCii 1278–80/GV 109–12). Since then, thanks to the 'democratisation' of art which allowed a general consumption of bourgeois 'cultural objects', reading and writing had become separated: 'Learning to read, and read well, has a positive side, but also a negative one, in that it enshrines the divorce between a small number of people writing and a large number who read without transforming what they read into *écriture*' (OCii 1278/GV 110). Writing as a baroque and parodying rhetoric could encourage people not only to read in a deeply critical way but to 'fissure the very representation of meaning' (OCii 1184/RL 66).

One way of encouraging this form of writing was to look to the non-Western Other, the Orient. So, the people's China, with its cultural revolution – despite state problems 'far from resolved' – offered the only way forward for a 'radical transformation' (OCii 1191 / RL 105). This (guarded) adherence to Maoist theories of cultural revolution was reiterated implicitly, but more forcefully, in the *TQ* special number on Barthes, in his own article 'Writers, Intellectuals, Teachers' (OCii 1194–210/RL 309–31). Of course, this political pro-China perspective and interest in dialogue between intellectual and proletariat dovetailed with the Maoisation of *TQ* politics in the wake of the establishment of the 'Movement of June 1971'.[10] But the ironic critique of the hysterics of Maoist political language evident in the special number of *TQ* on Barthes at the same time was to prefigure the indifference, if not disappointment, with the visit to China in 1974, evident in Barthes's 'No Comment' silence (OCiii 32–3). Throughout this 1971–4 period, his attempts to use a literary and rhetorical language to 'fissure' bourgeois symbolisation would move to a more utopian and dreamy 'atopics'.

Highly Micheletian in terminology, 'rêve' is a central feature of what Diana Knight has seen as Barthes's 'spatial' utopianism.[11] As Robert Kanters underlined, Barthes's 'dream' was to 'write in Japanese without knowing Japanese'. The opening pages of *Empire of Signs* stressed the 'dream' of knowing a foreign communicating system whilst escaping the recuperation of the signifying system (OCii 747–8/ES 6) – an apt description of his calligraphy and drawings from 1971 onwards.[12] As psychoanalysis became for Barthes a celebration of the anti-psychiatric drives of creativity, so 'rêve' turned a Bachelardian view of the structures of thought into a proactive device of disalienation. Indeed, Françoise Choay's review hailed *Empire of Signs* as able to escape the 'bitterness of polemical writings, the weight of theoretical writings' with a composition which was full of 'mobility, precision, lightness and happiness'; but her conclusion was that it was in relation to the West that Barthes's study had to be seen.[13]

The very title *Empire of Signs* seemed to hark back to a golden, pre-industrial and ultimately dreamed Japan. However, the utopianism of Barthes's ethnographic novel on Japan still could be seen to be operating a subtle critique of Western culture. Utopianism is not simply an escape, but can represent, particularly in times of censorship, an attack on one's own real world. In Barthes's case, utopianism had none of the hysteria of directly political discourse; it did not moralise, and (unlike Voltaire) it did not allegorise. But this utopianism was not concerned either (as in a Montesquieu) with a tangible reality: it was the *fictional* status of Japan which performed the critique. It was precisely because this Japan did *not* exist that it was a critique of Western symbols. Thus, Barthes formed a complex mixture of the utopian (deliberately idealised) and imaginary: a 'fictional utopia', if such a tautology may be permitted. Indeed, the introductory words had stressed that 'to challenge our society without having thought the limits of language' (OCii 750/ES 8) with which to challenge it would be derisory. Replicating the isolation which had been crucial in the experiences of the three 'logothets' Sade, Fourier and Loyola, Barthes now took a real place, fictionalised it and then, and only then, erected it as a utopia. Thus, for the philosopher and writer Roger Laporte in *Critique*, *Empire of Signs* was 'literally, revolutionary'.[14] Fully Gidian, Barthes enjoyed seeing a society as spectacle, and one which showed its scaffolding. Since Japanese relied on the visual link in its written language (the sign is 'motivated' in some sense), to judge Japan as écriture was to remain with the ideographic nature of Japanese culture. Thus, it was a short step for Barthes to find the gestures of writing in social phenomena such as pachinko, food or bunraku.

A good example of 'rêve' as utopian critique from this period was in Barthes's reading of Fourier. The International Situationists' interest in Fourier in the mid-1960s had been an important impetus to the publication of Fourier's *Complete Works* in 1967, which Barthes reviewed in *Critique* in 1970.[15] His interest in Fourier had been evident in a footnote in 'Authors and Writers' in 1960, on the writer's system as 'spectacle' (OCi 1279 n. 1/not in CE 145 n. 2), and then in relation to Sade and Newton and the powers of enumeration in his 1963 study of Bataille's *Story of the Eye* (OCi 1351/CE 246). But Fourier's relevance for the Barthes of 1970 was summed up in the 1963 interview in the *Cahiers du cinéma*, in which Barthes had first criticised Marxism for its failure to treat the 'personal' and signalled an interest in 'psychology'. Here he described how no 'big utopia' understood the notion of 'happiness':

what was needed was a 'micro-utopia' which could imagine 'psychological and relational utopias' (OCi 1162/GV 24).

Placing as epigraph to his 1970 article a quotation from Fourier, 'The aim of Harmony is not exclusively truth', Barthes was highlighting the critique of Marx and Engels: those who point out the failure of Fourier's system to be real or realisable are themselves 'bourgeois doctrinaires'.[16] Here was the crucial importance of 'rêve' for Barthes. Uncannily similar to Michelet's disregard for historical 'truth' – another reason why Michelet was 'a writer of tomorrow', as he put it in 1973 (OCii 1583/GV 207) – the enumerating and detailing of a perfect society became itself a way out of day-to-day alienation, be it having to eat couscous made with rancid butter or 'living in the unliveable'.

To understand fully the significance of Barthes's utopianism, particularly in relation to *Sade, Fourier, Loyola*, we must place it next to two pieces on two novels that Barthes wrote in 1971. They illustrate his interest in, and drastic attempts to find, 'rêve' in this post-1968 period. His review of Pierre Loti's *Aziyadé* in *Critique*, in which he celebrated 'drift' ('dérive'), and also his tiredness with novels such as Fromentin's *Dominique* will illustrate how trying to find 'pleasure in the classics' was fraught with difficulty.

Barthes seemed to find Fromentin's countryside novel *Dominique* a hard case. Barthes's article, originally a preface to an Italian edition of the novel, was (surprisingly) the penultimate piece in the *New Critical Essays* (OCii 1392–400/NCE 91–104). 'After reading Marx, Freud, Nietzsche, Mallarmé', who, he wondered, could appreciate the aphoristic dialogues in this novel? 'Reactionary', 'sad', 'indefectibly sensible, conformist, pusillanimous even, nailed to its heavy psychological signified, prisoner of a well-written form of enunciation, outside of which the signifier, the symbol, voluptuousness have great difficulty in fusing', Fromentin's novel of love lacked 'rêve' above all.

Barthes had of course 'dealt' with stuffy and 'readerly' texts before and found something scandalous and surprising in them; but for once he seemed singularly incapable of turning this writing round. Having exhausted political, urban/country, psychological and theatrical themes in search of 'rêve', he tried the body. But even here there was little to celebrate: 'In modern terms, we will say that Fromentin's text [. . .] has its signifier immediately *stolen* by the signified.' And though this signifier (the body) comes back in the form of physical illness, *Dominique* was a 'novel without sex'. The only interesting point Barthes could find was that the title in French is both masculine and feminine in this 'old-fashioned/backward-looking ['passéiste'] novel'. But, even though he found the language the most astonishing aspect of the novel, he seemed tired of the novel's 'correct' nature. 'I did not want to say necessarily that this novel should not be read', he concluded (sailing close to the wind here; he is after all writing the preface to the Italian translation of the novel), for there were 'corners of pleasure, which', he said using a dialectic of love, 'are not necessarily distinct from the alienations alluded to'. Thus, by concentrating on these 'corners' in the deficient areas – the incantation of some of the sentences, the 'light delicate voluptuousness of the countryside descriptions' like romantic paintings, the phantasmic, almost erotic, plenitude involved in all 'retreats' (in an allusion to the logothets of *Sade, Fourier, Loyola*) – we could just about read *Dominique*, he suggested:

> A conformist life is detestable when we are on the lookout ['état de veille'], that is when we speak the crucial language of values; but in moments of tiredness, of sagging ['affaissement'], of the strongest urban alienation or dizziness from language, a backward-looking 'rêve', such as life in the 'Trembles' region, is not impossible. (OCii 1400/NCE 104)

This was an important admission. The 'laziness' and 'irresponsibility' that this 'rêve' gave 'us' was a prelude to the political and ideological 'detachment' which was to mark the final stage of Barthes's career.

Such a view must be contrasted with the manner in which he treated 'rêve' in the famous article on Pierre Loti's novel *Aziyadé*, brilliantly described by Philippe Roger in a recent tribute to the article in the fiftieth anniversary special number of *Critique*.[17] As well as trying to come to terms with a rather 'traditional' story and suggest why it was also 'modern', Barthes applied the *S/Z* idea of a hole at the centre of the novel, a hole which allowed him to choose the aspects of Loti's novel worth retaining.

What he called in Fromentin's novel an 'outdated/backward-looking image' was here put to positive use. The kind of pre-capitalist, non-possessive aspect of Loti's novel, called 'disinheritance' and glimpsed (implicitly by Barthes himself) in Marrakech one summer, was, once found in the descriptions in the novel, to be celebrated: 'the grass growing between the stones on the road, the black cypress trees against the white marble' and finally (reminding us of Michelet's walking habits) in cemeteries, which were places not so much of death as of 'debauchery' and 'drift' ('dérive') (OCii 1411/NCE 118–19). The comment on grass growing resembled the haïku quoted (written?) by Barthes in *Incidents* (OCiii 1270/I 57). Not only did the 'incidents' that Barthes found in Loti's novel hark back to his own literary fragments written in Morocco, but the theme of 'disinheritance' was one which was to return, in different guises, throughout the 1970s. The ethos of 'not wishing to grab' in *A Lover's Discourse*, the photograph of A. Philip Randolph in *Camera Lucida* showing 'no impulse of power', were set in motion by the 'nothing', Zen-like void, at the heart of *Aziyadé*:

> Thus a minor author, out of fashion and clearly not interested in theory (yet a contemporary of Mallarmé, Proust) brings to light the most devious logic of écriture: for wanting to be 'he who is part of the painting' is after all to write simply that one is written, an abolition of the passive and the active, of the expressed and the expressing, of the subject and the uttered, precisely where modern écriture is trying to look for itself. (OCii 1408/NCE 116)

Thus, Barthes's wistful and poetic 'rewriting' of Loti's novel was a prelude to the final, autobiographical and romanticist, phase of his career. The fragment number 12 'The Journey, the Sojourn' (OCii 1408–9/NCE 117–18) (and doubtless others) seemed to be at least as much about Barthes's own experiences in Morocco as about *Aziyadé*.

Thus, Barthes's critical practice in 1971 was wavering between 'rêve' and the sometimes fruitless search for 'rêve'. This was linked to the dimensions in which utopia was articulated. If Barthes's utopianism was a spatial one – 'utopia' after all means 'no place' – it is important to stress also its *temporal* nature. In response to the critical final question from Bellour, which suggested that Barthes's strategy, like Mallarmé's, was to 'close himself off' from the world by 'fetishising the text', Barthes replied: 'I don't think that *waiting* is *closing* oneself off' (OCii 1016/GV 86). Though he justified this spatially – the decentred, empty nature of Japanese culture – the temporal was crucial to his utopian point of view:

> This void [. . .] is both necessary and transitory; in my view it is the present postulation of the ideological combat in our society: it is too late to keep the text as fetish, as the classicists and romantics did; it is *already too late* to cut the text-fetish with the knife of castrating knowledge as scientists, positivists and certain Marxists do; it is *still too early* to cut the break, to cross out science, without it appearing, in relation to what we call the political real, as a second castration [. . .]. (OCii 1016/GV 87)

I have translated 'coupure de la coupure' here as 'cut the break', on the basis that, in another interview in 1970, he had referred to the modernist epistemological 'break' of the mid-nineteenth century in the same term (OCii 993).

It is probably sufficiently clear by now that Barthes's temporal view of utopia can be part of a critique of any attempt to find a further 'break' in modernity (i.e. of a *post*modernity). What appears to be a 'coupure' in Barthes's work – he realised that the only way to overcome the alienation of language and its hijacking by myth was to steal back – was a continuity, or at most a more assertive reiteration, of the pessimistic perspective of 'Myth Today'. The defining feature of this continuity was the schizoid manner in which he swung, constantly, between a pessimistic and optimistic view of the possibilities of liberating language from alienation. *Sade, Fourier, Loyola* would seem, then, to represent an example of the latter.

Untying the Signifier: Between Writing and Quoting

The best way out is through.
Robert Frost

Not content with Michelet and Balzac as examples of writers on the cusp of modernity, Barthes now chose to look at Sade, Loyola, then Fourier in a similar perspective. Though all writers of long before 1848, and thus liable to be part of classical writing in the 'degree zero' schema of things, all three were taken as key elements in a liberation of language by rebirth. This questioning of the rigid schema of the 'degree zero' history of literary language, form and thought pointed to the contradiction at the beginning of *Writing Degree Zero*. The opening words concerning Hébert's swearing clearly showed Barthes's preoccupation with history and ethics in language; but why include discussion of the changes in language during the French Revolution in a book whose remit was partly (as we saw) to challenge the view that there was *any* significant change in writers' attitude to language during and immediately after the French Revolution?

If the section on Fourier was the most utopian of the three, it was not the most scandalous. It is perhaps tempting to see the piece on Loyola, 'How to Speak to God', published in *TQ* in 1969, as influenced by the notion of silence of a Blanchot or the mysticism of a Bataille. But, in fact, it was in relation to Camus and Michelet that references to Loyola appear in Barthes's early writing. Camus had, he said in 1944, refused to give up 'style', to make the ' "jump" ' of a Loyola in the latter's 'sacrifice' of the intellect (OCi 63). Barthes's article could be seen as a critique of Camus's view, showing how Loyola, on the contrary, was profoundly interested in language.

The reference to Michelet and Loyola is an intriguing one. Michelet was, of course, the arch anti-Jesuit. In *Michelet* Barthes noted that one of Michelet's bugbears had been the idea of 'Grace', because it sent history 'to sleep'. So the fad for novels in Spain at the time of Cervantes and Loyola encouraged Michelet, said Barthes, to see this period of Spain as absent from the organic movement of history, because the novel, 'arbitrary' and 'full of illusion', a 'phantasmagoria of miracle', was an 'absorbing power' inspiring 'sleep' which turned away from history, and therefore justice (OCi 276/MI 56).

Even before its combination with Sade in book form, an article on Loyola could only have been seen as a challenge to Barthes to undermine the most influential of Jesuit thinkers. Then again, if Barthes's aim was to 'fissure' the symbolic of bourgeois and petty-bourgeois society, what better way than to show how one wing of this thought – Jesuit mysticism – had been founded by a practitioner of 'écriture'. Barthes made this point obliquely at the beginning of the 'Loyola' section of the book version, in an introductory passage, 'L'écriture', added to the original *TQ* version.[18]

Barthes reiterated his critique of bourgeois and classical conceptions of writing which isolated the functions of language, reducing them to the content they expressed and then finally considering the form only in as much as it allowed this content to appear clearly. He suggested that this was one way in which bourgeois ideology maintained hegemony:

> Classical ideology practises in culture the same economy as bourgeois democracy in politics: a separation and a balancing of powers; an ample but surveyed terrain is given over to literature, on condition that this space is isolated and in hierarchical opposition to other spaces; it is in this way that literature, whose function is worldly, is not compatible with spirituality; one being a detour, ornament, veil, the other being immediate(d), bare: that is why you cannot be both a saint and a writer. (OCii 1069/SFL 39–40)

His aim was to go right to the heart of the beast (as it were), and to show precisely how a founder of bourgeois ideology, Loyola, was indeed part of literature, and practised what he called the 'seriousness of form'. [H]owever "spiritual" ', Barthes declared, Loyola's *Exercises* 'are founded in writing'. With great skill and dexterity, Barthes then proceeded to show how.

Not content with showing how Loyola was a 'novelist', how the *Exercises* were written like a novel, Barthes placed Loyola's writing on a par with Baudelaire's hashish smoker (OCii 1079/SFL 54). Doubtless inspired by his seminar on Balzac in 1969, Barthes concluded in a manner which undermined the alienation of language inherent in the '1848' theory: it was partly our reading methodology which needed changing. Whereas the classical Racine seemed impenetrable to the modern mind, and had to be 'distanced' to be barely appreciated, Loyola, predating the classical period by a century, could be reappropriated. However, it is perhaps the differences between the two pieces on Sade in *Sade, Fourier, Loyola* that best illustrate developments in the period 1967–71.

The sheer shift in Barthes's style between 'Sade I' and 'Sade II' with regard to the fragments is striking. It is almost as if the trilogy of 'Sade I', 'Loyola' and 'Fourier' showed a static perception of three pre-modernist writers, only for the final essay, 'Sade II' to move up a gear, and provide the crucial example of how logothetical status was dependent on the modern critic (Barthes), rather than inherent in the text. Thus 'Sade II' acts as a kind of final statement on the three preceding essays, supplementing the tidy trilogy but also knocking it out of step. Why else split the two pieces on Sade?

Clearly, the subject matter in the two is very different (apart from their being about Sade, of course). 'Sade I', written around the same time as the work on *Sarrasine*, is bound up with the 'effect of the real' and narration (OCii 1052/SFL 16). The aim is to show Sade's writing as language (OCii 1058–60, 1065/SFL 26–8, 36): Sade is erotic not in his descriptions but in the manner in which he ' "reasons the crime" '. Sade was subversive not because he had recounted debauched scenes but because he made these poetic:

> We begin to realise that transgressions of language have a power to offend which is at least as strong as moral transgressions, and that "poetry", the very language of the transgression of language, is in this way always contestatory. From this point of view not only is Sade's writing poetic, but Sade took all precautions to make sure nothing could be done with this poetry: pornography today will never be able to recuperate a world which exists only in proportion

> to its writing, and society will never be able to recognise a writing which is structurally linked to crime and sex. (OCii 1064/SFL 34)

Thus, Barthes considered in 1967 that 'inside the Sadian novel there is another book, a textual one woven with pure writing', which determines everything that happens in the 'imaginary aspect' of the first. It is not a question of narrating, but of 'saying that you are narrating'. Sade scandalised because the myth of romantic inspiration did not like being told that it was (no more than) an act of putting things together. Those, said Barthes, who declared Sade boring were missing the importance of someone who achieved what Mallarmé later called the 'union of a book and its self-critique':

> The Sadian combination [. . .] can appear monotonous to us only if we send our reading off in an arbitrary fashion, away from Sade's discourse and towards the 'reality' which it is supposed to be representing: Sade is boring only if we become fixated by the crimes reported, instead of the performances of the discourse. (OCii 1065/SFL 36)

The conclusion of 'Sade I' was that Sade is tedious unless we read him critically; not exactly the same as *S/Z*'s, but essentially emphasising the same point: 'it is on the level of meaning, not of the referent, that we should read Sade' (OCii 1065/SFL 37).

If we compare the measured composure and tentative nature of 'Sade I' with the manner in which 'Sade II' explodes (if this unfortunate term can be excused), we will only have half of the reasons behind Barthes's decision to divide his writing on Sade into two. The whole tone of 'Sade II' is different. As well as a supplement to the trilogy of the book's title, it marks a new departure for the world of writing, displaying a writing as pastiche, as parody. '[I]sn't the best form of subversion that which disfigures, rather than destroys, the codes?' (OCii 1129/SFL 123), suggested Barthes at the beginning of 'Sade II'. In splitting his work on Sade, he was evidently aiming to highlight his new-found act of (literary) subversion.

Against the 'endoxa' of bourgeois ideology – considered hegemonic, as our earlier discussion of the two 1971 essays 'Mythology Today' and '*Pax Culturalis*' showed – Barthes wanted to set up theft as the only possible response. Since shocking was not the 'most profound subversion', there had to be an alternative weapon against the 'doxa', a 'paradoxal' discourse. Though 'Sade I' had shown that such a weapon could be developed 'only by founding a new language', 'Sade II' no longer considered the link between crime and sex specifically important:

> Sade's greatness is not to have celebrated crime, perversion, or to have used a radical language for this celebration; it is to have invented an immense discourse, based on his own repetitions (not those of others), paid out in details, surprises, journeys, menus, portraits, configurations, proper names, etc.; in short, counter-censorship, starting from that which is prohibited, now became the use of the novelistic. (OCii 1131/SFL 126)

'Sade II' showed that it was now not only the story-line which can be shown to be perverse, but also the form of the language being used: 'Sade too knows that the perfection of a perverse posture is inseparable from the phrasal model which serves to utter it' (OCii 1154/SFL 160). Thus, building on the 'rewriting' begun in *S/Z*, the novelistic now became not just a literary strategy: '*invention* (and not provocation)', declared Barthes, 'is a revolutionary act'. 'Sade II' shows Barthes more adventurous in his acts of 'invention', rewriting Sade, concentrating on the theatre and performance evident in Sade's work.

Sade himself had indeed been involved in producing plays whilst in prison, as Peter Weiss's play *Marat/Sade* amply showed. One reviewer of *Sade, Fourier, Loyola* insisted on the centrality of 'theatralisation' as a 'process which allows writing-production'. In what can only be described as an early attempt to 'rewrite' Barthes, Pierre Duvernois's review in *Critique* stressed the highly political nature of the project: to work at a destruction of bourgeois language whilst accepting that this must be done via language.[19] For Duvernois, *Sade, Fourier, Loyola* went beyond the recuperation that saw *Empire of Signs* as a decentred text. Barthes's new book was written in such a way as to make it unclassifiable.

The idea suggested above of a utopian/critique dialectic in *Empire of Signs*, in which Barthes moved away from the real all the better to criticise it, was alluded to by Jacques-Pierre Amette in his incisive (at times, itself poetic) review of *Sade, Fourier, Loyola.*[20] The 'unblocking' operated by Barthes was carried out with pleasure, and was all the more revolutionary because it was a 'double movement' which combined irony with solid reasoning, a musical finesse and fluidity of speech: 'getting carried away' was placed alongside an 'analytical rigour'.[21] Barthes's subversive skill was, said Amette, to have demonstrated that Sade's language was so different from his contemporaries' (the 'classics' according to the orthodoxy), Loyola was read so much by bourgeois culture *in spite* of his 'style', and Fourier was seen as so ridiculous in his sensual imaginings that to put the three writers together was to show the censorship that bourgeois society, in different ways, had operated. Barthes had shown how writing could be 'revolutionary, terrorist, not recuperable by the petty-bourgeoisie'. Gennie Luccioni made a similar point: Barthes had shown Sade and Fourier as truly revolutionary writers because not 'recuperable', due to society's inability to digest them.[22] Jean Ormesson reiterated this by calling *Sade, Fourier, Loyola* an 'essay of modern rhetoric', which used 'classical recipes under new masks'. Noting Barthes's importance to *TQ*, he wondered what Mao Tse-tung would think of Barthes's sympathies with Sade.[23] Even Claude Jannoud welcomed *Sade, Fourier, Loyola* as a 'new humanity' breaking through, 'perhaps truer than the old one'.[24]

The examples of Barthes's 'rewriting' of Sade are numerous. One example follows 'The Handkerchief' (1138/137), where Barthes 'rewrites' this 'scene' in 'The Furnishings of Debauchery' (1141–2/140–2); and at the end of 'Scene, Machine, Writing' (1152/156), he works Sade's text into his own erotic scene. Then, in the final sentence of 'Bringing Order', it becomes unclear *who* is describing the 'structure of pleasures' (1155/161). Having made the joining of his and Sade's texts explicit in 'Grammar', Barthes's addition and 'rewriting' appear at the end of 'Silence' when, anachronistically, he describes how silence in the Sadian orgy avoids resembling petty-bourgeois eroticism (1158/166). Finally, in 'biographeme' 9 (OCii 1167/SFL 176), Barthes incorporated into his prose a passage from Sade. These rewritings of Sade's texts do not simply point to the erotic in Barthes's early 1970s' writing, but show an overall political writing strategy. The narrative of Barthes's text – including the formal nature of the 'author of these lines' interventions – clashes superbly with the baroque style of the whole of 'Sade II'. Thus, not only had Barthes succeeded in breaking the taboo he saw in 1967 (that of talking about *and* linking sex and language), but he had also established a strategy for the novelistic which undermined bourgeois artistic concepts of genius, ownership and originality. In the wake of 'Sade II', the rewriting technique was extended to Fourier, when he described how Fourier *would* have liked the idea (in the Moroccan king's court) of a 'director of royal Scents' (1172/183).

It was the sheer pleasure with which Barthes reassessed, if not rewrote, these three figures of pre-modernity which is striking in *Sade, Fourier, Loyola.* Precisely this pleasurable aspect of his work dominated the critics' almost overwhelming and unanimous welcome of *The Pleasure of the Text.* However, much of the debate around this apparent celebration missed the essentially schizoid and dialectical view of culture with which Barthes was working in 1973. If we do not underline the pessimistic and alienated nature of language (as well as the more 'voluntarist' pleasures to be found by the 'reader-writer'), we cannot explain fully the final phase of his career. Before we look at this phase in the final chapter, we must consider the influence of Nietzsche, for a more nuanced view of 'pleasure'.

Pleasure and the 'Slight Return' of Nietzsche

> Nothing is new, everything comes back; it is a very old complaint.
>
> Roland Barthes

> For all that one is led to interpret the thought of a mind which one seeks to understand and make understood, no-one leads the interpreter to parody him to the same extent as Nietzsche [. . .] one always makes him say either more or less than he says.
>
> Pierre Klossowski

To undertake a theoretical reflection on the pleasure of the text has a tactical value.

Roland Barthes

We have seen, through this chapter, a somewhat pessimistic diagnosis of social, ideological and linguistic alienation dominating Barthes's thought in the early 1970s. This is not to say that all of his writing from this period makes for depressing reading, as the 'rewriting' of Sade showed. Hopefully, it is sufficiently clear from this book that Barthes, ever the dialectician, ever the Gidian, was able to overturn and re-establish, if only textually, a guarded form of pleasure in the midst of a world gone mad. This is the significance of *The Pleasure of the Text*: a somewhat desperate attempt to find pleasure amidst a world both alienated and alienating. This dialectical attitude was not reflected in the reviews, however.

Angelo Rinaldi in *L'Express* saw the book's demand for a 'gratuitous and unproductive *jouissance*' as 'revolutionary'.[25] Barthes wrote in such a creative way, as a novelist would write about life, that his theories often had more warmth than fictional characters: 'the latest paradox of the great master', the review was subtitled, 'to be readable is no longer a crime'. Jean-François Josselin considered this 'little book' to be 'immense' in its ability to describe and undermine the literary experience: Barthes was a 'voluptuous explorer'.[26] For Dominique Rolin, Barthes was like a conductor of an orchestra digging up and bringing to life unknown 'scores', like Mallarmé wanting a new relationship between stage and audience but now between writing and reading; and *pace* those who accused Barthes of coldness and inhumanity, *The Pleasure of the Text* placed the 'I' at the centre.[27] Maurice Nadeau's review seemed to mark a renewal of their friendship and shared concerns, after a lengthy period of literary estrangement, and led to their working together on '(Where) is Literature Going?' in 1974 (OCiii 57–69). Adorned with a cartoon of Barthes wearing and holding flowers, with a peace sign on his sleeveless cardigan, Nadeau's review considered Barthes's criticism of the left's tendency to censure pleasure as a move 'towards the hippies'. Leaving behind the 'recreation' of Balzac which had hidden the literary work behind a 'knowledge and terrorising practice', Barthes's treatise of pleasure was itself a pleasure to read, which would disappoint 'linguists and semioticians' and force them to find their pleasure elsewhere.[28] In true Barthesian spirit and *Critique* tradition (evident in the reviews of Barthes's other three books since 1970), Jean Moreau ambitiously 'rewrote' Barthes's own text.[29] Perhaps the most influential welcome was Bernard Poirot-Delpech's in *Le Monde*, which, before Nadeau's review, saw Barthes's book as his 'little kama-sutra'.[30] As Calvet pointed out, Delpech's was followed by a deluge of reviews, a phenomenon not seen since *Mythologies*.[31]

Underlining Barthesian interest in the Orient, Poirot-Delpech illustrated Barthes's radical inversion of the reader–author relationship with a Chinese proverb: 'It is no longer the eater who has the taste of rice, but the rice which has the taste of the eater.' But the review sounded a word of warning. Though not of Barthes's making, the danger was that students might marvel at the 'ease' with which Barthes the magician performed his 'trick', and be tempted simply to copy the maestro instead of establishing their own 'pleasures' of reading: ' "doing" Barthes as Dad might "do" [the traditionalist criticism of a] Lanson'. This last point was an important one in terms of 'influence' and freedom, which went to the heart of Barthes's decentred view of cultural practice. It is no surprise or coincidence that, in an interview in April 1973, soon after this review, Barthes reiterated his opposition to the notion of 'influence' (see OCii 1699, also OCi 1450–2/GV 25–9).

Claude Jannoud in *Les Nouvelles littéraires* concluded that there was no doubt that Barthes was a writer on a par with Valéry, Proust, Breton and Butor.[32] The influence of Barthes was now unmistakable. Pierre-Jean Faunau suggested that, with the disappearance of the 'author-person' and the criticism of decipherment in favour of the 'rigorous and voluptuous lover' of *écriture*, Barthes was 'one of this new race of writers', with whom it was a question of letting fragments enter our lives: 'we have to live with Barthes'.[33]

There were a number of important exceptions to the general praise of *The Pleasure of the Text*. The only piece to take a more pessimistic approach was that by *Tel Quel*ian Jacques Henric. Following Barthes's

'Supplement' (see OCii 1589), he saw Barthes as a great figure of modernity who managed to predict which direction fashion would take long before others: *The Pleasure of the Text* had quickly been declared a 'gadget' by Barthes in the 'Supplement' for fear of a stereotype appearing.[34] The anonymous reviewer in *Pourquoi pas?* considered Barthes's 'conversion' from his 'destruction of letters' of the previous twenty years to the 'pleasure [of reading literature] to the wagon of the revolution' as 'pitiable opportunism'.[35] Maurice Chapelan in *Le Figaro* felt none the wiser after a reading that had just one pleasure: the book was only one hundred (small) pages long.[36] Jean-Paul Aron, one-time friend of Barthes and colleague at the EHESS, was no less sceptical; he joked: 'I like Barthes for the reasons that he objects to', without suggesting what these might be.[37] Highly complex, Aron's review *seemed* to be suggesting that Barthes was leaving himself open to an easy recuperation by the university system. This was echoed in *Clés pour le spectacle*: in avoiding ideology at all costs, Barthes's praise of pleasure risked his own ideology falling into that of the 'ruling class'.[38]

Barthes's antipathy to the cultural police of left-wing Maoist thought was indeed to be an important element in his final text to be significantly marked by May 1968. *The Pleasure of the Text* was as much against the populist and philistine *proletkultism* of Maoist revolutionary rhetoric as it was against bourgeois cultural hegemony. Already in his piece on Fourier in 1970 Barthes had dared to 'defend' money (OCii 1102–3/SFL 85–7). In the original *Critique* article, he had tempered such a view, heretical to a Maoist-dominated proletarianism, with some proletarian ones of his own. He had asked in the original article, somewhat rhetorically, whether it was possible for a class to have a view of 'happiness' which was different to that of the class immediately above it, whether happiness was already a class idea, and what was the political mechanism of 'citation' and finally the cultural mechanism of revolution. He cut these questions out of the book version, in what can only be described as a further distancing from Maoist revolutionary fervour.[39]

The questioning of Marxism continued in 1973. Barthes's entry in the *Encyclopedia Universalis*, 'Theory of the Text', showed, skilfully and tactfully, the limits of linguistics and semiology and the need for the two epistemes of Marxism and psychoanalysis to undermine their 'imperialism' (OCii 1678–9/T 34). Yet no sooner had he posed the 'historical materialism' of Marx, Engels, Lenin and Mao and the psychoanalysis of Freud and Lacan than he proceeded to underline their ossified nature. In line with the view that the left had abandoned pleasure to the right, Barthes was beginning to see these radical discourses as becoming heavily stereotyped. 'Asphyxiated' by the 'idiolects' of what was once his own language, he vaunted in a 1973 interview his 'infidelity' to Marxism and psychoanalysis (OCii 1702).

He did not simply abandon these two crucial epistemes of modernity, but wanted to invent a new language for them (OCiii 347). How was a human subject, dissolved into language, still 'traversed' by these two determinant categories? Before we look at this question in the final chapter, we must consider Barthes's growing fascination with Nietzsche. For not only did Nietzsche provide a further episteme through which to consider the subject, it was precisely at this time of growing political disengagement that Barthes began to engage systematically with Nietzsche's ideas.[40]

Now, as Michael Moriarty has pointed out, the 'will to power' in language, which Nietzscheanism might inspire, stood in opposition to a Barthes deeply conscious of the oppression operated by language.[41] However, if we are to see the 'late Barthes' as a kind of 'moralist' – concerned with how people live out their lives – then we must consider the interest in, as Barthes himself put it in 1973, this 'formulator and liberator of a certain pluralism, of a pluralist thought' (OCii 1703). Gregory Ulmer has looked at Barthes's Nietzschean phase in relation to the fetish.[42] But there seemed to be some more fundamental influences from Nietzsche.

Nietzsche's views on theatre and tragedy had informed Barthes in the early phase of his career from the 1930s through to the 1950s. The German philosopher did not really reappear, however, until *Criticism and Truth*, and in the critique of historical 'fact' in the 'Discourse of History': what Barthes was doing with 'text' was the equivalent to what Nietzsche had done with truth (OCii 1678/T 34). But if there was a 'Nietzschean phase' as Ulmer suggests, it was most noticeable in *The*

Pleasure of the Text. Indeed, it is difficult not to see that work – despite seemingly rejecting the Nietzschean idea of hedonism as a form of pessimism (OCii 1523–4/PT 57) – as an attempt to rectify the fact that 'there has been no equivalent of Nietzsche in France', a writer who 'dares to discourse from spark to spark, abyss to abyss' (OCii 1007/GV 72).

In the 'war of languages', whilst insisting on the fictional and sacerdotal status of intellectuals, Barthes, like Georges Bataille, saw bourgeois and petty-bourgeois culture as a 'flattening' ('aplatissement') of value. Here Michelet's and Nietzsche's nineteenth-century pessimism dovetailed with Barthes's own post-1968 'boredom'. It was from this point that Nietzsche became an important and regular reference, prompting many of the formulations which Barthes would borrow in his rediscovery of Michelet, in the 'generalising of the subject' and the subject as 'fiction' (OCii 1525–6/PT 61–2). All of these, as we shall see, were crucial elements in the post-1974 phase of Barthes's career.

Douglas Smith's recent study of Nietzsche's reception in France stresses the resurrection of the German philosopher which took place in the early 1970s, through thinkers such as Sarah Kofman, Pierre Klossowski and Gilles Deleuze. There is little doubt that Barthes's growing interest in Nietzschean thought was mediated by Klossowski and Deleuze, both amply cited in *A Lover's Discourse.*

According to Alain Arnaud, Barthes had known Klossowski as early as 1948, playing piano duets with him at a time when the latter was writing on Sade; and had, according to David Macey, introduced him to Michel Foucault at the start of the 1960s.[43] Klossowski's work on Nietzsche – a collection of important essays in 1963, the organisation of the Royaumont conference in 1964, published in 1967, and finally his *Nietzsche and the Vicious Circle* in 1969 – was to influence 'the death of the author' theorist considerably, in relation to the self and its disintegration in the acts of pleasure and '*jouissance*' in reading. '[I]t is', Douglas Smith notes, 'the self-cancelling logic of Nietzsche's work which permits its appropriation', and Klossowski demonstrated how his interpretation left Nietzsche open to an 'expropriation'.[44]

Klossowski's angle on the German philosopher showed – against the pessimism typical of standard views of Nietzschean 'eternal return' – that, in order to live, we needed a relation to the contemporary plurality of the singular event through its infinite repetition. He demonstrated the tension in Nietzsche's thought between science and aesthetics, and the latter's pyrrhic triumph: if both science and art were seen as 'errors' by Nietzsche, stressed Klossowski, at least art, as a simulacrum, was a self-conscious construct ('willed error'). In short, Klossowski underlined the fundamentally mythological belief at the heart of Nietzschean philosophy, based on desire, parody and fiction rather than reality: what Smith calls 'a ludic suspension of the principle of reality'. Klossowski held that parody extended to eternal return – that even eternal return is a parody which deprives everything it touches of any coherence, 'from history to the individual', a 'creative fiction which challenges the very notion of truth'. This notion must have impressed Barthes, who, twenty years before, had insisted on the singular nature of history, but had gone on to see change – in fashion at least – as cyclical. He had theorised the simulacrum as evidence of bourgeois cultural hegemony, only to realise, in a 'dialectic of love', that these 'degraded' forms were a mirroring of people's psychic reality, not simply signs of the alienating nature of commodities.

Deleuze's views, very different from Klossowski's work on Nietzsche, also influenced Barthes. Like Klossowski, Deleuze insisted on the 'reversal of platonism', leading to the 'rehabilitation of the simulacrum'.[45] But Deleuze's mix of psychoanalytical and Marxian categories posed Nietzsche's 'Nomadic thought' as a form of 'counter-culture', both subversive and recuperable. *Anti-Oedipus*, published in 1972, described the revolutionary potential of schizophrenia, seeing both the (highly Barthesian) tendency of a subject to move from one code to another and self-critique as elements of this condition. However, repetition was perhaps the key Nietzschean theme for Barthes. As a return itself from Barthes's early work, on both fashion and historiography, the post-1968 period saw him questioning again the contradictions between change and structure, and between singular and general phenomena.

Barthes had seen the fracturing of the symbolic order as nihilistic in the 'nearly Nietzschean sense' (1015/85). But over the next two years, as disappointment with China set in, he began to see all culture as 'subject to an unremitting repetition' (OCiii 1188/RL 100), a fact attributed to the lack of innovation from a petty-bourgeoisie in whom models were 'repeated' and 'flattened'. Even this returning was itself a repetition of bourgeois culture. Here was the Barthesian bugbear of the 'stereotype' (OCii 1190–1/GV 103–4).

So it is no coincidence in this period that he began to celebrate the figure of the spiral (OCii 1200/RL 318). It appears in articles on language (OCii 1609/RL 124), on the abstract painter Requichot (OCii 1630–2/RF 217–20), and especially in the 1971 preface to the new edition of the *Critical Essays* (OCi 1168/not in CE). The spiral was a way of accommodating both Nietzsche and Hegel, if not Nietzsche and Marx (see OCii 1289/GV 126): it was progressive without being teleological, dialectical without totalising, repetitive without constructing a stereotype. Since even modernity was now being repeated – 'for a hundred years, we have been in repetition' (OCii 1211/RL 56) – the spiral became the figure within which Barthes could criticise modernity.

If 'to get past' the stereotype was an 'unrealistic desire' – for language, not fully dialectical, allowed us to move only in 'two-steps' (OCii 1200/RL 317) – then the only way of undermining the stereotype was precisely to celebrate repetition, to repeat as if citing, in a spiral fashion. The haïku, the quotation, were both examples of a void (of the referent in the former, of 'genius' in the latter). The new task for Barthes was to find a 'new' semiology, 'not in order to be original, but to pose the theoretical problem of repetition' (OCii 1292/GV 129). Thus, like psychoanalysis and 'rêve' before it, repetition now became a source not of alienation as such, but of creativity. This was the philosophical basis of his re-reading and now rewriting strategy.

The aphoristic status of the following from *S/Z* pointed to a concern with 'eternal return': 'those who fail to re-read are forced to read the same story everywhere' (OCii 565/SZ 16). This is augmented in his analysis of a Poe story in 1973, where he described codes as the 'already-seen, already-read and already-made' (OCii 1672/SC 288). Structurally similar to the manner in which boredom with Racine at the end of the

1950s became a textual performance strategy which attempted to undermine Racine, the ethos of repetition and citation developed at this time. Thus, by applying the Nietzschean notion of 'eternal return' and 'flattening' to the consumption of literature, Barthes could insist on the pleasure of re-reading and (re)writing.

Rewriting and copying could be extended to other Nietzsche-inspired writers. In good *TQ* fashion, the acts of rewriting and copying were to be the opposite of spontaneity for Barthes: 'spontaneity is the field of the *immediate*, of the *already-said*'. Rather than give the signified the freedom to return, thereby allowing, paradoxically, closure and the consequent lack of freedom, he wanted the freedom of the signifier: 'return of words, of plays on words, of proper names, of quotation, etymologies, reflexivities of discourse, of typography, of blanks, of "combinations" ("*combinatoires*"), of refusals of language', anything which allowed us to read in the central text the crucial idea of all writing: 'everything circulates' (OCii 1420/RL 72). The notion of circulation, so crucial to Bataille, was now central to Barthes's definition of the avant-garde (OCii 1597/RF 153). Clearly, it was inspired by a post-1968 materialist critique of creative 'genius', originality, ownership, inheritance – in short, of capitalist social relations in intellectual and creative matters – and promoted instead sharing, stealing and unoriginality. But it was also inspired by Bataille's notion of the void. Against the 'full' nature of repetition and stereotype, 'the void' represented the opposite. Rather than an absence, the void was 'more like the new, the return of the new (which is the opposite of repetition)' (OCii 1284/GV 118). Who better then to illustrate circularity and the repetitive void of the signifier than Bataille himself? In the 1973 piece 'The Outcomes of the Text', Barthes's contribution to the commemorative conference on Bataille, he analysed the surrealist's text 'The Big Toe'. Noting Bataille's Nietzschean obsession with italics, Barthes proceeded quite gratuitously then to parody this obsession (see OCii 1620–2/RL 247–9).

The 'flattening of values' and 'boredom' that Barthes was experiencing in this period were accompanied by the 'boredom' of 'consuming' avant-garde, unreadable texts alone; and it was in opposition to this that Barthes resurrected the 'pleasure' of re-reading classics. Though in

1971 he had not been able to see how one could write 'like that', in a classical fashion – knowing how one can*not* write was perhaps to know one's modernity, he suggested – Barthes's 'rather sad realisation' went on to found the final phase of his career. It was to be precisely a classical writing of the old literary themes – love, the diary, Proust, photography and memory – that would dominate. Unlike modern texts, which of course could not (yet?) be 'rewritten', the classics were now ripe for a 'rewriting' strategy. Here was the interest in one of Barthes's favourite novels by Flaubert, *Bouvard et Pécuchet*: a copy of a copy.

Thus, Barthes had transposed the Klossowskian view of Nietzschean thought into his critique of French culture. This did not exclude paradoxes and parodies of repetition, of course, evident for example in the triumphant manner in which *The Pleasure of the Text* saw Robbe-Grillet as *already* present in Flaubert, Sollers *already* in Rabelais (OCii 1504/PT 20). In an interview in 1972, published in the new weekly newspaper emerging from 1968, *Politique-hebdo*, Barthes set out his view of appropriate action (OCii 1473–7/GV 150–6). Theorising the destruction of bourgeois control, a language of 'transformation' and 'production' needed to be promoted. In short, despite the alienation of language and its social divide, artists and writers needed to undermine language from the inside, by reassembling and 'combining' the elements of (bourgeois-controlled) language with which to subvert its controllers. Certain that there was an (inevitable) divorce between intellectuals and the 'mass' of French workers, because of language, Barthes's view was that there must be a different focus: 'One of the century's historical tasks is to know how the petty-bourgeoisie can itself become a progressive class. I think that if we do not manage to answer this question, history risks standing still for a long time' (OCii 1476/GV 154). Barthes implied a certain *détente* in attacks on petty-bourgeois culture, a prediction which largely proved correct in France, and he reiterated this by quoting Brecht in *The Pleasure of the Text* (OCii 1509/PT 29–30) on peaceful moments between skirmishes, in which one could sit down and enjoy a beer. Barthes thus seemed to foresee the social changes of the coming years. From 1974 onwards, France (and Western Europe) saw a relative, though dramatic, subsidence in ideological, political and social challenge, a 'downturn'.

Recognising the interviewer's point that the activities based on the 'nihilism' of a Nietzsche were practised only by 'narrow groups', Barthes now accepted that, though the esoteric destruction of meaning was necessary, it could not be an attempt to reach the 'masses'. The following comment was an important indicator of his later writing on the discourse of love: 'French society, on the cultural level, is so subjected to the models of petty-bourgeois culture that, in order to reach a large audience, one has to compromise oneself (and one's action) in these models' (OCii 1477/GV 156). For, in writing about one of the key elements of social interaction, Barthes was widening his appeal to a greater section of society. At the same time, he now 'returned' to the more aesthetic and literary concerns of his earliest writings.

6

Biography, Democracy, Loss

Literature is like a religion for me.
Roland Barthes

Won't a 'Scienza Nova' have to express both the brilliance and the suffering of the world, that in it which both seduces and outrages me?
Roland Barthes

IT IS PERHAPS NO coincidence, in relation to the 'late Barthes' at least, that 'romancier', 'romance' and 'romanticism' have the same etymology. When asked in 1975 if he considered himself a failed novelist, Barthes quickly replied 'or future novelist, who knows?' 'A century ago', he added, 'I would have been walking through life holding the notebook of a realist novelist' (OCiii 313/GV 203). Though heavy with (self-)irony, these words suggest an important change of direction in the last six years of his life.

His work on pleasure had instigated a new attitude. 'Pleasures', he suggested in an interview in March 1973, 'are finite in number'; 'and', he added, 'it will certainly be necessary for a disalienated society, if it ever happens, to pick up in another place, spiral fashion, certain fragments of bourgeois social graces' (OCii 1695/GV 172–3). More than simply a reiteration of the 'pleasure in the classics' or a 'pleasure of the text', such a comment indicated a new concept of his role, which we might describe as depoliticisation, or at least depolemicisation. The difference between Calvet's 1973 assessment, which had insisted on the political aspect, and Stephen Heath's 1974 characterisation of 'displacement' as the central Barthesian ethos reflected this shift well.

Of the *nouveaux philosophes* in 1976, the most important were often disillusioned leftists, either Maoists (Bernard-Henri Lévy, André Glucksmann) or anti-Stalinist Marxists such as Jean-François Lyotard. Their rise was mirrored in Barthes's and Sollers's dining with President Giscard, evidence of what some have called *TQ*'s 'turn to the right'.[1] Barthes's own 'detachment' ('décrochage') from politics had begun, as he had suggested, in ignoring Japan's economic system in *Empire of Signs* and been 'accentuated' in *The Pleasure of the Text* (OCiii 332/GV 230).

Indeed, to some, Barthes's appointment in 1977 to a chair of semiology at the Collège de France, though not as the Minister of Education as predicted by Paulhan in 1955, was still a sign of recuperation by the institution. In a review of *Leçon*, Barthes's inaugural lecture, and the proceedings of the conference on Barthes at Cerisy in 1977, Kenneth White, the Scottish poet, pointed to the contradiction in Barthes's desire not to be 'fried' into a particular image: accepting a chair of semiology was surely to fall into this trap.[2] White objected too to the politeness with which Barthes had been treated at Cerisy, suggesting ironically that a table-tennis tournament would be next on the list of activities organised by Antoine Compagnon. The whole conference, he said, had highlighted Barthes's inability to escape the 'confected' and 'closed-doors' nature of the French language. In practice, semiology only turned 'round in circles': to 'cheat' was an admirable strategy, but it could not then allow a 'cortège' to follow (rather sycophantically, implied White) Barthes's every turn. Support for the inaugural lecture did seem to confirm White's point.[3]

One important development within his 'detachment' was the increasing affective *at*tachment to friends and family. The collection and publication in 1979 of his writings on Philippe Sollers, *Sollers Writer*, was inspired, it seems, by the desire to defend his best friend against the hostile critics.[4] It showed Barthes to be prepared even to 'readmit' the author (OCiii 960/SW 92). But the crucial event in his last years was the death in 1977 of his mother, with whom he had lived all his life.

In 1971, Barthes had explained his attachment to his mother, as 'she who removes social alienation' (OCii 1309). Her loss was a crucial moment in his late career: after 1977 his writing was characterised by a sense of loss, and by a concern with memory worthy of a Patrick

Modiano novel. To see the final phase of Barthes's career as 'romantic' is not a facile critique of *A Lover's Discourse*, but, on the contrary, to consider (and in some sense experience) suffering at the level of memory and loss, and appreciate the dialectic of these two: that is, how to overcome loss via memory. It is no coincidence then that this period saw Barthes emphasising his interest in (German) romantic music.

This 'romantic' phase was not simply a function of his growing interest in the great writer of memory, Marcel Proust, but the crowning of a life-long fascination with the romantic historian Jules Michelet. Precisely during the period of growing Nietzschean 'detachment', Barthes rediscovered the significance of the nineteenth-century historian. Michelet was 'modern' because he had not only searched for an effective link with the past and a new science of life, but also taken sides on behalf of, and given a voice to, those excluded in and by history. The radical democrat of nineteenth-century popular culture provided lessons for the Barthes of a century later. Indeed, describing Barthes's view of the liberal (as well as totalitarian) nature of the signifier in 1978, Jacques-Alain Miller deemed him a 'democrat'.[5]

However, the 'dissolution' of the subject through psychoanalysis meant that, in Barthes's work, it was not a romantic and individualist 'genius' of the nineteenth-century self which impressed, but a collective and unidentifiable source of knowledge which 'circulated'. How do we relate to the past, creatively and critically, without falling into the traps of bourgeois and romanticist individualism? Michelet, the voice through which the 'people' could speak, provided the answer. Central to Barthes's views on writing and reading, and cultural practices in general, this 'democratic' concept of creativity was defined by the (seemingly egotistical, but paradoxically selfless) act of writing one's *own* biography.

The idea of writing a biography of himself (as opposed to an autobiography) went back to 1971. Throughout the period 1971–4, we can see presages of *Roland Barthes*, from the 'biographemes' in *Sade, Fourier, Loyola* to the highly ironic autobiographical interview, 'Réponses', in *TQ*, which declared that 'all biography is a novel which does not dare say its name' (OCii 1307). An interview in 1972 thought we 'ought perhaps to redo biographies as *écritures* of life' (OCii 1306/GV 149). Then *Le Monde* in 1973, inquiring about his writing practices, saw Barthes base the interest in the self on sound theoretical premises: 'Insignificance, we must not forget, is the place of real significance. That's why I consider it fundamental to examine a writer's working practices' (OCii 1710/GV 177). The same year Barthes had reviewed Sollers's monumental work, *H*.[6]

If this review was indicative of the course Barthes wanted to follow after *The Pleasure of the Text* in terms of a modern 'beauty' (see that book's opening paragraph), then the manner in which he insisted that the critical reaction to *H* was part of *H* itself (OCiii 958–60/SW 92) prefigured the auto-critique of *Roland Barthes*. Indeed Philippe Dulac, in direct contradistinction to White, criticised the satirical *Roland Barthes sans peine* for not seeing that Barthes's writings already contained a 'sufficiently mocking autocritique'.[7]

Self-critique was an obvious element in his growing 'detachment'. Following a course of psychoanalysis with Roland Havas in 1975, Barthes had begun to dissolve his own subjectivity. In his last article in *Communications*, the 'subject' who came out of the cinema was to be found – in Lacanian fashion – in a multiplicity of places: 'he', 'I', 'one' were the terms of reference (OCiii 256–9/RL 345–9). Part of this dissolution was to admit the 'dialectic of love' into the very things which he had criticised so strongly in the previous five years: the stereotype, the 'trap', the 'glued': what he called a 'dual rapport', both 'narcissistic and maternal'. Moves to accept contradiction in the face of 'doxa' were also the point at which 'maternal space' (to borrow Knight's term)[8] and the 'photogrammes' became part of the project of investigating photography in *Camera Lucida*. Even Brecht's 'critical distance' was now questioned, in favour of a dialectic of love:

> There is another way of going to the cinema (other than being armed with the discourse of a counter-ideology). [. . .] That which I use to take my distance with regard to the image, there it is, is that which fascinates me: I am hypnotised by a distance; and this

distance is not critical (intellectual); it is, as it were, an amorous distance. (OCiii 259/RL 349)

Then Brecht's reading of Hess's 'detestable' speech was undermined by an 'erotic of the text' (OCiii 260–7/RL 212–22): 'The destruction of the monstrous text uses here an amorous technique', mobilising not 'the reductive weapons of demystification' but rather 'caresses, amplifications, the ancient subtleties of literary scholarship'. This was, in short, a critique of bourgeois thought from within bourgeois culture itself: 'where else?', asked Barthes rhetorically (OCiii 262–3/RL 216). Of course, there is nothing more 'retro' than to subvert bourgeois democracy by pointing to its extreme (but logical) aberrations via a pleasure of parody and recycling.

The other side of the attempt to 'dissolve the subject' was to reject (therefore to examine) the manner in which the self was constructed; hence an acute sense of 'image' in the 'late Barthes'. But the constant displacements described by Heath could not achieve this dissolution; for to displace oneself constantly is, of course, to end up with the image of a 'displacer'. Therefore, the self had to use a 'tactical suspension': all attempts to undermine a 'fixed' image were 'provisional', suggested Barthes, transposing his Bachelardian critique of science and social theory to the self. This provisionality, once applied to the self, implied that the 'fatigue' noted at the end of the previous chapter could in fact be a corrosive, and paradoxically active, element in the attempt to undermine 'image'.

I want to show in this final chapter that, far from becoming progressively self-obsessed (as some might superficially suggest), the dissolving of the subject in Barthes's writing was like Michelet's writing of history. It attempted, democratically, to open out the possibility of reflection, and, at the same time, allowed each self to see itself shifting: a kind of Gidian practice of writing – both fictional and literary – but open to all and sundry. This does not stop us noting how Barthes's writing, on a 'macro' scale across his career, had moved him from the 1950s' spectator and critic on the periphery of cultural phenomena – watching from the ringside and intervening from the sidelines – to the 1970s' star entering and taking up the acting and action with the critical spotlight firmly on him: always, of course, in the most unassuming of ways.

By the mid-1970s, Barthes was clearly writing in a self-assured, literary way. One need look only at his poetic (but still ironic and self-conscious) preface to Brillat-Savarin's *Physiology of Taste* (OCiii 280–94/RL 250–70). At one point he exclaimed (for the sake of the alliteration, it is pointless to translate): 'cadavre exquis, confit, candi, en confiture!' (287/259). Both the 'mysticism of pleasure' and the sheer number of interviews in 1975, one of which put forward the view that the best way to avoid 'solidification' was to 'pretend to write in a classical style' (OCiii 318/GV 209–10), betrayed a self-conscious maturity. Though linked to a 'dissolved' subjectivity, this made *Roland Barthes* a key element in the rise to distinctly literary prominence.

Writing the (Gidian?) Self

> I worry about not knowing who I am; I don't even know who I want to be; but I do know that I have to make a choice. I feel in me thousands of possibilities, but cannot resign myself to want to be just one of them. And it frightens me, every moment, every word I write, to think that this is one more indelible trait of my image which is taking hold.
>
> André Gide

> The old opposition, between subjectivity as an attribute of impressionist criticism, and objectivity as an attribute of scientific criticism, is no longer of any interest.
>
> Roland Barthes

The decision to republish his 1942 article 'On Gide and his Journal' in the *Magazine littéraire* special number in 1975 does not seem to have been Barthes's.[9] Jean-Jacques Brochier's introductory comments, disagreeing with Barthes's view of the article as 'soft wishy-washy humanism', suggest that the idea was the magazine's. Indeed, as Brochier pointed out, many of the themes in the 1942 article were being replayed by Barthes in 1975. But why might Barthes now wish to downplay this Gidian connection?

Philippe Roger suggests that the fragment on Gide in *Roland Barthes*, 'Abgrund' (OCiii 170–2/RB 99), was highly ironic about attributing a Gidian influence – in Roger's view, for fear of appearing 'weighed down', if not 'old-fashioned'.[10] After all, to be a Gidian is indeed a contradiction in terms, not only because it is difficult to sum Gide up, but because the Gidian ethos was for others to be 'protean' and not enslaved to any one system or style. It is under this paradox that we shall consider *Roland Barthes*. Inspired by Gidianism, but not cancelled out or 'recuperated' by it, *Roland Barthes* must be read then for its self-irony.

The similarity between Barthes's 1942 article on Gide and his biography of himself thirty years later is uncanny; all of the following comments on Gide from 1942, then, can be considered as applicable to *Roland Barthes*. First, the 'dialogue' that Barthes found in the meeting of Gide's *Journal* and his works would be replicated in *Roland Barthes*, as would Gide's uncertainty about the status of the details considered too insignificant for a novel. In spiral fashion, Barthes would go on in 1975 to raise Gide's preoccupation with the self outside of 'art' and make himself (Barthes), in Nietzschean fashion, into an object of literary analysis.

Strikingly similar to the use of the third person in *Roland Barthes*, and to the suggestion that it be read as if spoken by a character in a novel, Barthes's 1942 article had shown how Gide always wanted to be one of the characters in his own novel. Describing Gide's diary style as 'sentences halfway between creation and confession', Barthes had prefigured his own writing style in *Roland Barthes*. Approving Gide's belief that it was from the artistic point of view that his *Journal* should be judged critically (and pointing ahead to the style of presentation in *A Lover's Discourse*), Barthes had considered that Gide's critical works, the 'most profound parts of himself', needed to be read like certain editions of the Bible with a synopsis of references, or like the *Encyclopedia* with notes in the margin (OCi 24/BR 4). The 'life as literature' of the 'late' Barthes was evident in his views on Gide in 1942.

Also, the slippery and ironic self-presentation of *Roland Barthes* owed much to Barthes's original view of Gide as an ever-changing 'simultaneous being'. Gide took 'aesthetic pleasure in slowly revealing the tiny changes in his nature' (26/6). Indeed, he had noted, the self could be 'corrected' by the autobiographical nature of the diary, in this 'mystical' 'dialogue' of a soul 'looking for itself' (OCi 23–4/not in BR). As with the slipperiness with 'systems' in *Roland Barthes,* Gide's 'perpetual setting the record straight of himself' was contradicted by never 'giving himself' fully in a work: as Barthes put it in 1942, 'Gide's discoveries have never meant rejections'. Did this mean Gide's thought was 'neutral'? 'With this man', he had answered, 'we never know': 'he places himself in such a way that he is ahead of you in appreciating his weaknesses, so that it is difficult to impute them to him. We do not know if this is done voluntarily but without warning, without telling us if it is conscious or not.' Everything in Gidian thought was 'linked to movement'. Thus the truth of people was in their 'impulses', and conflict within the self meant the search for truth was more important than its finding. Indeed, stressed Barthes, it was this 'escape' from all dogmas and opinions which allowed Gide's diary to be a work of art. All the above comments on Gide's diary from 1942 are possible descriptions of *Roland Barthes.*

This is not to say that *Roland Barthes* simply replayed (Barthes's early view of) Gidian themes. On the contrary, there is a sense in which the book represents, in spiral fashion, an attempt to 'disalienate' the self from the contradiction in which Gidian writing had left it. As Barthes noted, he wanted to imagine a utopian society in which the 'amateur', a creation 'in theory', was 'disalienated' (OCiii 323/GV 217). In this sense, *Roland Barthes* evolved Gidian dialectical subjectivity into a dissolved, imageless 'pleasure of writing'. This move from a purely individual to a social concern, collapsing the opposition in Gidian thought between the individual and the social, was, as we shall see, an important component in Barthes's 'democratic' cultural practice.

'Image', not surprisingly, was at the heart of the warm reception given to *Roland Barthes. Le Monde* had welcomed *Roland Barthes* by asking a series of writers, such as Sollers and Claude Roy, to talk about *their* Barthes.[11] Then, as if to heap irony on the fact that this number of the

'Ecrivains de toujours' series on Barthes was written by Barthes, Barthes reviewed his own biography of himself.

'Barthes to the Power of Three' (OCiii 253–5) appeared in what might be described as a special number of *La Quinzaine littéraire*, divided between Barthes and China. The front cover read: 'Barthes assesses the "Barthes" by Barthes'.[12] Barthes's 'review', prefaced by Nadeau and followed by extracts from the 'book of the fortnight', joked that Barthes – he was still writing in the third person – was the 'only person unable to speak *really* about himself'; 'this', he continued, 'was the "disappointing" significance of the book' (254–5).

Clearly, this 'stunt' served to highlight the playfulness of the idea not only of Barthes writing his own biography, but also that there was one on him at all. After all, the series up till then had dealt exclusively with the 'greats' of literature and thought. To place 'Barthes' here whilst (I choose at random) Marx, Nietzsche, Racine, Sand were absent from the ninety-six already published in 1975 was perhaps difficult to defend.

The second half of this number of *La Quinzaine littéraire* was devoted to reviews of recent books on China, most of which underlined the human rights and socio-cultural failure of Maoist rule. Though not as powerful as Solzhenitsyn's, these revelations about forced labour camps only added to the disillusionment with left-wing revolutionary thought besieging former May 1968 activists. Thus, the 'review' of *Roland Barthes* and attention to China's failed experiment were a fitting combination. It underlined forcibly the end of Barthes's (mild) blindness to the 'excesses' of Maoist China, attributable, in part at least, to those sinologists who were (mis)informing *Tel Quel*.[13]

The importance of Barthes in 1975 was such that *Critique* carried two separate reviews in the same number.[14] Alain Rey's 'The Body in Mirrors' saw *Roland Barthes* as 'an arrangement of reflections', which, though 'flat', were nevertheless profound, because they showed how a reflection of the self was impossible. Barthes's skill was to have established an image of the self which moved continually in and out of sight: 'Present and turned away, going into the distance, he gets larger.' The second review was by Jean-Louis Bouttes, a student from Barthes's seminar at the EPHE, to whom a fragment of 'To the Seminar' had been dedicated. In 1974, Bouttes had written in the *Arc* special number on Barthes on truth, lies and falsehood, providing Barthes with a number of ideas which resurfaced in *Roland Barthes*, particularly the notion of 'stupidity' ('bêtise') (see OCiii 133, 179/RB 51, 110).[15] Since a number of 'conversations' in *A Lover's Discourse* are attributed to Bouttes, and mentioned in *Roland Barthes*, there is the distinct impression that his review acted as a reply and supplement to Barthes's 'biography'. Indeed, thanking not just Bouttes but also Roland Havas and François Wahl 'for the text', in the same breath as a list of others 'for the pictures' (OCiii 82/not in RB), suggested that *Roland Barthes* was, for Barthes, a fulfilment of the Brechtian desire of having people 'think through' his mind, and vice versa. We will return to this in a moment.[16]

Many reviews insisted on the literary aspect of *Roland Barthes*. Jean Duvignaud considered it a complex Nietzschean 'poetry of fragments', more like Proust than Gide.[17] Camille Bourniquel underlined that, 'above all', Barthes was a 'writer, and in the end, fairly conscious of this fatality'; this 'pastiche' of the self suggested a certain irony that the glorious collection 'Writers of all time', concerned with biography and exegesis of dead authors, should find its *chef-d'oeuvre* in a living writer writing about himself.[18] More a 'voyage', a 'homage and a trap' for Jean-François Josselin, *Roland Barthes* was not an analysis or a 'digest' of the books written by Barthes, which would have 'allowed us to talk about them without having read them'. Like the *Argos* (continually changing its constituent parts – a favourite structuralist metaphor), this 'funny old novel, absolutely imaginary' jumped 'over the wall of classifications and stereotypes', like an 'infinite dance' giving us the metronome to which 'to waltz'.[19] More theatrical than literary, *Roland Barthes* was 'a living germination' for Robert Kanters: Barthes was putting his own 'character' 'on stage', with the 'little anecdotes' as part of 'the production's scenery'.[20] Kanters's favourable review finished on an important point. 'Nicer' and 'more tormented' than Barthes's 'openly touted intellectual arrogance', the book showed 'tangible emotion', 'dramatic' and 'youthful' memories from a man who 'disliked his body'. Barthes, he said, was admitting his 'susceptibility' to the bourgeois way of life.

Thus, *Roland Barthes* became part of a heated debate over the political role of the intellectual in post-1968 France. Jean Thibaudeau, who had conducted the *TQ* autobiographical interview with Barthes in 1971 just before his departure from the journal, was now the reviewer of the interview's results in book form.[21] Discussing Barthes's reply to the *Le Monde* questionnaire on the role of the intellectual (OCiii 76/GV 196–7), published just as *Roland Barthes* was finished in November 1974, Thibaudeau praised Barthes's conception of the intellectual for its political consequences. '[T]o encourage *everyone* to see themselves as very real actors in what is happening and to understand how the ideas that "lead the world" are governed, would be to increase considerably revolutionary chances', he declared. Barthes's reply to *Le Monde* – that the intellectual was treated like a sorcerer, magically undermining ideological interests, and, under the threat of liquidation by Fascism, 'decomposing bourgeois and petty-bourgeois ideology' – was a critique of the intellectual, said Thibaudeau, from the 'inside'. Since intellectuals were 'beings in language', any decomposition of dominant ideology had to take place from *within* bourgeois language, and had therefore to accept its analytical, as well as utopian, status. Thibaudeau now went on to show how *Roland Barthes* performed this. If the fight against Picard was part of modernity's revolutionary contribution to May 1968, Barthes was now outwitting the State's attempts to recuperate the intellectual as a 'great thinker'. *Roland Barthes* showed that Picard had been right all along to see Barthes as an 'impostor'; and with his refusal, evident since *The Pleasure of the Text*, to stick to the level of the 'politicist', Barthes's persistent use of a 'textual' Brecht was an indication that class struggle needed allegiances, said Thibaudeau. Finally, in literary terms, Barthes had, in exemplary fashion, transformed the 'schizoid' split, 'I/he', into a historical project, a split which was both incurable and the condition of human artistic practices. Twenty years after *Writing Degree Zero* had challenged Sartrian hegemony, Barthes had become the 'explicit figure' of a new literature, one which 'class struggle wrote positively'.

Not surprisingly, Thibaudeau's forthright, above all revolutionary, praise raised objections. In the same journal three months later, Jean-

Claude Dupas challenged this revolutionary view of Barthes.[22] Referring to 'Reproach by Brecht to Roland Barthes' in *Roland Barthes*, Dupas regretted that, when placed next to the definition of ideology in *The Pleasure of the Text* – 'ideology passes over the text and its reading like a face going red (certain people in love might find this redness erotic)' (OCii 1510/PT 31) – Barthes's distinction between politics and pleasure made ideology into nothing more than an 'addition, a supplement to the soul, remaining exterior to the text, without participating in it'. Furthermore, wrote Dupas, *Roland Barthes* claimed a '*jouissance* of ideology as secondary perversion', no longer seeing it as 'alienating' (OCiii 174/RB 104). Following the view that the expression 'dominant ideology' was 'quite rancid' from overuse (OCiii 163/RB 89), and that the 'subversion of all ideology was at stake' (OCii 1511/PT 32–3), Dupas concluded that the 'desire for rest' in Barthes's thought since 1973 amounted to nothing more than saying that 'taking power was a matter of getting hold of words'. He thought this a dubious understanding of political and ideological power, peddling 'the illusion of the "autonomy" of its functioning'.

Following Dupas's article, Thibaudeau placed his reply under the title 'Roland Barthes is not a Marxist'. Twenty years after the joust with Paulhan in which Barthes had been accused of being a 'Marxist', here was Thibaudeau saying the opposite: clearly Barthes's 1955 'mythology' 'Am I Marxist?' still had currency in 1975. Thibaudeau's reply was nevertheless of interest. Putting forward a modernist conception of literature and culture, he denied that ideology was the 'last word in the literary debate'. Dupas's inference that there was a 'reflection' of ideology in literature, though based on Marx' and Engels's views in *The German Ideology*, had also been used by Stalin's cultural thug Jdanov, with the dire consequence of the 'socialist realist' doctrine. Preferring Gramsci's conception of ideology to Marx's, Thibaudeau considered a political – as opposed to an economistic and sociological – definition of ideology far more appropriate in today's world. Thibaudeau's rather curious view of Solzhenitsyn as 'merely a puppet of the West' notwithstanding, he set out why Barthes was important to this debate.

Barthes had consistently and publicly vaunted the brilliance of one of the finest Marxist thinkers of the century without perverting Brecht's work by making a 'totalising commentary' on it. Taking from Brecht a taste for intelligence, humour, freedom, deciphering and friendship, Barthes's free thinking inside petty-bourgeois and bourgeois ideology was to Thibaudeau 'no less useful and brave than the exemplary manner in which Brecht had had to go through the darkest years of the Communist movement'. Thus welcoming the manner in which *Roland Barthes* was an 'exploration' of 'bourgeois individualism', Thibaudeau concluded that 'one cannot transform anything without coming into contact with it.'

This debate is important for a number of reasons. First, it illustrated the various political conclusions being drawn on Barthes's work in the mid-1970s. Second, it placed the 'self' at the heart of the debate. Finally, and most importantly for us here, it illustrates the fundamentally *literary* fashion in which *Roland Barthes* was being considered. Before we look at the final effort of 'literarisation', we must consider the Brechtian ethos of Barthes's ideas and writing practice suggested by Thibaudeau, and insist upon the thoroughly 'democratic' fashion in which Barthes saw a practice of writing.

Democracy, Voice and the (Eternal) Return of Michelet

> Often when I write, though I don't say it, I rely on the impressions I have in relation to students.
>
> Roland Barthes

Barthes's Hellenistic training in youth – evident above all in his appreciation of Gide, his inspired view of ancient Greek theatre and his work on rhetoric – is nowhere more evident than in this period. If *A Lover's Discourse* is greatly indebted to Plato, then Socrates influenced this 'return to sources', in a reversal of philosophical fortunes. Barthes's piece published in the *Arc* special number, 'To the Seminar' (OCiii 21–8/RL 332–42), involved a Socratic maieutic as much as a Bataillean concept of 'circulation'. Indeed, the teaching method claimed by

Barthes in this article confronted the ancient and the modern in these words from Michelet: 'I have made sure never to teach anything except what I did not know [. . .] I had transmitted these things as if now part of my passion: new, lively, burning things (and charming for me), like the first attractions in love' (OCiii 27/RL 340).

As if part of a Fourier-type phalanstery, the seminar was for Barthes a utopian space, which, though linked to the world, also resisted it. This 'partial utopia' allowed a circulation of ideas free from the constraints of traditional – and alienated, because quantified – academic requirements. Here, at the heart of the academy paradoxically, Barthes could establish a place for a practice of writing which, both democratic and free, questioned the rigid and hierarchical schemes of scholarship.

Though humanist in its preoccupation, this ethos was also concerned with a gratuitous and potentially nihilist conception of 'production for nothing'. Antoine Compagnon's attempt at the Cerisy conference to show Montaigne as a major influence on Barthes, and Rey's view that the very structure of *Roland Barthes* was a 'fervent homage' to Montaigne (the great Renaissance essayist who had listed somewhat arbitrarily his rigorous and playful self-interrogations in the *Essays*), both suggested that the humanist lineage running through French writing, from Montaigne to Gide, was being kept alive by Barthes.[23] However, this did not take account of the radical democracy with which Barthes viewed the act of writing.

Picking up on his activism in the popular theatre, Barthes put forward, in an interview with Nadeau in 1974, some stern beliefs about writing:

> Since the development of bourgeois democracy alongside technical progress and mass culture beginning about a hundred and fifty years ago, there has been [. . .] a clear split, and an awful one in my view, between the reader and the writer; on one side you have just a handful of writers, [. . .] and on the other, the great mass of readers. And those who read don't write. This is the problem, isn't it? Those who read don't write. (OCiii 67)

The intricate link between reading and writing was an important theme of Barthes's democratic view.

Talking about the act of reading for a conference on writing in 1975, he declared that it would be impossible to 'liberate reading, if, at the same time, we did not liberate écriture' (OCiii 383 / RL 41). Clearly, this could be taken to be words spoken by a writer who wanted to have more alert readers, rather than a desire to widen out writing as a social practice for all. But Barthes's notion of 'amateur' and 'DIY' ('bricoleur'), in music, painting and theory as well as writing, was informed by the perhaps utopian desire for all to participate.

From the Michelet quotation in 'To the Seminar' to his emphasis on the material and physical act of writing, Barthes stressed the need 'to avoid mastery'. In the appropriately named journal *Pratiques*, he believed there were two ways of achieving this (OCiii 337–42/GV 233–42). One had to practise either a 'flawed, elliptical and drifting/skidding ['dérivant/dérapant'] discourse', or, at the other extreme, a discourse which had an excess of clarity in its presentation of knowledge. However, it was evidently the more 'amateur' aspect of the former, both clumsy and passionate, that he favoured:

> We know of societies where there was an impressive numerical relationship between writers and their audience. In the same way, classical music, up until the nineteenth century, was listened to above all by those who played. Today it is not the case. That's why I give so much importance to the role of the 'amateur', who has to give back a value to the productive function which commercial circuits have reified. (OCiii 342/GV 240)

No doubt influenced by the (limited) control over the body that the recent legalisation of contraception in France had meant for French women, this 'production', said Barthes in an interview the same year, gesturing towards a Sadian and Bataillean idea of 'expenditure', must be 'for nothing'. '[P]erversion is the search for pleasure which is not made profitable by a social finality or cash; for example the pleasure of love which is not calculated ['comptabilisé'] in view of procreation' (OCiii 333/GV 232).

The question of modesty and democracy was linked intricately to the idea of 'circulation'. In a wonderful piece, paradoxically brilliant in its modesty, Barthes ended an interview in 1974 with a quotation from Brecht, which, amongst other things, makes the claim in John Fuegi's recent biography that Brecht 'stole' many of ideas from his friends look rather stupid.[24] Asked whether he thought he had changed since *Writing Degree Zero*, Barthes replied that, in 'imaginary' terms, barely at all, for language was still the crucial theme in his writing:

> But what has changed in me, fortunately, is other people, because I am also this other which speaks to me, which I listen to and which moves me along. How happy I would be if I could apply to myself this idea from Brecht: 'He used to think in other people's heads; and in his own other people than himself thought.' That is true thought. (OCiii 74/GV 195)

One example of this might be *The Pleasure of the Text*: 'others' (friends and conversations) were cited as its origin (OCii 1700).

Thus, the Lacanian psychoanalytical dissolution of the subject was tied tightly to the democratic critique of 'genius', of the romanticist notion that the individual was a fount of creativity. For Barthes (and, of course, for Brecht too) creativity was both collective and unattributable. This critique of romanticism evident in much of Barthes's early writings, especially on theatre, became (spirally?) modified in the 1970s. For example, it is difficult not to place the account of poverty in relation to the Moroccan boy in the 'Brecht and Discourse Analysis' article (OCiii 265–6/RL 219–20) with the final paragraph of 'Features and Faces' of 1953. In the preface to Brillat-Savarin, Barthes 'returned' to discussing 'popular language' (OCiii 286/RL 259). Similarly, Gérard Miller's book on Pétain, in looking at sexual impulses as historical matter, was a Micheletian 'art of resurrection' (OCiii 277).

Thus the return to Michelet, part of a general trend, was a crucial aspect of the 1970s, especially for the writing of the 'novelistic'. Michelet had not been treated at length since 1959. After the post-war studies, there had been a general revival of interest in the nineteenth-century historian in the 1950s – not just from Febvre and Barthes, but by historians such as Paul Viallaneix, alongside the publication of Michelet's diaries. But this interest appeared not to be sustained through the sixties. It was not until the wake of the events of May 1968 that Michelet was fully 'resurrected'.

A crucial publication in this area was that by Seuil of a new edition of Michelet's *L'Étudiant*. This series of lectures at the Collège de France from 1847–8, first published posthumously in 1877, comprised twelve lectures on youth and education, of which only three had been given. Michelet's classes were stopped at the beginning of 1848 by ministerial decree, only for him to be suspended from the Collège in 1851; such was the social and political turmoil of 1848–51.[25] The significance of the title and the book's contents in the wake of May 1968 was central to its republication. In his preface to this new edition, Proust specialist Gaëtan Picon underlined the extraordinary similarity between Michelet's view of youth and students in 1848 and the demands by the student uprising of the previous months. Calling his first section 'The Student, Marx and the Month of May', Picon spelled out the uncanny similarities between Michelet's lessons and the recent tumultuous events.[26]

Following Picon's intervention, there was a spate of publications and events on Michelet to commemorate the centenary of his death. First, in February 1973 a special number of *L'Arc* on Michelet appeared, organised by eminent historian Jacques Le Goff and featuring Barthes's essay 'Michelet Today' (OCii 1575–83/RL 195–207), followed by a special number of *Europe* (November/December 1973) and a conference at the Collège de France. The following year, a series of events was organised by the Society for Romantic Studies, including a programme on French radio, *Resurrection of Michelet*, involving a debate in which Barthes and well-known experts on Michelet took part.[27]

Barthes's comments in the discussion showed the importance of Michelet's writing to his own ideas at this time. Insisting on the ethnological and 'utopian scientific' aspect of Michelet's writing, similar to the unitary discourse of a Fourier, Barthes suggested that, in contrast to Fourier, Michelet's attempts to allow the 'Other' of contemporary society to speak (the people, women) were dependent on his 'refracting and hallucinatory' writing. Indeed, despite his petty-bourgeois ideology, Michelet's discourse, continued Barthes, was 'full of holes, discontinuous'. Its 'beauty' was that it was full of 'sharp bends and chicanes', which, once passed, brought the reader to an 'absolutely sumptuous, free, modern, emancipated and, to a great extent, enigmatic body of writing'. Michelet's 'singular' modernity, continued Barthes, was that he took on a 'complete femininity'. As a historian and a naturalist deploying an 'immense anamnesis', he remembered all temporalities from his own subjective place of writing; and though circular and mythical, his use of fragments of memories or historical and natural dreams from throughout his life was not 'impressionistic'. Finally, said Barthes, progressively less able to understand his own century, Michelet's history of his century was *the* pre-eminent book of the nineteenth century, precisely because it was full of the deepest despair and of boredom 'with a capital B'.[28]

Barthes's comments here illustrated the Nietzschean and writerly preoccupations we looked at in the previous chapter. These continued in his next article on Michelet, which displayed Barthes's growing importance for Michelet studies. Following the transcriptions of the papers given at the Collège de France conference published in the *Revue d'histoire littéraire de la France*, the very journal which, we will remember, had severely lambasted his book on Michelet, Barthes wrote his view of the contemporary relevance of Michelet. 'Modernity of Michelet' (OCiii 41–3/RL 208–11) is a brilliant essayistic piece which saw Michelet as a precursor of modernity for three reasons. First, Barthes was impressed by the historian's acts of 'resurrection' of past lives. Second, Michelet had made important epistemological discoveries. Finally, he had been biased in favour of the people.

Prefiguring Nietzsche and Bataille, Michelet's work was paradoxical for Barthes. It was, he said in line with the comments on Nietzsche in *The Pleasure of the Text*, too early to 'cite' Michelet; we were not 'mature or educated' enough to cut Michelet's writing into 'fragments', to 'detach' ('décrocher') him from his petty-bourgeois ideology, to read him 'against the grain', in the way we could with Diderot. Patricia Lombardo has suggested that 'nothing could be less timely than his romanticism', implying that Barthes rejected Michelet's romanticism;[29] this tallied with his critique of romanticism in the theatre and the novel in the 1950s. All this was a sign of Michelet's ambiguous modernity for Barthes, both post-1848 and late twentieth-century: 'we are still theologians, not dialecticians' (OCiii 43/RL 211). Neither classical nor after Marx, Freud and Nietzsche, Michelet was in a no-man's land – all the better for a Barthes finding writing as a way out of, and an account of, alienation.[30]

The return to Michelet in this period is important for our understanding of Barthes's preoccupations in this final phase. If the 'dialectic of love' had been a Micheletian aim to 'refind my contemporaries', this was an important aspect of his work on photography in *Camera Lucida.* But first, we must consider how Barthes proposed, in response to the 'flattening' of culture he was perceiving, to bring back the 'values' with which to counter the 'degrading' of culture by the petty-bourgeoisie. Curiously perhaps for one who was accused of a terrorist and highly detached view of cultural matters, he now applied himself to a writing form and subject – love – which suggested an accommodation with the deficiencies of bourgeois society.

Music, Silence, Zen: Love

> Many are the delicious things, Nathaniel, for which I have been consumed with love.
>
> André Gide

As Barthes moved towards a novelistic conception and performance of self, he also began to revel in the peacefulness of music. The semiological schemas and diagrams typical of the 1960s, indicative of a 'babble of language', now gave way to musical notation. For example, 'Rasch' displayed how language, both written and spoken, could become a form of music (OCiii 295–304/RF 299–312). The celebration of the Japanese haïku and Loyola's silence notwithstanding, he now began to see a combination of Zen and music. Music, as his praise of his one-time singing tutor Charles Panzéra showed, could place the body via the voice in relation to its 'tastes' (OCii 1441/RF 276). The ethereal nature of music, first noted in modernity by the Cubists, was perfect for questioning the general and particular nature of 'taste', especially given the dissolved nature of the subject. Why, *Roland Barthes* had asked (OCiii 184/RB 116–17), did we like certain things? Thus, allowing an immediate (i.e. unmediated) communion between the body and a source of pleasure (OCiii 303–4/RF 311–12), an ephemeral pleasure destroyed only by the adjective (OCii 1436/RF 268), music was paradoxically a silence. In his tribute to the theorist of performative language Emile Benveniste, he described music as having 'a language, a syntax, but no semiotic'; it seemed to represent a utopia, away from the 'babble' of connotation.

There was an important political point here too. His 'no comment' response in 'On China' might have been a tacit rejection of a political opposition to Western society in the guise of the 'Orient' as 'other'. It was also indicative of a Zen-like 'detached' silence on other matters, such as the novel. His 1973 review of Sollers's *H* suggested that its use of fragments now dispensed him from having 'a thesis to defend' (OCiii 956/SW 84–5)

This silence and mystical hiding from meaning found its significance at the end of *A Lover's Discourse* in a further rendition of 'no comment' and in the 'refusal to seize hold' of the 'other' as loved one, which, paradoxically and according to a Tao motto, guaranteed one's deeds would be perennial (OCiii 677 n.8/LD 232–4). The asceticism at the end of *A Lover's Discourse*, highly reminiscent of Gide's *Fruits of the Earth* in both style and content, suggested further debts to Gide with the latter's deep interest in Goethe. And if Michelet had written at length on love in 1868, we should not be surprised that Gide had written a Platonic dialogue on the virtues of gay love (*Corydon*).

Barthes's best-selling book, both at the time and today, *A Lover's Discourse* has had sixteen imprints, selling more than 150,000 copies.[31] The reactions confirmed this popularity. Aline Arénilla saw it as a 'painful and subtle, rich and sensitive' book.[32] Despite the apparent lack of politics pointed out by Louis-Jean Calvet,[33] many on the left were impressed. Though disappointed by Barthes's recent lunch with right-wing French President Giscard and tired of his avant-garde posturing, Catherine Backès-Clément, Communist philosopher and former student of Barthes's, had enjoyed reading this 'precious and romantic' writer.[34] She admitted her surprise at being 'touched' by the manner in which this 'soft left' intellectual managed to make something as impersonal and general as love relevant to the individual. Alain Poirson in *Humanité*, despite reservations on Barthes's view that language was 'fascist' and on the refusal to take up party positions, admired the 'endurance and vitality' of an intellectual whose changes in direction were a 'great example of the dialectic', indicative of his durable relevance to modernity. Despite the subject matter, no 'theoretical compromise or regression' was evident: the Brechtian, moralist stance allowed for a liberation via hedonism, allowing the imaginary to be stimulated by love.[35] Above all, it was a 'provocative' book, which would scandalise the puritans, surprise the libertarians by its asceticism, and please Communists not afraid of feelings. The hard left was no exception, as the Trotskyist weekly *Rouge* showed.[36]

Though insisting on the Brechtian influence, with the chapter titles acting like 'placards' announcing each new 'tableau', Calvet found it hard to find anything political in *A Lover's Discourse*. He did not accept that though love was relevant to women's and gay liberation, it could be posited outside of 'time and space'. Love was an utterance, but 'anchored in a practice', both social and psychoanalytical. Disappointed by the comment in Barthes's inaugural lecture that flesh was 'outside of power', Calvet was wondering whether, in junking structuralism, Barthes was now left with only the 'simulacrum', and had lost the political – Brechtian and Marxian – conception of the sign.

However, Barthes's subtle moves were the most endearing feature of his latest book. Hector Bianciotti in the *Nouvel-Observateur* summed up what many were saying: that Barthes always seemed to manage to take an 'exiled' word such as love – at a time in the mid-1970s when it was 'not so much sexuality but sentimentality' that was 'indecent' – only to 'remove the crust of aberration and contempt' and to make it fashionable. Barthes's book was 'turning its nose up' at the 'spirit of the times'.[37]

Indeed, arch-critic of the *nouveau roman* Pierre de Boisdeffre noted how Barthes's great principle was always to wrong-foot the reader and the adversary.[38] This success did not exclude the odd ironic comment. Mathieu Galey finished his review in *L'Express* asking the 'unforgivable question' of how many of all those who had bought the book had actually read it.[39] If *A Lover's Discourse* was a mere bedside read, Galey joked, then Barthes's 'trendiness' made his Collège de France seminar into the twentieth-century equivalent of the literary salon; and the 'caustic spirit' behind an image of melancholy, produced in alphabetical order, made *A Lover's Discourse* into the structuralist version of a medieval love-letter.

There were two reviews, once again, in *Critique*. For Philippe Roger – clearly in reference to *Roland Barthes – A Lover's Discourse* was Barthes's first book which had the 'coalescence' of its subject, which, in love and in a 'retro kitsch', was a gift 'materially dedicated to the reader'.[40] Was it like Stendhal's study?[41] With the dialectician absent, the petty-bourgeois attacked in *Mythologies* was pulled out of 'opprobrium', with almost Poujadian 'tautological bliss' and politics, concluded Roger. For Roger, the Sade expert, Barthes's model was Sade's *120 Days*. Claiming at one point that the *Nous deux* love magazine was 'more obscene than Sade' (OCiii 625/not in LD 178), Roger stressed that Barthes's major political point was that anything out of date was obscene, and could not be 'recuperated as spectacle'. Furthermore, the idea of killing oneself because the loved one had not phoned was obscene when compared to those starving in the world or fighting for liberation. Here, said Roger, was the source of Barthes's 'stupidity' ('bêtise'): perhaps the only way to read *A Lover's Discourse* was to treat it as the first Barthes text ever.

Thus, the theatrical nature of *A Lover's Discourse* was established, and its conversion to the stage was not long in appearing, directed by Pierre Leenhardt at the Théâtre Marie-Stuart in Paris. Discussing this in an interview in *L'Express* in April 1978 called 'Barthes on Stage' (OCiii 899–900), Barthes noted that Leenhardt's production had added pieces which had a much more youthful and happy aspect than his own version. Despite his rather sarcastic comments on the book version, Mathieu Galey's review of the production was enthusiastic: 'for once the theatre makes a good reading'.[42] The popularity of *A Lover's Discourse* was such that, said Galey, Barthes had been read on the beaches of St Tropez over the summer. Thus, 'poor dear Barthes had been transformed into a product of consumption for the soaring band of hungry cultural snobs'. Luckily, Leenhardt's production gave Barthes the 'humanity' which others had taken from him. The review in *Humanité* was less favourable, suggesting that once the body appeared the idea of 'voice off' in the original text had been compromised.[43] Clearly, this was of great significance. If Barthes did leave the theatre but maintain the performative spirit at the heart of his writing, as Jean-Pierre Sarrazac has recently suggested,[44] this was paralleled by *Roland Barthes* putting the subject on stage under spotlight. Barthes's appearance on 29 April 1977 on Bernard Pivot's influential culture programme *Apostrophes* added to the theatrical myth. Before the famous media coup of a Duras in 1984, Barthes, the skilful media and interview performer, won over hearts and minds here on national television, as a number of critics pointed out.[45] Jean-François Josselin considered that the 'photogenic' Barthes had put his fellow interviewee Françoise Sagan 'into the shadows'; and though a 'prof.', his 'novelistic book', thought Josselin, suggested that 'we were witnessing perhaps the birth of a hero and his immediate double, its creator'.[46]

What retains us in an account of Barthes the 'novelist', however, is the thoroughly literary nature of Barthes's enterprise. For Jean-Jacques Brochier, this was 'one of most beautiful novels of love'.[47] Pierre Gamarra in *Europe* underlined how the mix of 'poetic invention and professorial erudition' and the 'simulation' (rather than description) of the language of love meant that the novelistic sources led onto 'another novel', not necessarily avoiding 'the traditional French psychological' novel.[48]

Indeed, *A Lover's Discourse* made no attempt to hide its 'novelistic' nature. 'How this book is constructed' declared that the 'horizontal discourse' had 'no transcendence, no salvation, no novel (but lots of the novelistic)' (OCiii 463/LD 7). 'The lover is so stupid', declared Barthes at one stage, that he or she dare not appear in public 'without a serious mediation: novel, theatre or analysis (at the end of tweezers)' (624/177).

The 'stupidity' of being an intellectual who sentimentalises was also clearly linked to the feeling of stupidity of writing a novel, or rather of thinking about putting oneself in that position. Indeed, it is difficult not to see *A Lover's Discourse* as a 'writing with' Goethe's epistolary story, as it followed *Werther* to the end, from the 'quoted' nature of the discourse ('It is thus a lover who speaks and who says') to the regular use of X (469, 499/ 12, 41). For example, the final phase of Barthes's study mirrors the final phase of *Werther*, but supplying a happier ending (664/219). At one stage, Barthes mentioned this palimpsestic addition, doubling up the Xs when quoting *Werther*: describing how 'Werther complains about Prince Xx', was Barthes implying X to the power of X (509/52)?

For once, the text used the past historic in this narrative of meeting a lover – only later on to underline the significance of the past historic in such accounts (637/193–4). Furthermore, despite the Barthesian view that the third person is 'nasty' ('méchant)' (630/185), the story is sometimes told in the 'he'. The mix of the past historic with the perfect (normally mixed in French only when speech is used) serves to underline the narrative nature of the passage. The nature of love is linked centrally in Barthes's view of Goethe's novel and the different levels of meaning depending on who is speaking:

> It is only when one leaves the confidence for the final narrative that the rivalry becomes acute, bitter, as if jealousy originated in the simple move from I to he, from an imaginary discourse (saturated by the other) to a discourse of the Other – whose Narrative is the statutory voice. (OCiii 595/LD 144)

Thus love, like fiction, is dependent on the question of where the narration originates.

Furthermore, in line with the 'democratic' dissolution of the subject, Barthes made his treatise on love appropriate to everyone. Diametrically opposed to, but curiously reminiscent of, Michel Butor's unnerving novel *The Modification*, which places 'Vous' as the central character, *A Lover's Discourse* uses a pluralised 'I' which tends to coincide with the third person employed earlier. At the end of 'The Heart', with X announcing his or her departure, there is no telling to whom the 'I' refers specifically (509/52). By the time of 'The World Desired', the narrative in the 'I' and present tense is placed between quotation marks to start with, tentatively (and with no reference at all in the margin), then removed after the first section (539/87–8). Then, as if to illustrate the 'feeling of absence' of the subtitle of this section, the narrative moves into a non-quoted section, though still in the 'I'. The effect of this fragment between apostrophes is contrasted strongly with the rest of the section, in order to show how the narrator (who is it? Barthes? the lover? any one of us?) can be alone and isolated, even – or especially – in a crowded place such as a café. It also marks the burgeoning desire to write the narrative of a novel, a narrative which finally arrives in 'Faults'.

As the novel-writing takes shape, it is no coincidence that *A Lover's Discourse* initiates the romantic aspect of memory which characterises Barthes's final book, *Camera Lucida*:

> I could easily have spoken ('discourir') for years about love, but I could hope only ever to catch the concept of it 'by its tail': by flashes, formulas, surprising expressions, all dispersed across the great flow of the Imaginary; I am in the *wrong place* of love, where love is blinding: 'The darkest place, according to a Chinese proverb, is always under the lamp.' (OCiii 515/LD 59)

In discussing the use of the past historic in describing a love event, he adds in parenthesis that 'the being of photography is not to represent, but to recall' (637/194). In fine Micheletian style this contains the paradox of (hi)story-telling: 'the whole reconstituted scene operates like the sumptuous montage of an ignorance':

> Though the amorous discourse is only a speck of dust of figures which move around in an unpredictable order in the manner of a fly meandering around a room, I can assign to love, at least retrospectively, in an imaginary fashion, an ordered development: it is via this *historical* phantasm that I sometimes make it into an adventure. (OCiii 641/LD 197)

However, what is at stake in the lover's discourse is the attitude towards the past and the future, which neither gives him/us everything, nor predicts an outcome. In short, there is a freedom to invent, to 'romanticise' in a manner reminiscent of Fourier's utopian obsessions with detail:

> One day I will remember the scene, I will lose myself *in the past.* The lover's tableau, equal to the first ravishing, is made up only of after-events: it is the *anamnesis* which finds only insignificant totally undramatic events, as if I was remembering the time itself and the time only: it is a perfume without support, a texture of memory, a simple fragrance; something like a pure expenditure, which the Japanese haïku alone has learnt to say, without recuperating it into any destiny. (OCiii 661/LD 216)

The imperfect tense is the tense of memory; not a 'resurrection', which Michelet might have used, but an 'exhaustive luring of memory'. And, stresses Barthes, the lover's discourse is not a Proustian 'static comprehension' of the past, but a spectacle of a memory forming itself:

> This theatre of time is the very opposite of the search for lost time; because I remember pathetically, on the spot, and not philosophically, discursively: I remember to be happy/unhappy – not in order to understand. I don't write, I don't lock myself away to write the great novel of recaptured time. (OCiii 662/LD 217)

Despite the final line of the above, *A Lover's Discourse* is precisely the novel which tries to look at how our emotions are constructed and played out. It is not quite the 'dialectic of love' which characterised many of Barthes's twists and turns from the 1950s, but, as Hector Bianciotti called it, a diary or a novel 'in negative'. The photographic dimension to love was an apt one. If looking for love itself is a way of remembering the past, it was the memory and pain of loss which now came to dominate his final years.

Vita Nova: Life as Literature

There is properly no history; only biography.
Ralph Emerson

Photography has the same relationship to History as the biographeme to biography.
Roland Barthes

The death of Barthes's mother was a crucial moment for the end of his own life. The suggestion by some that Barthes's month-long 'slide out of life' after the accident had been encouraged by his depressed state after his mother's death had been prefigured in *A Lover's Discourse*, in the section 'Ideas of Suicide' (OCiii 663–4/LD 218–19). But the fragment immediately following, '*Tel*' ('*Thus*') (665–7/220–3), was fitting in its following on from suicide, for it was to point to a possible solution in the memory of his mother in *Camera Lucida*.

'Tel', though devoid of adjectives and a kind of Zen-like 'no comment' and silence, was paradoxically to become the obverse of his view that 'One Always Fails to Speak of What One Loves Most', the article sitting in Barthes's typewriter when he died. For in avoiding adjectives, 'Tel', stressed Barthes, allowed you ('toi', referring to his mother?) to escape the 'death of classification'. Also it included an obliteration of meaning, implying (in Lacanian terms) one's standing outside of the 'symbolic order', analogous therefore to the pre-oedipal oneness with the mother, what Barthes called in *A Lover's Discourse* – in a rather Zen, if not hippy, fashion – 'a dream of total union'. Therefore, in *Camera Lucida*, the 'Tel' nature of photography would allow Barthes to feel, artificially and imaginatively of course, in short fictively, that his mother was alive for him.

In *Camera Lucida* there is a constant battle between the feeling of loss and the inability to remember an image on the one hand, and the refinding of an image but destroying it with adjectives on the other. This dialectic is evident in Barthes's piece on the photographer Richard Avedon, also called 'Tel', published in January 1977 (OCiii 691–3).

Tacitly gesturing towards the North African belief that photography locks the soul in – admirably described by Michel Tournier in his novel *La Goutte d'Or* –, *Camera Lucida* is an attempt to breathe life into the photographs. Photography becomes a project of 'resurrection', related to refinding his mother, with all the pain, irony and suffering that Diana Knight has brilliantly shown to be involved in the (possible) invention of the photograph of his mother, which the book, apparently, does not allow us to see.[49] Now the affective and deeply historical sensibility of a Michelet found its relevance for Barthes.

Nancy Shawcross has argued persuasively the thoroughly *modern* concerns in Barthes's writing on photography.[50] Comparing his ideas with those of Baudelaire, Benjamin and Duras, as well as the scientific theory of Einstein on time, matter and relativity, Shawcross's study begins to examine the importance of what I have called the earliest – or ambiguous, because in the transitional moment – modernism of a Michelet. Her conclusion is that, thoroughly modern, Barthes's aim is to show that photography *proves* history.

Thus, far from the 'discourse of history' invoked by postmodernism, Barthes affirmed, if not in a 'vulgar' materialist way, the 'untreatable reality' of what has existed. This profoundly 'documentalist' view of history replicated the work of Michelet, the first historian to use documents to write the history of the French Revolution. Thus, in an interview in 1979, Barthes underlined his transportation back to 1822, not *in* photos but *before* a photo (OCiii 1238/GV 357).

Though Shawcross does not include in her account Barthes's earliest thoughts on photography, 'Features and Faces' and 'Child-Stars', written at the same time as *Michelet*, her study shows that the problematic at the heart of Barthes's writing on photography was informed by Michelet. The fact that the latter was himself photographed by Nadar and that Barthes had been fascinated by representations of Michelet's face – in paintings and photos – suggests a further connection between Michelet and photography.[51]

Shawcross's view of *Camera Lucida* seems to highlight a number of the crucial themes we have noted throughout Barthes's career. Her statement that it is the singular – rather than general, scientific and purely theoretical

– view of photography which characterises Barthes's final book suggests that, during the last years of his career, as we noted, he brought back in spiral fashion themes which predominated in the earliest phase of his career. This is not simply the relationship to history and time, but what we might call *le vécu*, the lived subjective experience in relation to the past. Michelet was for Barthes not simply the first 'photographer', as Chantal Thomas implies,[52] but the first to place – before Marx, before Nietzsche, before Bataille – the singular in relation to the general, precisely as the photographic technique was being first discovered. Thus, Barthes's investigation of photography was not simply a spatial one – the relation of the individual to the whole – but a temporal one which (paradoxically) considered the individual in general terms:

> I have always wanted to *argue* my feelings; not to justify them, even less to fill the textual stage with my individuality; but on the contrary to offer, to tender this individuality to a science of the subject; the name of this science does not matter, as long as it reaches (which hasn't happened yet) a generality which does not reduce nor squash me. (OCiii 1119/CL 18)

However, by the end of the first section of *Camera Lucida*, Barthes had realised that he had lost thereby the '*eidos*' of photography: 'a subjectivity reduced to its hedonistic project could not recognise the universal'.

Always wary of synthesis, the conclusion of the book suggested that this overcoming of contradiction was impossible. Is it possible to talk about *anything* – especially the nearest and dearest – in general terms without losing the particular individual's place within this? Apart from rehearsing the photographic version of the contradiction of change and structure, this question was the ultimate Zen-Buddhist concern. Is there not a sense in which *Camera Lucida* is an attempt to stop photography being a 'pure analogy of existence', as he hinted in 1975 (OCiii 317/GV 208)?

Despite the return of various crucial themes in this final period, Barthes ended his writing career with an innovation. If the final phase was characterised by a deeper lackadaisical attitude, then the feeling that language was 'fascistic' – in that it *obliged* one to speak – now became in a 1979 interview the demand for the 'right to laziness' (OCiii 1082–7/ GV 338–45). The strong feelings of loss and alienation at this time in Barthes's life were amply illustrated by his posthumous diary 'Soirées de Paris', published with *Incidents* (OCiii 1273–86/I 71–116), which detailed a three-week period of failed meetings and unrequited love at exactly the same time as the interview on 'Laziness'. The fact that Barthes now seemed to be keeping a diary – something which he had abhorred in earlier periods of his life – was of immense significance, for the theme of biography now became central to his concerns. An interview in *Le Nouvel-Observateur* in 1979 on Chateaubriand underlined not only his preference now for the classics rather than the modern aspects of French literature (OCiii 1088–91/GV 346–50), but also his view of the art and desirability of writing biography. Combined with his writing of a diary – not the first effort: he had written a diary briefly whilst he nursed his mother on her deathbed in the summer of 1977 – this attention to the art of biography was but a prelude to his ultimate act of 'literarisation'.

On 15 April, noted repeatedly with extreme precision in the manuscript reproduced in the *Complete Works* (OCiii 1299–307), Barthes decided (and made this decision itself textual) to start his life anew. Following Dante, Vico and Michelet, he now wanted a *vita nova*. Though it is never explicit in his work, my view is that this *vita nova* was to be a Nietzschean conversion of his old life into what Alexander Nehamas has called 'life as literature'.[53]

If we trace the date of the *vita nova* decision in relation to Barthes's writings and publications of this period, we can see its germination in interviews directly preceding 15 April 1978. They began to hint at the full literary status that he had come to have for himself: 'I am, in terms of studies, a purely literary person' (OCiii 891). Indeed, and not surprisingly, this pose was full of Nietzschean paradoxes. At the end of the *Humanité* interview in March 1978, he heralded the return to the old forms of the diary and the novel. However, he stressed that to renew the link with the past might be renouncing 'the demands of modernity', but it was also making oneself more 'popular' for one's historical age: 'So this turn, this change of practice *and image* has to be lived inside not as a simplistic return to old-fashioned forms, but as a new conception of the modern itself. Whatever one writes, it must be in touch with the "contemporary"' (OCiii 898, my italics).

Alongside the lessons at the Collège de France in the academic year 1978–9 on 'The Preparation of the Novel', his first piece to appear after 15 April 1978 was 'At the "Palace" this Evening' (OCiii 824–6). Published in *Vogue for Men* in May 1978, this wistful account of his visit to a dance displayed an imagined and fictionalised appearance of Proustian proportions; and it was mirrored in Barthes's cameo appearance as Thackeray at a dance in André Téchiné's film on the Brontë sisters. This was followed by the brilliant, Proustian lecture given at the Collège de France in October 1978.

Russian-doll-like in its levels of reference, the piece on Proust's decision to write a novel, not published until 1982 (OCiii 827–36/RL 277–90), was not simply the moment when the third form – a hybrid of novel and essay – was posited as a solution to the 'suffering' of *Camera Lucida*, as Shawcross has pointed out.[54] It also marked Barthes's objectification of his life within the literary. In discussing Proust's 'decision' to write a novel, he was 'postulating' his own 'novel to be written' (OCiii 835/RL 289). This attitude culminated in 'Deliberation', his last piece in *TQ* (OCiii 1004–14/RL 359–72). Both a 'diary' – begun in July 1977 just as his mother was dying – and a reflection on the diary form from the vantage point of two years later, this reflection was referred to in 'Soirées de Paris' in the most literary ways, via a *mise en abyme* (OCiii 1275/I 79–80). Deciding whether this diary was actually publishable and ending with the view that it was perhaps no longer anything like a 'journal', these musings on his own life had themselves quite clearly become part of the 'literary'.

Though Barthes's drastic 'literary' decision was trauma-inspired, this is not to say that there were no hints of it earlier his early career – as the Gidian nature of *Roland Barthes* showed; only that the loss of his mother was a crucial moment in this decision. The *vita nova* decision to aestheticise his own life was surely the ultimate act of one so in love with writing.

Afterword

Our interpretation of history will be both materialist with Marx and mystical with Michelet.

Jean Jaurès

The world can only be described if capable of transformation.

Bertolt Brecht

THOUGH BARTHES'S DEATH IN 1980 displayed none of the literary myth of a Victor Segalen – committing suicide with a copy of *Hamlet* opened at the appropriate page by his side – the numerous obituaries testified to the Barthesian 'myth' that had been created. It was perhaps a fitting tribute that these acted also as reviews of his last book, *Camera Lucida.*[1] There is not, however, enough space here to consider this first episode in Barthes's posthumous life. But we can make some general points about the conditions of this afterlife.

The theorist of the 'Death of the Author' was in fact acutely aware of his *own* status as author, of the appropriate strategies and tactics to be employed, be they journalistic, academic or textual, in a fashion which was not so much *mauvaise foi* as an acknowledgement of the 'performative contradiction' within a politics of language. Perhaps there is another irony here: the theorist of textual 'disinheritance' is constantly plagued, posthumously, by arguments over ownership and authority.[2] Thus, Barthes might have theorised 'the Death of the Author', but his own life as writer was subject to the vicissitudes of alienation.

Being in a contradictory generation, dying the same year as Sartre but clearly not part of his generation, and too old to be considered part of the Foucault/Althusser one either, helped put Barthes in a curious materialist position. Having written to supplement his meagre resources in the 1950s – a production for 'something', if ever there was an example – Barthes became the champion of writing 'for nothing'. Leaving allusions to the Research Assessment Exercise to one side, this points not simply to a 'gratuitous', Gidian writing practice but to a political libertarian ethos: I am going to write for nothing *in order* to show that the pleasure it involves is not recuperable by an alienating society which reifies production.

However, unless one believes in a spiritual afterlife, a consideration of Barthes after 1980 would sit outside of the phenomenon/myth structure used in this book. This dialogic approach is traversed by a crucial contradiction of modernity: the relationship between self and society. Exacerbated by the imponderables of writing and publishing, this contradiction raises the question of the nature of biography. Is it history, literature, fact, fiction or none of these? Does its generic status, and its parametrically defined methodology, depend on the subject, the object or the medium?

It should be sufficiently clear from this study what a consideration of a writer's life such as Barthes's should *not* be. A hagiographic, purely mythical approach would not only be a failure to understand our own relationship with the past, but also a gross disservice. Is making 'life into literature' not the ultimate 'petty-bourgeois' act, in that it changes culture into nature? Surely, an approach to Barthes's writing should be either *with* and/or against, but not *for* Barthes? The 'pleasure in the classics' ethos may help us to appreciate apparently repellent texts, to read Sade without boredom; clothes could now be seen as a challenge to the fashion system, part of a subtle, unhysterical 'taking sides' which, anti-totalitarian and against exclusion and alienation, acts as a 'resistance to history'. Such considerations ought to take place *via* Barthes. But a dialectical view of what Nietzsche called this 'mild madness which is language' – not simply involving love or erotic pleasure, but a profound ambivalence – makes Barthes into a source of radical questioning.

If we are to be fully and dialectically linked to our moment, then our criticism must rest on that moment, which, today, is dominated by talk of a '*post*modernity'. What the apparently *post*modern 'literary' critique of social sciences and literary studies had accomplished, it seems now, was (in Barthes's work at least) nothing more than the *modernisation* – not *post*modernisation – of the humanities. If the twentieth century had seen fine art, music, theatre and poetry all thoroughly reassessed by artistic revolutions which had begun in the second half of the nineteenth century and ended with the *nouveau roman*, then sociology and literary criticism were now ripe for such a treatment. Thus, the *nouvelle critique* and cultural studies have operated on the uncorrected positivism of the historical and human sciences. The problem is, what are we left with?

When asked at the Cerisy conference in 1978 about the embarrassment of admitting that one is *either* an idealist *or* a materialist, Barthes suggested that 'swinging' between both sides of this 'terrible bar' might save him: 'if I am in extreme idealism, I will then immediately also be in extreme materialism'.[3] This epistemological hedging of bets has become the academic norm today within cultural materialism.[4] The deployment of a multiplicity of determinants, in which none is privileged over the rest, seems to be returning us (what else after Nietzsche?) to an unadulterated romanticism. Nietzsche's 'variant of romantic anti-capitalism'[5] cannot hide the curious mix of utopianism, reformism and mysticism in current intellectual thought. Indeed, as Susan Sontag has suggested, once the veneer of semiologist has fallen, Barthes will appear as a *promeneur solitaire* (BR 8). For the diversity of his writings cannot hide the narrowness of his concerns. The 'dialectic of love' – and its 'dialectic of two-terms' – has left open a synthesis of theory and practice, out of which springs the 'undecidability' of Barthes's own writings and of literature in general.

However, to consider Barthes purely a 'romantic' would be to misunderstand his relationship to science, explanation, justice and liberation. Marxism – and other theories of alienation and liberation, such as psychoanalysis – cannot be part of an *historical* romanticism. Therefore, to a theory of the ideology of the imagination in romanticism, as analysed recently by Forest Pyle,[6] we need to add the very temporal 'dialectic of love'. Such a contribution to Romanticism would not be simply an ideological 'forging of unity' against 'fissure', but an account of attempts to overcome alienation in the here and now. We might 'have to live in the unliveable', but surely it was precisely the ability to dream which Marx and Engels found important in Fourier: how *could* the world be different?

Barthes's necessarily paradoxical battle with alienation – both philosophically and personally – suggests that his utopian response was a powerful *combinatoire*, which, as ever in Barthes, was in the form of a question. How do we *simultaneously* place the self, the singular, the particular, in relation to an alienated and alienating world, whilst maintaining a general and generalised notion of explanation (and therefore transformation)? Literature was, ultimately, Barthes's reply.

However, the dialectic of science and romanticism raises another question: is it *possible* to be utopian after Marx? After all, the apparent triumph today of the free market across the globe only serves, in the final instance, to underline Marx's dialectical view of the 'gravedigger'. If it is possible, then Barthes's utopianism underlines the contradiction – what he sometimes called the 'blockage' – in history.

Such a *post*-romanticism might encourage us, following Brecht, to 'liquidate and theorise', or to dream, following Benjamin's account of French Revolutionaries shooting at clocks or the Bolshevik idea of stopping the sun from rising. Unfortunately, though, obscenities will not be enough to signal that change is happening. Perhaps this unpredictable aspect of language is the resistance to – and above all the 'reserve' of – history.

Notes

Introduction

1. *NNRF*, October 1955, 803.
2. See S. Burke, *The Death and Return of the Author* (Edinburgh, Edinburgh University Press, 1992).
3. I have tried to argue this point elsewhere; see A. Stafford, 'Barthes and Michelet: Biography and History', *Nottingham French Studies* 36:1 (Spring 1997), 14–23.
4. See *The Bookseller*, 4615.
5. L. Marcus, *Auto/biographical Discourses* (Manchester, Manchester University Press, 1994), 255.
6. Not only is the main character called Roland, but his hero, Randolph Henry Ash, is clearly modelled on (and frequently quotes) Jules Michelet.
7. S. O'Brien, 'Feminist Theory and Literary Biography', in William H. Epstein (ed.), *Contesting the Subject. Essays in the Postmodern Theory and Practice of Biography and Biographical Criticism* (West Lafayette, Indiana, Purdue University Press, 1991), 123–33.
8. P. Roger, *Roland Barthes, roman* (Paris, Grasset, 1986), 15; A. Brown, *Roland Barthes: The Figures of Writing* (Oxford, Clarendon Press, 1992).
9. Y. Velan, 'Barthes', in John K. Simon (ed.), *Modern French Criticism. From Proust and Valéry to Structuralism* (Chicago, University of Chicago Press, 1972), 311–39.
10. C. Calligari, 'Tout dire', in *Collective, Prétexte: Roland Barthes/Colloque de Cerisy* (Paris, 10/18, Union générale d'Éditions, 1978), 9–39.
11. See D. Smith, *Transvaluations. Nietzsche in France 1872–1972* (Oxford, Clarendon Press, 1996), 20–2.
12. R. Barthes, 'Phénomène ou mythe?', *LLN*, December 1954, 951–3 (not republished in OC). See G. Duhamel, 'Le Phénomène Rimbaud', *Les Nouvelles littéraires*, 21

October 1954, 1; R. Etiemble, *Le Mythe de Rimbaud. 1 Genèse du mythe 1869–1949* (Paris, Gallimard, 1954).

13. See for example the 'biographemes' in *La Règle du jeu* 1 (May 1990), 52–80; see also P. Mauriès, *Roland Barthes* (Paris, Gallimard, 1992); J. Kristeva, *Les Samouraïs* (Paris, Gallimard, 1990); F. Gaillard, 'Roland Barthes: le biographique sans la biographie', *Revue des sciences humaines* 98:4 (Oct./Dec. 1991), 85–103.
14. See S. Khilnani, *Arguing Revolution. The Intellectual Left in Postwar France* (New Haven, Connecticut, Yale University Press, 1993), 14.
15. See for example the special number of *Communications* 63 (1996) on Barthes; and A. Lavers, *Roland Barthes: Structuralism and After* (London, Methuen, 1982).
16. L. Hill, *Marguerite Duras. Apocalyptic Desires* (London, Routledge, 1993), 7–8.
17. See for example D. Miller, *Bringing Out Roland Barthes* (Berkeley and Los Angeles, University of California Press, 1992).
18. Jean Cau, *Croquis de mémoire* (Paris, Julliard, 1985), 188.
19. D. Knight, *Barthes and Utopia. Space, Travel, Writing* (Oxford, Clarendon Press, 1997).
20. For an excellent account in Barthes's work, see M. Moriarty, *Roland Barthes* (Oxford, Polity Press, 1991).
21. J. G. Merquior, *From Prague to Paris. A Critique of Structuralist and Post-Structuralist Thought* (London, Verso, 1986), 247.
22. M. Kofman, *Edgar Morin. From Big Brother to Fraternity* (London, Pluto, 1996), 8.
23. B. Comment, *Roland Barthes, vers le neutre* (Paris, Christian Bourgois, 1991).
24. See *Le Monde*, 9 May 1970.

Part One

1. J. Culler, *Roland Barthes* (Glasgow, Fontana, 1983), Ch. 1.
2. A fuller account of this period is given in Ch. 3 of Louis-Jean Calvet, *Roland Barthes: A Biography*, trans. Sarah Wykes (Oxford, Polity Press, 1994). All references to this biography are henceforth to the English translation.
3. His paper at the conference – published as 'A Brief Sociological Study of the Contemporary French Novel', *Documents* 2 (February 1955) (OCi 465–70) – described the 'fundamental aspects' of the 'literary economy' as the 'submission of the body of producers (novelists) to the distributing body'; and concluded that '[t]he rights of an author are generally a salary in disguise' (OCi 465). René Wintzen's introduction to this conference quoted Barthes's view of the exploited, if not proto-proletarian, status of the writer: '[A] book is now nothing more than a commodity subject to the laws of commerce, and the writer, to quote Roland Barthes, is an employee on a reasonable salary who does overtime with other companies in order to survive (journalism, radio, television, translations etc.)' (*Documents* 2, 178–9).

4. See F. Dosse, *Histoire du structuralisme 1* (Paris, La Découverte, 1991), Ch. 22, 237–50.
5. P. Bourdieu, *Homo Academicus*, trans. Peter Collier (Oxford, Polity Press, 1988), xviii–xix, xxii.

Chapter 1

1. Cited as an epigraph to Barthes's editorial in *TP* 12 (March/April 1955) (OCi 484).
2. P. Roger, 'Barthes in the Marx Years', *Communications* 63 (1996), 39–61.
3. In an interview with Bernard-Henri Lévy in 1977, Barthes claimed to have written 'just two' articles whilst in the sanatorium (OCiii 747/GV 260).
4. See L.-J. Calvet, *Roland Barthes. 1915–1980* (Paris, Flammarion, 1990), English translation, *Roland Barthes: A Biography*, by Sarah Wykes (Oxford, Polity Press, 1994), 76–7.
5. The articles for the latter constituted a regular two-weekly series (see OCi 393–7, 407–21, 427–9, 432–4), which ended in October 1954 with the beginning of the regular column of mythological studies in *LLN*.
6. See the 1979 interview with M. Padova, 'Vie et mort des revues' (OCii 1095–6); and Calvet, *Biography*, 63–4.
7. Barthes was, according to Rebeyrol, 'socialist, utopian, humanist' (interview between A. Stafford and P. Rebeyrol, 14 October 1992). See also Calvet, *Biography*, 23.
8. M. Nadeau, *Histoire du surréalisme* (Paris, Seuil, 1945).
9. Nadeau's memoirs, *Grâces leur soient rendues* (Paris, Albin Michel, 1990), devote a chapter to his first meeting with Barthes in 1947, 'Un souvenir de Montmorency: Roland Barthes' (311–22).
10. Nadeau, *Grâces*, 312–15, 187; Nadeau, *La Littérature présente* (Paris, Corrêa, 1952).
11. See Calvet, *Biography*, 72–3, 102, and more generally A. Callinicos, *Trotskyism* (Buckingham, Open University Press, 1990), 28–38.
12. Calvet, *Biography*, 103.
13. *Ibid.*, 64, 80–1.
14. 'Le degré zéro de l'écriture', *Combat*, 1 August 1947, 2. See Diana Knight, *Barthes and Utopia. Space, Travel, Writing* (Oxford, Clarendon Press, 1997), 3–4, 123
15. See Nadeau's introduction to the second article (*Combat*, 26 September 1947, 2) which described the interest generated by the first; called originally 'Responsibility of Grammar' by Barthes, it was published under Nadeau's chosen title, which removed the reference to Sartrian 'responsibility' (OCi 79–81). Some aspects of this second article have been incorporated into *Writing Degree Zero*, see for example OCi 170/WDZ 62–3.
16. See J.-P. Sartre, *Qu'est-ce que la littérature?* (Paris, Gallimard, 1948).
17. Barthes reiterated this point more firmly three years later in 'Triumph and Rupture of Bourgeois Writing' (*Combat*, 9 November 1950, 4): 'Bourgeois ideology lasted free of fracture until 1848, without the slightest ripple from a Revolution which gave the

bourgeoisie political and social power, but not intellectual power which it had held for a long time before. From Rousseau to Chateaubriand, from Laclos to Stendhal, bourgeois writing, if not style, needed only to pick up again and continue through the brief spell of troubles. And the romantic revolution, always said to be a great challenge to form, sensibly held onto the writing appertaining to its ideology.'

18. Trotsky wrote: 'From the time of the Renaissance and of the Reformation which created more favourable intellectual and political conditions for the bourgeoisie in feudal society, to the time of the Revolution which transferred power to the bourgeoisie (in France), there passed three or four centuries of growth in the material and intellectual force of the bourgeoisie. [. . .] The bourgeoisie not only developed materially within feudal society, entwining itself in various ways with the latter and attracting wealth into its own hands, but it weaned the intelligentsia to its side and created its cultural foundation (schools, universities, academies, newspapers, magazines) long before it took open possession of the state' (L. Trotsky, *Literature and Revolution* (London, Bookmarks, 1991), 216–17).
19. See S. Khilnani, *Arguing Revolution. The Intellectual Left in Postwar France* (New Haven, Connecticut, Yale University Press, 1993), 24–8.
20. R. A. Champagne, *Beyond the Structuralist Myth of Écriture* (The Hague/Paris, Mouton, 1977), 82.
21. Compare Sartre, *Qu'est-ce que la littérature?*, 106–7 with 117.
22. Published in *Combat*, 9 November 1950, 4.
23. In *Qu'est-ce que la littérature?* Sartre even considered surrealism, this 'Trotskyist safety valve', as an 'aberration' in the history of committed art and literature (see 151, 296–304).
24. See J. Ehrmann, 'On Articulation: The Language of History and the Terror of Language', *Yale French Studies* 39, special number, 'Literature and Revolution', 1967, 15–16.
25. See *LLN*, July 1953, 591–9.
26. Calvet, *Biography*, 105. J.-B. Pontalis, 'Le degré zéro de l'écriture', *Les Temps modernes*, November 1953, 934–8.
27. M. Blanchot, 'Plus loin que le degré zéro', *NNRF* 9 (September 1953), 485–94.
28. 11 June 1953, 17–19.
29. G. Venaissin, 'Jean Cayrol, romanicer du point zéro; *Critique* 84 (May 1954), 414–20.
30. J. Piel, 'La fonction sociale du critique', *Critique* 80 (January 1954), 1–13.
31. 'Du degré zéro de l'écriture au point de congélation de la critique', *Preuves*, July 1953, 87–90.
32. See the 'Présentation' of the first number, republished in part in M. Nadeau, *Le Roman français depuis la guerre* (Paris, Gallimard, 1963), 213–15.
33. See D. Mortier, *Celui qui dit oui, celui qui dit non ou la Réception de Brecht en France (1945–56)* (Paris/Geneva, Champion/Slatkine, 1986), 91.
34. P. Roger, *Roland Barthes, roman* (Paris, Grasset, 1986), 314.

35. See Calvet, *Biography*, 78.
36. Contrasting Barthes's approach with the 'academic' study by Oscar Haac, Febvre, currently editing Michelet's unpublished diaries, praised the manner in which Barthes placed himself 'inside' Michelet, and considered that Barthes was uncannily accurate in his unorthodox view of the historian; L. Febvre, 'Michelet pas mort', *Combat*, 24 April 1954, 1 and 9. Compare this favourable review with that of Jean Pommier, who doubted the accuracy of Barthes's views; J. Pommier, 'Baudelaire et Michelet devant la jeune critique', *Revue d'histoire littéraire de la France*, October/December 1957, 544–7.
37. See 'Le parcours d'une écriture', *Le Magazine littéraire*, October 1993, 22.
38. See A. Stafford, 'Constructing a Radical Popular Theatre: Roland Barthes, Brecht and *Théâtre Populaire*', *French Cultural Studies* 7 (1996), 33–48.
39. See B. Dort, 'Brecht en France', *Les Temps modernes* 171 (June 1960), 1858.
40. B. Dort, 'Du combat au constat', *Revue des revues* 1 (March 1986), 54.
41. Hence Barthes's editorial in *TP* 18 (April 1956), which showed the shortcomings and 'recuperability' of avant-garde theatre. This search for a political theatre was an important development from 1953, when Beckett's *Godot* (though clearly apolitical) had been considered appropriate popular theatre material. Compare OCi 1224–5 and 413–14 (CE 67–70).
42. See *NNRF* 25 (January 1955), 167.
43. 'Mythologie perpétuelle', 'Les Martiens et la presse', 'Les Martiens et l'église', 'Nouvelles mystifications', 'L'opération Astra', 'Conjugales' and 'Phénomène ou mythe?', *LLN*, December 1954, 944–53. Only 'Conjugales' has been republished in the *Oeuvres complètes*.
44. See *LLN*, March 1955, 394n. Calvès was another of Nadeau's Trotskyist comrades from before the Occupation.
45. *LLN*, November 1955, 666–72.
46. *LLN*, December 1955, 817–18.
47. See 'The Cruise of the *Batory*', *LLN*, October 1955, 512 (OCi 644/ET 98, with minor editing). Barthes would have had every reason to protest, since his friend Bernard Dort was one of those called up.
48. These articles by Calvès are to be found, respectively, in *LLN* July/August 1955 (179); November 1955 (660); October 1955 (500); November 1955 (660–1).
49. See Roger, *Barthes, roman*, 323–44.
50. J. Guérin, 'Notes', *NNRF*, June 1955, 1118–19.
51. Calvet, *Biography*, 118–20.
52. J. Guérin, 'M. Barthes se met en colère', *NNRF*, October 1955, 802–4.
53. A brief exchange with François Mauriac might also be mentioned. Barthes's early witty satire, 'The Writer on Holiday', which spoke of a 'certain great writer' in *Mythologies* wearing 'blue pyjamas', had named this writer in the original article as François Mauriac (compare *France-Observateur*, 9 September 1954, with OCi 581/M

31). In his weekly column in *L'Express* called 'Bloc-notes', and having seen Barthes's article in *France-Observateur,* Mauriac replied to Barthes, and appeared unusually angry at the mocking of his placing a photo of blue pyjamas at the foot of an earlier 'Bloc-notes'. Barthes's article was, he wrote, 'a nasty piece of paper', 'unworthy' of the author of *Writing Degree Zero* and the 'stunning' *Michelet*; and though he enjoyed 'combative journalism', Mauriac could not understand why Barthes had chosen Gide and himself as 'adversaries'. See 'Bloc-notes', *L'Express,* 18 September 1954, 12.

54. A. Brown, *Roland Barthes: The Figures of Writing* (Oxford, Clarendon Press, 1992), 26–32.
55. See R. Klein, 'Images of the Self: New York and Paris', *Partisan Review* 2 (1973), 295–301, in which Klein noted the contradiction between 'Racine is Racine', and the 1963 article for the *Times Literary Supplement* 'Criticism as Language'. Klein's view was that Barthes's critique of bourgeois formalism in 'Racine is Racine' which exposed bourgeois ideology's abstraction of historical reality in its 'common sense' refusal of critical/philosophical interpretation, was contradicted by 'Criticism as Language', in which Barthes adopted 'the very formula he earlier derogates'. Here, writes Klein, Barthes's intention was to defend a mode of structuralist criticism 'whose aim is to liberate literature from the tyranny of meaning to which "bourgeois" culture submits it' (294–5).
56. Precisely what Barthes did in the footnote to his review of a production of Labiche's *Le plus heureux des trois, TP* 19 (July 1956), OCi 552 n1.
57. This ambiguous, dialectical relationship to myth is implicitly suggested by Rick Rylance's contrast of *Mythologies* with Richard Hoggart's *The Uses of Literacy.* The 'dialectique d'amour' fits with Rylance's view that, devoid of the 'moral earnestness' of Hoggart's book, *Mythologies* 'finds pleasure as well as cant in the consumer world' (see R. Rylance, *Roland Barthes* (Hemel Hempstead, Harvester Wheatsheaf, 1994), 62–3).

Chapter 2

1. See A. Lavers, *Roland Barthes. Structuralism and After* (London, Methuen, 1982), 7–11.
2. See F. Dosse, *L'Histoire en miettes: des* Annales *à la* nouvelle histoire (Paris, La Découverte, 1987), 95–105.
3. Quoted in F. Dosse, *Histoire du structuralisme 1* (Paris, La Découverte, 1991), 255.
4. See H. S. Hughes, *The Obstructed Path: French Social Thought in the Years of Desperation 1930–1960* (New York, Harper Torch, 1966), Ch. 1.
5. P. Roger, *Roland Barthes, roman* (Paris, Grasset, 1986), 289. His knowledge of Nietzsche can be traced, according to L.-J. Calvet, *Roland Barthes: 1915–1980* (Paris, Flammarion, 1990), English translation, *Roland Barthes: A Biography* by Sarah Wykes (Oxford, Polity Press, 1994), 33, back to 1935, a relatively 'early' date in France for the German philosopher. In his biography of Michel Foucault, David Macey (*The Lives of Michel Foucault* (London, Vintage, 1994), 34) suggests that

Nietzsche was known in France in the first half of the twentieth century predominantly via literary authors – Paul Valéry, Gide and Camus – precisely Barthes's reading diet during the 1930s and the war years.

6. Calvet, *Biography*, Ch. 3.
7. Richard Howard's translation is, unfortunately, taken from the partial republication in *Le Magazine littéraire*, February 1975, 24–8. Victim of a minor editing process (one large and three smaller fragments are omitted), the article was judged by Barthes in 1975 to be 'out of date' (p. 24); and those passages excised seem to reinforce the humanism of the article; see OCi 23–5, 28.
8. For a brief account of Gide's 'materialism' see Maurice Nadeau's preface to A. Gide, *Romans. Récits et soties. Oeuvres lyriques* (Paris, Gallimard, 1958), xxi.
9. Marty's designs recreated the ancient Greek theatre's portrayal of humanity as a 'lone and upright thing, innocent, excluded, obstinate and happy', and, in contrast to the 'useless and indiscreet scenery of bourgeois drama', it promoted acts of 'interrogation' (OCi 71).
10. Roger, *Barthes, roman*, 323–43.
11. M. Moriarty, *Roland Barthes* (Oxford, Polity Press, 1991), 45.
12. See *TP* 1 (March 1953), 1–6.
13. An extended version of his address to the Avignon ATP, 'The Popular Theatre Today', described the blue-collar nature of the participants, 'a building apprentice, a skilled worker, a post-office employee' (OCi 443).
14. See for example his view that Brecht showed the 'power of men over the artificial servitudes of their History' at the end of the 'Notice' for Brecht's *Complete Works* in French (OCi 496); see also OCi 755, 1229.
15. Moriarty, *Barthes*, 45.
16. Compare the first paragraph (OCi 1241/CE 91) with the original article in *Arguments* 6 (February 1958), which has an extra paragraph on how Robbe-Grillet was wrong to encourage the 'confusion' (p. 6).
17. Roger, *Barthes, roman*, 323–34.
18. *Ibid.*, 336.
19. Jean Paris's study of *Hamlet*, warmly welcomed by Barthes in 1953, was an early influence on Barthes's conversion of play to text. A proto-structuralist analysis of Shakespeare's play, Paris's study encouraged Barthes to see a great Elizabethan tragedy as akin to a detective novel (OCi 233–5).
20. Pontalis's review of *Writing Degree Zero* in *Les Temps modernes* sums up well the voluntarism–determinism swing evident in Barthes's views on literary writing (p. 937).
21. A. Brown, *Roland Barthes: The Figures of Writing* (Oxford, Clarendon Press, 1992), 76–9.
22. See E. Wilson, *To the Finland Station* (London, Collins/Fontana, 1974), Chs 1–4, 9–32.
23. H. Juin, 'Michelet mangeait l'Histoire', *Combat*, 1 July 1954.
24. This is repeated by Duvignaud in his review: 'Michelet was a sort of Shakespeare of the past'; *NNRF* 19 (July 1954), 126.

25. Compare 'Voltaire, le dernier des écrivains heureux?', *Actualité littéraire*, March 1958, 15, with OCi 1239/CE 89.
26. Quoted in P. Thody, *Roland Barthes: A Conservative Estimate* (London, Macmillan, 1977), 49n; U. Eco, *Misreadings*, trans. William Weaver (London, Picador, 1994), 1–2.
27. 21 September 1957.
28. September 1958.
29. July/August 1957, 113–19.
30. 21 March 1957.
31. 25 April 1957; 3 April 1957.
32. 13 March 1957; June 1957.
33. November 1957, 123–4.
34. August 1957.
35. June 1957, 306–9.
36. December 1957.
37. 20 September 1957; 23 June 1957.
38. 9 March 1957. Barthes had reason to bear a grudge against Coiplet for the review of *Michelet par lui-même*; see 'Michelet extravagant', *Le Monde*, 10 April 1954.
39. Compare *LLN*, November 1954 (793), with OCi 583, and January 1955 (153) with OCi 594.
40. 28 August 1957.
41. 12 April 1957.
42. 28 March 1957.
43. 30 March 1957.
44. 22 March 1957.
45. See Calvet, *Biography*, 126.
46. 12 April 1957; October 1957.
47. 7 February 1958.
48. 18 September 1957.
49. 31 July 1957.
50. I have not had the space to consider Maurice Blanchot's review (ironically in the *NNRF*), a sophisticated account of Barthes's Hegelian-Marxian attempt to explain the nature of ideology; see 'La Grande tromperie', *NNRF* 5 (1957), 1061–73.
51. See Andrew Leak's critical guide to *Mythologies* (London, Grant and Cutler, 1994), Ch. 4.
52. See H. White, *Metahistory: The Historical Imagination in Nineteenth-Century Europe* (Baltimore, Maryland, Johns Hopkins University Press, 1973), Ch. 3, 149–58.

Part Two

1. R. Lourau, *Auto-dissolution des avant-gardes* (Paris, Editions Galilée, 1980), 74.
2. P. de Boisdeffre, *La Cafétière est sur la table, ou Contre le Nouveau Roman* (Paris, Table Ronde, 1967), 67–77.

3. A. Robbe-Grillet, *Pour un nouveau roman* (Paris, Editions de Minuit, 1963), 55.
4. See Y. Buin (ed.), *Que peut la littérature?* (Paris, Union Générale d'Editions, 1965), 57.
5. O. Burgelin, 'Le Double système de la mode', *L'Arc* 56 (1974), 8–16 (9).
6. See for example Victor Leduc's preface to *Structuralisme et marxisme* (Paris, Union Générale d'Editions, 1970), 7–12. At the same conference, Barthes was completely overlooked in Olivier Revault d'Allones's comments on Foucault's *Les Mots et les choses* and Henri Lefebvre's *Langage et société*, even though both appeared at exactly the same time as Barthes's *Criticism and Truth* (*ibid.*, 30). Barthes's reply to the question of existentialism's relevance in 1966, 'A Fertile Confrontation', was published in *Arts et loisirs* 26 (23–29 March 1966), 11 (not in OCii).
7. G. Mounin, *Introduction à la sémiologie* (Paris, Editions de Minuit, 1970).
8. A. Green, 'Les *Mythologies* de Roland Barthes et la psychopathologie', *Critique* 132 (1958), 105–13.
9. 'J'ai cherché à ouvrir une discussion', *La Quinzaine littéraire* 3 (15 April 1966), 14.
10. A point made by John Sturrock (ed.), *Structuralism and Since. From Lévi-Strauss to Derrida* (Oxford, Oxford University Press, 1979), 54–5.

Chapter 3

1. The original article provides a number of intriguing photographs of actors in costume as illustrations of his views, and under which Barthes added brief comments; see *TP* 12 (March/April 1955), 64–76.
2. See Barthes's comment in 1961 in 'French Avant-Garde Theatre': 'one good review by an important bourgeois newspaper, we used to say a few years ago, was worth a million adverts' (OCi 916).
3. The proceedings of this conference are collected in Collective, *Situation de la critique. Actes du premier colloque international de la critique littéraire* (Paris, Syndicat des Critiques Littéraires, 1964).
4. *Ibid.*, 147–62, followed by a discussion (177–83).
5. Writing in 1963, Gilbert Durand criticised Barthes's use of Bachelard in 'Myth Today' in a manner which prefigured Barthes's own later literarisation of the real. Rejecting Barthes's Saussurian model, which, putting myth on the second level of meaning, considered it 'second' to language, Durand insisted that myth was 'always first in all senses of the word': 'poetry like myth', he concluded in contradistinction to the conclusion of 'Myth Today', 'is inalienable'. See G. Durand, *Les Structures anthropologiques de l'imaginaire* (1963) (Paris, Bordas, 1969), 457–9.
6. See M. McAllester, 'Polemics and Poetics: Bachelard's Conception of the Imagining Consciousness', *Journal of the British Society for Phenomenology* 12:1 (January 1981), 3–13.
7. See L. Goldmann, *Pour une sociologie du roman* (Paris, Gallimard, 1964), 15; and his partial retraction in the face of criticism in the 1965 preface, 16–17.

8. See G. Thomson, *Aeschylus and Athens. A Study in the Social Origins of Drama* (London, Lawrence and Wishart, 1946). First published in 1941, Thomson's study, an impressive attempt to link drama, sociologically and anthropologically, to socio-economic change, was republished in abridged form in a pamphlet called 'Marxism and Poetry' (London, 1946).
9. R. Jones, *Panorama de la nouvelle critique en France de Gaston Bachelard à Jean-Paul Weber* (Paris, SEDES, 1968), 28; see Ch. 4 on Barthes and Goldmann (221–50, esp. 235–7, 249).
10. Interestingly, in his review of *On Racine*, Hubert Juin considered that exactly the opposite was the case; *On Racine* was interesting for what it said not about Racine but about Barthes and modern criticism. See H. Juin, 'Autour de Racine', *Les Lettres françaises*, 18–24 July 1963, 2; see also Robert Kanters's similar view that the 'Racinian Eros' and the 'Micheletian Eros' revealed more of 'a Barthesian Eros' than anything else ('Roland Barthes et le mythe de Racine', *Le Figaro littéraire*, 10 August 1963).
11. Barthes's contribution to this renewal of interest was noted in René Girard's review, 'Racine, poète de la gloire', *Critique* 20 (1964), 483–506, and by André Bonzon in 1970; see Introduction to A. Bonzon, *La Nouvelle critique et Racine* (Paris, Editions Nizet, 1970), 18.
12. See Guy Dumur's comment in 1972 that it would be impossible for a director of Racine plays *not* to take note of Barthes's analysis of *Bajazet*; G. Dumur, 'Racine à Pigalle', *Nouvel-Observateur*, 6 March 1972.
13. P. Bourdieu, 'Homo Academicus', *Le Monde aujourd'hui*, 5 November 1984.
14. J.-L. Baudry, 'La Tragédie racinienne: une oeuvre ouverte', *TQ* 15 (Autumn 1963), 65–7.
15. R.-M. Albérès, 'La "Nouvelle Critique" ', *Les Nouvelles littéraires*, 22 August 1963.
16. S. Doubrovsky, *Pourquoi la nouvelle critique* (Paris, Mercure de France, 1966), 1.
17. See 'M. Roland Barthes et la "critique universitaire" ', *Le Monde*, 14 March 1964.
18. See 'M. Barthes et la "critique universitaire" ', two extracts of letters from Guitton and Fluchère, *Le Monde*, 28 March 1964 (9).
19. See M. Diéguez, 'Roland Barthes and the Degree Zero of Writing', in *L'Ecrivain et son langage* (Paris, Gallimard, 1960), 133–48.
20. See *Le Monde*, 7 April 1964 (11), 11 April 1964 (13).
21. See also *Le Monde*, 23 October 1965.
22. *Le Figaro littéraire*, 7–13 and 14–20 October 1965, respectively. (The latter appears in OCi 1563–5/GV 38–42.)
23. Robert Poulet, 'Qu'est-ce que la critique?', *Rivarol*, 24 February 1966, an article which seemed to prefer Barthes, rather surprisingly, to Picard. Interestingly the same Robert Poulet wrote an article in *Les Nouvelles littéraires* three weeks later (10 March 1966) which, far from praising Picard, gave him nevertheless the edge over Barthes. It rejected both the subjectivity of 'new criticism' and the scientific claims of university criticism, in favour of a living 'art' of criticism which, without method,

relied on 'taste' – a position which Picard and Barthes would certainly have agreed to reject!

24. *Le Nouvel-Observateur*, 3 November 1965.
25. *Le Monde*, 6 November 1965 (13); see also the supportive comments of M. Chessen (*Le Monde*, 20 November 1965) and Y. Bellenger (*Le Monde*, 27 November 1965), who ironically called herself one of Barthes's 'gullible admirers'.
26. 'Les anciens et les modernes', *Le Français dans le monde* 39 (1966), 46–8.
27. A point reinforced by Lucette Finas's review of *Criticism and Truth*, 'Barthes, ou le pari sur une nouvelle forme de raison', *La Quinzaine littéraire* 3 (15 April 1966). This concluded (rather poetically itself) that Barthes's substitution of desire for beauty was part of his return to the 'mythical sources of literature [. . .] towards Homer and Aeschylus, about whom we know nothing, about whom we know everything because their voice is reaching us' (15).
28. This was the title of Jean Bloch-Michel's review of *Criticism and Truth* in *Le Nouvel-Observateur* (30 March 1966, 34–5); for Bloch-Michel, Barthes was far more 'academic' than Picard because he did not 'raise his voice'.
29. *Les Nouvelles littéraires*, 21 April 1966.
30. *Options* 7–8 (1966), 40–2; *Les Lettres françaises*, 24 March 1966, 3–4.
31. 'La lettre et le symbole', *Esprit* 5 (May 1966), 1113–16; see also Y. Bertherat, *Esprit* 5–6 (May/June 1964), 1202–4.
32. *Le Nouvel-Observateur*, 13 April 1966.
33. F. Dosse, *Histoire du structuralisme 1* (Paris, La Découverte, 1991), Ch. 11.
34. H. Lefebvre, 'Sur le structuralisme et l'Histoire', *Cahiers internationaux de Sociologie* (July/December 1963), republished in Lefebvre, *L'Idéologie structuraliste* (Paris, Éditions Anthropos, 1975), 13–44 (19).
35. D. Knight, *Barthes and Utopia. Space, Travel, Writing* (Oxford, Clarendon Press, 1997), Chs 1 and 2.
36. E. Wilson, *Adorned Dreams. Fashion and Modernity* (London, Virago, 1985), 57–8.
37. See F. Braudel, 'Histoire et sciences sociales', *Annales* 4 (Oct./Dec. 1958), 725–53.
38. See *LLN*, July/August 1957, 118.
39. See F. Dosse, *Histoire du structuralisme II* (Paris, La Découverte, 1992), 33.

Chapter 4

1. See G. Poulet (ed.), *Les Chemins actuels de la critique* (Paris, Union Générale d'Editions, 1966).
2. M. Cournot, 'La zuppa Pavese', *Nouvel-Observateur*, 22–28 June 1966.
3. See 'Les Artistes devant la politique', *Arts* 10 (1–7 December 1965), 10–11; 'Les réactions sur Céline' and 'Le degré 007 de l'écriture', *Nouvel-Observateur* 15 (1965), 27–8, and 57 (1965), 28–9, respectively, none of which appears in the *Oeuvres complètes*.

4. For the enormous difference between a *historical* materialist and a *cultural* materialist view of May 1968, compare C. Harman, *The Fire Last Time: 1968 and After* (London, Bookmarks, 1988), with K. Reader (and K. Wadia), *The May 1968 Events in France. Reproduction and Interpretation* (London, Macmillan, 1993).
5. P. Combes, *La Littérature et le mouvement de mai 68* (Paris, Seghers, 1984), 24–8.
6. See Gorz's early 1968 belief that no crisis was likely in the 'foreseeable future', quoted in Harman, *Fire Last Time*, 4.
7. See Combes, *La Litterature*, 273–8.
8. J. Culler, *Roland Barthes* (Glasgow, Fontana, 1983), Ch. 1.
9. See M. Moriarty, 'Rhetoric, Doxa and Experience in Barthes', *French Studies*, May 1997, 169–82.
10. M. Mannoni, 'Psychoanalysis and the May Revolution', published in France in July 1968 and republished in translation in C. Posner (ed.), *Reflections on the Revolution in France: 1968* (Harmondsworth, Penguin, 1970), 215–24.
11. E. Roudinesco, *La Bataille de cent ans. Histoire de la psychanalyse en France 2* (Paris, Seuil, 1986), 398.
12. *Ibid.*, 397.
13. See in Poulet, *Les Chemins actuels*, D. Noguez, 'Choix bibliographique', 285–309 (306), and R. Jean, 'Une situation critique', 101–7 (102–3).
14. O. Hahn, 'Il y a toujours un système', *L'Express*, 23 April 1964.
15. M. Galey, 'Etre ou ne pas être romancier', *Arts*, 8 April 1964.
16. J.-P. Faye, 'Une Critique fabuleuse', *Les Lettres françaises*, 2 April 1964.
17. P. Sénart, 'La Critique: De Barbey D'Aurevilly à Roland Barthes', *Combat*, 16 July 1964.
18. G. Genette, 'L'Homme et les signes', *Critique* 21 (1965), 99–114.
19. P. ffrench, *The Time of Theory. A History of* Tel Quel, *1960–1983* (Oxford, Clarendon Press, 1995), 2.
20. P. Forest, *Histoire de Tel Quel. 1960–1982* (Paris, Seuil, 1995), Ch. 1.
21. See ffrench, *Time of Theory*, Ch. 2.
22. Forest, *Histoire de Tel Quel*, 168–9.
23. *Ibid.*, 195. Barthes's rather sardonic piece on the critics' general failure to criticise de Gaulle's *Memoirs* had joked about the view of the general as a 'writer', whilst mocking mildly but explicitly the 'young review' *TQ* and its notion of a 'writer's gift'; see 'De Gaulle, the French and Literature' (OCi 830–2).
24. Curiously for two writers in the Seuil literary stable, Barthes and Sollers did not meet until 1963, according to L.-J. Calvet, *Roland Barthes: 1915–1980* (Paris, Flammarion, 1990); English translation, *Roland Barthes: A Biography*, by Sarah Wykes (Oxford, Polity Press, 1994), 171.
25. L. Hill, 'Philippe Sollers and *Tel Quel*', in M. Tilby (ed.), *Beyond the Nouveau Roman* (London, Berg, 1990), 100–22 (102).
26. See Forest, *Histoire de Tel Quel*, 77, 92.

27. *Ibid.*, 83–4.
28. *Ibid.*, 176, 196.
29. See the articles collected in P. Sollers, *L'Écriture et l'expérience des limites* (Paris, Seuil, 1968).
30. See Léon Andréev's article on Soviet literature in *Le Monde* (9 August 1967, III) which regretted the manner in which 'Barthes and *Tel Quel*' had 'turned their backs on History'. Ironically, Barthes's 1965 reply on Céline (see n. 3 above) seemed to have placed him in the de Roux camp.
31. Poulet, *Les Chemins actuels*, 106.
32. See Forest, *Histoire de Tel Quel*, 198.
33. See ffrench, *Time of Theory*, 109–10, 116–18.
34. Published in *TQ* 43 (1970), 94–5, but not republished in OCii.
35. See also 'May 68' in *TQ* 34 (Summer 1968), 94–5.
36. Forest, *Histoire de Tel Quel*, 359.
37. See D. Attridge, G. Bennington and R. Young (eds), *Post-Structuralism and the Question of History* (Cambridge, Cambridge University Press, 1987).
38. L. Finas, 'Entre les mots et les choses', *La Quinzaine littéraire*, 15–31 May 1967, 3–4.
39. T. Todorov, 'De la sémiologie à la rhétorique', *Annales* 22 (Nov./Dec. 1967), 1322–7.
40. G. Luccioni, *Esprit* 35 (1967), 338–9.
41. Forest, *Histoire de Tel Quel*, 251–2, 258.
42. J. Kristeva, 'Le Sens et la Mode', *Critique* 24 (1967), 1005–31.
43. See R. Salado, 'Barthes/Baudrillard: la corruption de la théorie', in C. Coquio and R. Salado, *Barthes après Barthes: une actualité en questions* (Pau, Publications de l'Université de Pau, 1993), 148.
44. See P. Barbéris, 'A propos du *S/Z* de Roland Barthes', *L'Année balzacienne* 1971, 109–22 (110).
45. 'Voulez-vous jouer avec Balzac?', *Le Nouvel-Observateur*, 4 May 1970.
46. 'Roland Barthes, ou la critique devient rêve', *Combat*, 14 May 1970.
47. See Forest, *Histoire de Tel Quel*, 357–9; 'Sollers parle de Barthes', *La Quinzaine littéraire*, 1–15 March 1970, 22–3.
48. *Esprit* 38 (1970), 1199–202.
49. 'Balzac à l'encan [at the auction]', *Critique* 302 (July 1972), 610–22; Barbéris, 'A propos du *S/Z*'.
50. 'Deux points de vue sur *S/Z*: Balzac lu par Roland Barthes', *Le Monde* 9 May 1970 (supplement, III); Raymond Jean, 'Le "commentaire" comme forme "active" de la critique', and Pierre Citron, 'Une méthode qui accentue le côté subjectif de toute lecture'.
51. 'Roland Barthes et le lac des signes', *Le Figaro littéraire*, 18–24 May 1970.

Part Three

1. N. Shawcross, *Roland Barthes on Photography. The Critical Tradition in Perspective* (Gainesville, Florida, University Press of Florida, 1997), 65.
2. See F. Wagener, 'La rencontre de Erté et Roland Barthes', *Le Monde*, 13 December 1973 (21).
3. G. de Mallac and M. Eberbach, *Barthes* (Paris, Editions Universitaires, 1971), published the same year as the first journal devoted to Barthes, *TQ* 47 (1971).
4. *Le Monde*, 3 December 1971, 18. See D. A. F. de Sade, *Justine ou Les Malheurs de la vertu*, pref. Béatrice Didier (Paris, Librairie Générale Française, 1973), xxix.
5. Louis-Jean Calvet, *Roland Barthes. Un regard politique sur le signe* (Paris, Payot, 1973), 137–8, which concluded with a 'Short Barthian lexis' (161–81).
6. *Le Monde*, 14 February 1975; *Magazine littéraire*, February 1975.
7. M.-A. Burnier and P. Rambaud, *Le Roland Barthes sans peine* (Paris, Balland, 1978); J.-B. Fages, *Comprendre Roland Barthes* (Toulouse, Privat, 1979).
8. G. Petitjean, 'Les marginaux de la VIe section', *Nouvel-Observateur*, 9 November 1974; Petitjean, 'Les Grands prêtres de l'Université française', *Nouvel-Observateur*, 7 April 1975.
9. T. Todorov, 'La réflexion sur la littérature dans la France contemporaine', *Poétique* 38 (1979), 131–48 (142).
10. See G. Mounin, *Introduction à la sémiologie* (Paris, Editions de Minuit, 1970), 189–97, 11–13, 15, 227.
11. 'Le Formalisme français', in M. Riffaterre, *Essais de stylistique structurale* (Paris, Flammarion, 1971), Ch. 11, 261–85.
12. See P. ffrench, *The Time of Theory. A History of* Tel Quel, *1960–1983* (Oxford, Clarendon Press, 1995), 256–68.

Chapter 5

1. J. Kristeva, 'Comment parler à la littérature', *TQ* 47 (27–49), 33.
2. H. Rousso, *Le Syndrome de Vichy* (Paris, Seuil, 1987), Ch. 3.
3. P. Roger, 'Traitement de faveur (Barthes lecteur de Sade)', *Nottingham French Studies* 36:1 (spring 1997), 34–44; Diana Knight, *Barthes and Utopia. Space, Travel, Writing* (Oxford, Clarendon Press, 1997), 163–4.
4. M. Boughali, *L'Érotique du langage chez Roland Barthes* (Casablanca, Afrique-Orient, 1986).
5. *TQ* 45 (spring 1971), 101.
6. J.-F. Revel, 'Le fantasme anonyme', *L'Express* 19–25 October 1970, 137.
7. See *Tel Quel*ian Marcelin Pleynet's interview with the cinema journal *Cinéthique*, translated in S. Harvey, *May 68 and Film Culture* (London, British Film Institute, 1978), 153–4.

8. L.-J. Calvet, *Roland Barthes. Un Regard politique sur le signe* (Paris, Payot, 1973), 150–60.
9. Indeed, the 1970 preface to *Mythologies* had made an explicit reference to May 1968 (OCi 563/M 9).
10. See P. ffrench, *The Time of Theory. A History of* Tel Quel, *1960–1983* (Oxford, Clarendon Press, 1995), 183–6.
11. See Knight, *Barthes and Utopia,* Chs 1 and 2.
12. R. Kanters, 'Roland Barthes et le lac des signes', *Le Figaro Littéraire,* 18–24 May 1970.
13. F. Choay, 'L'emploi des signes', *La Quinzaine littéraire,* 1–15 May 1970, 5.
14. R. Laporte, 'L'empire des signifiants', *Critique* 302 (July 1972), 583–94.
15. See P. Combes, *La Littérature et le mouvement de mai 68* (Paris, Seghers, 1984), 282 n.32.
16. 'Vivre avec Fourier', *Critique* 281 (October 1970), 789–812. See Knight, *Barthes and Utopia,* 68.
17. P. Roger, 'Et ma liberté est illimitée', *Critique,* special number (1996), 754–62.
18. The opening section of Loyola in *Sade, Fourier, Loyola,* 'L'écriture' ('The Writing') (OCii 1069–70/SFL 39–40), was added in its entirety to the original 'How to Speak to God', *TQ* 38 (summer 1969), 32–54.
19. P. Duvernois, 'L'emportement de l'écriture', *Critique* 302 (July 1972), 595–609.
20. J.-P. Amette, 'Apprendre à lire', *La Quinzaine littéraire,* 1–15 January 1972, 15–16.
21. Amette's (shorter) review in *NRF* 230 (1972), 92–3, made this point even more forcibly: the 'jubilation' in Barthes's writing was 'a guarantee of the truly revolutionary content of his work' (p. 92).
22. G. Luccioni, *Esprit* 40 (1972), 885–7.
23. J. Ormesson, 'Logothètes et Littérature', *Les Nouvelles littéraires,* 24 Dec. 1971/2 Jan. 1972, 8.
24. Claude Jannoud, 'Roland Barthes réunit dans une même lecture Sade le maudit, Fourier l'utopiste et Loyola le jésuite', *Le Figaro,* 3 December 1971.
25. A. Rinaldi, 'Barthes réhabilite le plaisir de lire', *L'Express* 1128 (19–25 February 1973).
26. J.-F. Josselin, 'Texte-shops', *Le Nouvel-Observateur,* 6 March 1973.
27. D. Rolin, 'La volupté de lire', *Le Point,* 6 March 1973, 69.
28. M. Nadeau, 'Le petit kamasutra de Roland Barthes', *La Quinzaine littéraire,* 16–31 March 1973, 3–4.
29. Jean A. Moreau, 'Heurs', *Critique* 314 (July 1973), 583–95.
30. B. Poirot-Delpech, 'Pour une érotique de lecture: le petit kamasutra de Roland Barthes', *Le Monde,* 15 February 1973, 17.
31. See Calvet's review in *Politique-hebdo,* 15 March 1973, 21–2.
32. *Les Nouvelles littéraires,* 11 March 1973.
33. P.-J. Faunau, *NRF* 247 (1973), 95–7.

34. J. Henric, *Art-Press*, May/June 1973.
35. Anon., 'Lire? Mais quoi?', *Pourquoi Pas?*, 1 March 1973, 124–5.
36. M. Chapelan, 'Lecture(s) de Barthes', *Le Figaro*, 17 February 1973.
37. J.-P. Aron, 'Hédonolecte', *Cahiers du chemin*, October 1973, 134–42.
38. Anon., *Clés pour le spectacle*, 20 May 1973, 27.
39. See 'Vivre avec Fourier', 796–7.
40. References to, and quotations from, Nietzsche are often unattributed in Barthes's writing; see Andrew Brown, *The Figures of Writing* (Oxford, Clarendon Press, 1992), 85–6; see also S. Ungar, *Roland Barthes: The Professor of Desire* (Lincoln, University of Nebraska Press, 1983), 58–63.
41. M. Moriarty, *Roland Barthes* (Oxford, Polity Press, 1991), 137.
42. G. Ulmer, 'Fetishism in Roland Barthes's Nietzschean Phase', *Papers on Language and Literature*, 14:3 (1978), 334–55.
43. See A. Arnaud, *Pierre Klossowski* (Paris, Seuil, 1990), 188; and D. Macey, *The Lives of Michel Foucault* (London, Vintage, 1994), 120.
44. The following points are all based on D. Smith, *Transvaluations. Nietzsche in France 1872–1972* (Oxford, Clarendon Press, 1996), 152–62.
45. *Ibid.*, 168–84, 210–25.

Chapter 6

1. See P. Forest, *Histoire de Tel Quel. 1960–1982* (Paris, Seuil, 1995), 504–8.
2. K. White, 'Le cortège de Roland Barthes', *La Quinzaine littéraire*, 1 February 1979, 4–5.
3. See, for example, *Le Monde* 19 and 24 January 1977.
4. Forest, *Histoire de Tel Quel*, 558.
5. J.-A. Miller, 'Pseudo-Barthes', in Collective, *Prétexte: Roland Barthes/Colloque de Cerisy* (Paris, Union Générale d'Editions, 1978), 206.
6. Originally announced as 'Passage of Sensual Objects into Discourse', *Critique* 314 (July 1973), 582, the review was finally called 'Over the Shoulder', *Critique* 318 (November 1973), 965–76 (republished in *Sollers Writer* in 1979).
7. P. Dulac, *NRF* 313 (1979), 102–5.
8. D. Knight, *Barthes and Utopia. Space, Travel, Writing* (Oxford, Clarendon Press, 1997), Ch. 10.
9. *Magazine littéraire*, February 1975, 24–8.
10. P. Roger, *Roland Barthes, roman* (Paris, Grasset, 1986), 491.
11. *Le Monde*, 14 February 1975.
12. *La Quinzaine littéraire*, 1–15 March 1975; M. Nadeau and R. Barthes, 'Barthes puissance trois' (3–5).
13. See P. ffrench, *The Time of Theory. A History of* Tel Quel, *1960–1983* (Oxford, Clarendon Press, 1995), 188–9.

14. A. Rey, 'Le Corps aux miroirs', and J.-L. Bouttes, 'Faux comme la vérité', *Critique* 31 (1975), 1016–52.
15. J.-L. Bouttes, 'A travers et à tors', *L'Arc* 56 (1974), 57–62.
16. Calvet hints at the importance of Bouttes in Barthes's life from 1974 onwards L.-J. Calvet, *Roland Barthes: 1915–1980* (Paris, Flammarion, 1990); English translation, *Roland Barthes: A Biography*, by Sarah Wykes (Oxford, Polity Press, 1994), 191–2.
17. J. Duvignaud, *NRF* 269 (1975), 93–5.
18. C. Bourniquel, *Esprit* 445 (1975), 616–18.
19. J.-F. Josselin, *Nouvel-Observateur*, 24 February 1975.
20. R. Kanters, *Le Figaro*, 1 March 1975.
21. J. Thibaudeau, 'Situation de Barthes', *La France nouvelle*, 5 May 1975, 24–6.
22. J.-C. Dupas, 'Situation de Barthes', *La France nouvelle*, 25 August 1975, 19–20.
23. A. Compagnon, 'L'Imposture', in Collective, *Prétexte*, 40–64; Rey, 'Le Corps aux miroirs'.
24. J. Fuegi, *The Life and Lies of Bertolt Brecht* (London, HarperCollins, 1994).
25. J. Michelet, *L'Étudiant* (Paris, Seuil, 1970).
26. *Ibid.*, 9–28. In 1979 Barthes wrote a moving introduction to the catalogue of a memorial exhibition on Picon, who died in 1976, called 'Mémoire' (OCiii 1055).
27. Office de la Radio et Télévision Française (ORTF), Saturday 2 March 1974. The discussion is transcribed in P. Viallaneix, *Michelet cent ans après* (Grenoble, Presses Universitaires de Grenoble, 1975), 12–46.
28. See Barthes's comments in Viallaneix, *Michelet cent ans après*, 28–42.
29. P. Lombardo, *The Three Paradoxes of Roland Barthes* (Athens, Georgia, University of Georgia Press, 1989), 30–4.
30. The challenge of 'reading' Michelet for his modernity was taken up, and executed admirably, by Linda Orr in *Jules Michelet. Nature, History, and Language* (Ithaca, New York, and London, Cornell University Press, 1976).
31. See Forest, *Histoire de Tel Quel*, 556.
32. A. Arénilla, *NRF* 309 (1978), 113–15.
33. L.-J. Calvet, 'Grand' peurs et misères du discours amoureux', *Politique-hebdo*, 27 June/3 July 1977, 29.
34. C. Backès-Clément, 'Roland Barthes: le précieux et le romantique', *Le Matin*, 30 April 1977.
35. A. Poirson, 'La transgression sentimentale ou "Nous deux" contre Sade', *Humanité*, 21 April 1977.
36. See 'Parle-moi d'amour', *Rouge* 349 (14/15 May 1977), 10.
37. H. Bianciotti, 'L'amour en dentelles', *Nouvel-Observateur*, 25 April 1977.
38. *Le Point*, 27 June 1977.
39. M. Galey, 'La Carte du tendre de Roland Barthes', *L'Express*, 13–19 June 1977, 69–70.
40. P. Roger, 'C'est donc un amoureux qui parle et qui dit', *Critique* 361–2 (1977), 563–73.

41. An idea reinforced by the review by Maurice Chapelan in *Le Figaro*, which took the form of a letter from Stendhal to Barthes (*Le Figaro*, 25/26 June 1977).
42. M. Galey, 'Les élans du coeur', *Quotidien de Paris*, 22–23 April 1978.
43. Anon., 'Le paradoxe contre le comédien', *Humanité*, 29 April 1978.
44. J.-P. Sarrazac, 'L'invention de la théâtralité', *Esprit*, February 1997, 60–73.
45. Calvet, *Biography*, 221–2. See the significance of 'Apostrophes' for Duras in L. Hill, *Marguerite Duras. Apocalyptic Desires* (London, Routledge, 1993), 13–14.
46. J.-F. Josselin, 'Barthes et son double', *Nouvel-Observateur*, 9 May 1977, 38.
47. J.-J. Brochier, 'La solitude du discours amoureux', *Magazine littéraire*, June 1977, 63.
48. P. Gamarra, 'Discours amoureux – amour du roman', *Europe*, June 1977, 205–8.
49. Knight, *Barthes and Utopia*, 264–7.
50. N. Shawcross, *Roland Barthes on Photography. The Critical Tradition in Perspective* (Gainsville, Florida, University Press of Florida, 1997), Ch. 2.
51. See the original version of *Michelet par lui-même* ('Ecrivains de toujours', Seuil, 1954), 104–5, for the impressive double-page photo of Michelet by Nadar. Most unfortunately (and inexplicably), the republished *Michelet* (Seuil, 1988) and its English translation have removed this photo and other illustrations (other – unattributed – photos of Michelet).
52. C. Thomas, 'Barthes et Michelet: Homologie de travail, parallèle d'affection', *La Règle du jeu*, January 1995, 73–84.
53. Hinted at by Eric Marty, in an editor's footnote to 'Vita Nova' (OCiii 1300 n. 2).
54. Shawcross, *Barthes on Photography*, 64.

Afterword

1. See, for example, *Esprit* 7–8 (1980), and *NRF* 330 (1980).
2. See, for example, the court case against Bernard-Henri Lévy in 1991, not to mention the question of Barthes's correspondence, which (as Philippe Rebeyrol's holding alone shows) is voluminous.
3. Collective, *Prétexte: Roland Barthes/Colloque de Cerisy* (Paris, Union Générale d'Editions), 216.
4. For example, David Harvey has recently mobilised Barthes's '1848' theory to back up his cultural materialist argument for the existence of *post*modernity; see *The Condition of Postmodernity. An Enquiry into the Conditions of Cultural Change* (Oxford, Blackwell, 1989), 260–3.
5. See A. Callinicos, *Against Postmodernism. A Marxist Critique* (Oxford, Polity Press, 1989), 67ff.
6. See F. Pyle, *The Ideology of Imagination. Subject and Society in the Discourse of Romanticism* (Stanford, Stanford University Press, 1995), intro.

Bibliography

1 Books and Articles by Barthes

(a) Books

French references are given to the three volumes of Barthes's *Complete Works*, prepared by Eric Marty and published by Les Editions du Seuil:

R. Barthes, *Oeuvres complètes*, 3 vols.
tome 1: *1942–1965* (1993)
tome 2: *1966–1973* (1994)
tome 3: *1974–1980* (1995)

I have also used:
R. Barthes, *Michelet par lui-même* ('Ecrivains de toujours', Paris, Seuil, 1954).

(b) Articles, Letters, Interviews

The following is a list, in chronological order, of Barthes's writings used in this book which do not appear in the *Complete Works*, or are the original versions which differ significantly from those collected:

'Le degré zéro de l'écriture', *Combat*, 1 August 1947, 2.
'Mythologie perpétuelle', *LLN*, December 1954, 944–5.
'Phénomène ou mythe?', *LLN*, December 1954, 951–3.
'Georges Friedmann nous parle de théâtre' (propos recueillis par Roland Barthes), *TP* 22 (January 1957), 1–4.

'Les réactions sur Céline', *Nouvel-Observateur* 15 (1965), 27–8.
'Le degré 007 de l'écriture', *Nouvel-Observateur* 57 (1965), 28–9.
'Les artistes devant la politique', *Arts* 10 (1–7 December 1965), 10–11.
'Une confrontation féconde' (réponse à un interview de Pierre Hahn, titre: 'L'existentialisme vingt ans après: déclin ou renaissance?'), *Arts et loisirs* 26 (23–29 March 1966), 11.
'Vivre avec Fourier', *Critique* 282 (October 1970), 789–812.
'Lettre à Philippe Sollers' (25 October 1970), *TQ* 43 (Autumn 1970), 94–5.
'Sade, Fourier, Loyola', *Le Monde*, 3 December 1971, 18.

2 *Reviews of Barthes's Books*

Reviews of Barthes's books are presented in chronological order of the books' publication. The periodicals in which the reviews appear are in alphabetical order. The list of reviews here is certainly not exhaustive, but contains perhaps the most significant.

Le Degré zéro de l'écriture

Critique 80 (January 1954) (J. Piel).
LLN, July 1953 (M. Nadeau).
NNRF 9 (September 1953) (M. Blanchot).
L'Observateur, 11 June 1953 (J.-M. Caplain).
Preuves, July 1953 (C. Mauriac).
Les Temps modernes, November 1953 (J.-B. Pontalis).

Michelet par lui-même

Combat, 24 April 1954 (L. Febvre), 1 July 1954 (H. Juin).
Critique 88 (September 1954) (B. Dort).
Le Monde, 10 April 1954 (R. Coiplet).
NNRF 19 (July 1954) (J. Duvignaud).
Revue d'histoire littéraire de la France, October/December 1957 (J. Pommier).

Mythologies

Le Canard enchâiné, 13 March 1957 (M. Lebesque).
Christianisme social, October 1957 (anon.).
Cinéma 57, November 1957 (R. Guyonnet).
Combat, 25 April 1957 (A. Bosquet); 19 September 1957 (N. Ballif).

Critique 132 (1958) (A. Green).
La Croix du nord, 23 June 1957 (H. Platelle).
Demain, 21 September 1957 (J. Cathelin).
L'Echo du centre, 30 March 1957 (P. Vandromme).
Europe, August 1957 (J. Baumier).
L'Express, 22 March 1957 (T. Lenoir).
Le Figaro littéraire, 6 April 1957 (A. Alter).
France Catholique, 12 April 1957 (J.-P. Morillon).
France-Observateur, 21 March 1957 (M. Nadeau).
LLN, July/August 1957 (Y. Velan).
Libération, 3 April 1957 (C. Roy).
Le Monde, 9 March 1957 (R. Coiplet); 5/6 May 1957 (J. Lacroix); 28 August 1957 (E. Henriot).
Mercure de France, June 1957 (N. Vedrès).
La Nation française, 31 July 1957 (M. Vivier); 18 September 1957 (J.-B. Morvan).
NNRF 5 (1957) (M. Blanchot).
La Parisienne, June 1957 (M. Zéraffa).
La Pensée française, September 1958 (B. Voyenne).
Pourquoi pas?, 20 September 1957 (anon.).
La République libre, 7 February 1958 (G. Lefranc).
La Revue socialiste, December 1957 (A. Marissel).
Rivarol, 28 March 1957 (P.-A. Cousteau); 11 April 1957 (anon.).
Témoignage chrétien, 12 April 1957 (G. Venaissin).

Sur Racine

Arts, 22 May 1963 (R. Matignon).
Critique 20 (1964) (R. Girard).
Le Figaro littéraire, 10 August 1963 (R. Kanters).
Gazette de Lausanne, 14/15 September 1963 (G. Dumur).
Les Lettres françaises, 18–24 July 1963 (H. Juin).
NRF 134 (1964) (C.-M. Cluny).
Les Nouvelles littéraires, 22 August 1963 (R.-M. Albérès).
TQ 15 (Autumn 1963) (J.-L. Baudry).

Essais critiques

Arts, 8 April 1964 (M. Galey).
Combat, 16 July 1964 (P. Sénart).
Critique 21 (1965) (G. Genette).
Esprit 5/6 (May/June 1964) (Y. Bertherat).

L'Express, 23 April 1964 (O. Hahn).
Les Lettres françaises, 2 April 1964 (J.-P. Faye).
Le Monde, 8 April 1964 (P.-H. Simon).

Critique et Vérité/Picard debate

Esprit 5 (May 1966) (Y. Bertherat).
Le Figaro, 3 November 1965 (C. Mauriac).
Le Figaro littéraire, 7–13 October 1965 (R. Picard).
Le Français dans le monde 39 (1966) (G. Raillard).
Les Lettres françaises, 24 March 1966 (P. Daix).
Le Monde, 14 March 1964 (R. Picard); 28 March 1964 (E. Guitton, H. Fluchère); 7 April 1964 (M. Diéguez); 11 April 1964 (L. Goldmann); 23 October 1965; 6 November 1965 (B. Pingaud); 20 November 1965 (J.-B. Barrère, M. Diéguez, M. Chénu); 27 November 1965 (Y. Bellenger, H. Lecause); 5 February 1966; 9 April 1966 (J. Piatier).
Nouvel-Observateur, 3 November 1965 (J. Duvignaud); 30 March 1966 (J. Bloch-Michel); 13 April 1966 (R. Picard).
Les Nouvelles littéraires, 10 March 1966 (R. Poulet); 21 April 1966 (F. Nourissier).
Options, 7–8 (1966) (anon.).
La Quinzaine littéraire 3 (15 April 1966) (J.-P. Revel and L. Finas).
Revue des sciences humaines, Jan.–May 1965 (R. Picard).
Rivarol, 24 February 1966 (R. Poulet).

Système de la Mode

Annales 22 (Nov./Dec. 1967) (T. Todorov).
Critique 24 (1967) (J. Kristeva).
Esprit 35 (1967) (G. Luccioni).
Le Figaro littéraire, 24–30 July 1967 (C. Jannoud).
Gazette de Lausanne, 16/17 September 1967 (Y. Velan).
La Quinzaine littéraire, 15–31 May 1967 (L. Finas).

S/Z

L'Année Balzacienne (1971) (P. Barbéris).
Combat, 14 May 1970 (A. Bosquet).
Critique 302 (July 1972) (B. Vannier).
Esprit 38 (1970) (G. Luccioni).
Le Figaro littéraire, 18–24 May 1970 (R. Kanters).
Le Monde, 9 May 1970 (R. Jean and P. Citron).
Nouvel-Observateur, 4 May 1970 (J.-F. Josselin).
La Quinzaine littéraire, 1–15 March 1970 (P. Sollers).

Empire des signes

Cahiers du chemin 11 (15 January 1971) (G. Perros).
Critique 302 (July 1972) (R. Laporte).
Le Figaro littéraire, 18–24 May 1970 (R. Kanters).
Le Monde, 9 May 1970 (R. Jean).
Nouvel-Observateur, 4 May 1970 (G. Dumur).
La Quinzaine littéraire, 1–15 May 1970 (F. Choay).

Sade, Fourier, Loyola

Critique 302 (July 1972) (P. Duvernois).
Esprit 40 (1972) (G. Luccioni).
Le Figaro, 3 December 1971 (C. Jannoud).
Les Nouvelles littéraires, 24 December 1971–2 January 1972 (J. Ormesson).
NRF 230 (1972) (J.-P. Amette).
Paris-Match, 22 January 1972 (J.-L. Bory).
La Quinzaine littéraire, 1–15 January 1972 (J.-P. Amette).

Le Plaisir du texte

Art-Press, May/June 1973 (J. Henric).
Cahiers du chemin, October 1973 (J.-P. Aron).
Clés pour le spectacle, 20 May 1973 (anon.).
Critique 314 (July 1973) (J. A. Moreau).
L'Express 1128 (19–25 February 1973) (A. Rinaldi).
Le Figaro, 17 February 1973 (M. Chapelan).
Le Monde, 15 February 1973 (B. Poirot-Delpech).
Nouvel-Observateur, 6 March 1973 (J.-F. Josselin).
NRF 247 (1973) (P.-J. Faunau).
Les Nouvelles littéraires, 11 March 1973 (C. Jannoud); 15 April 1973 (R. Sabatier).
Le Point, 6 March 1973 (D. Rolin).
Politique-hebdo, 15 March 1973 (L.-J. Calvet).
Pourquoi pas?, 1 March 1973 (anon.).
La Quinzaine littéraire, 16–31 March 1973 (M. Nadeau).

Roland Barthes par Roland Barthes

Critique 31 (1975) (A. Rey, J.-L. Bouttes).
Esprit 445 (1975) (C. Bourniquel).
Le Figaro, 1 March 1975 (R. Kanters).
La France nouvelle, 5 May 1975 (J. Thibaudeau).

Le Monde, 14 February 1975 (J. Bersani et al.).
Nouvel-Observateur, 24 February 1975 (J.-F. Josselin).
NRF 269 (1975) (J. Duvignaud).
La Quinzaine littéraire, 1–15 March 1975 (M. Nadeau, R. Barthes).

Fragments d'un discours amoureux

Critique 361–2 (1977) (P. Roger, P. Mauriès).
L'Express, 13–19 June 1977 (M. Galey).
Europe, June 1977 (P. Gamarra)
Le Figaro, 25/26 June 1977 (M. Chapelan).
Humanité, 21 April 1977 (A. Poirson).
Magazine littéraire, June 1977 (J.-J. Brochier).
Le Matin, 30 April 1977 (C. Backès-Clément).
Le Monde, 8 April 1977 (B. Poirot-Delpech).
Nouvel-Observateur, 25 April 1977 (H. Bianciotti).
NRF 309 (1978) (A. Arénilla).
Le Point, 27 June 1977 (P. de Boisdeffre).
Politique-hebdo, 27 June/3 July 1977 (L.-J. Calvet).
La Quinzaine littéraire, 1 May 1977 (X. Delcourt).
Rouge 349 (14/15 May 1977) ('Le Can').

Leçon

Le Monde, 24 January 1977 (anon.)
NRF 313 (1979) (P. Dulac).
La Quinzaine littéraire, 1 February 1979 (K. White).

Sollers écrivain

Nouvel-Observateur, 8 January 1979 (H. Bianciotti).

La Chambre claire

Esprit 7–8 (1980) (C.-H. Rocquet).
NRF 330 (1980) (P. Dulac).

3 Books and Journals devoted to Barthes

(a) Published before 1980

Burnier, Michel-Antoine and Patrick Rambaud, *Le Roland Barthes sans peine*, Paris, Balland, 1978.

Calvet, Louis-Jean, *Roland Barthes. Un regard politique sur le signe*, Paris, Payot, 1973.
Collective, *Prétexte: Roland Barthes/Colloque de Cerisy*, Paris, Union Générale d'Editions, 1978.
Fages, Jean-Baptiste, *Comprendre Roland Barthes*, Toulouse, Privat, 1979.
Heath, Stephen, *Vertige du déplacement: lecture de Barthes*, Paris, Fayard, 1974.
Mallac, Guy de and Margaret Eberbach, *Barthes*, Paris, Editions Universitaires, 1971.
Thody, Philip, *Roland Barthes: A Conservative Estimate*, London, Macmillan, 1977.

(b) Published after 1980

Boughali, Mohamed, *L'Érotique du langage chez Roland Barthes*, Casablanca, Afrique-Orient, 1986.
Brown, Andrew, *Roland Barthes: The Figures of Writing*, Oxford, Clarendon Press, 1992.
Calvet, Louis-Jean, *Roland Barthes: 1915–1980*, Paris, Flammarion, 1990; English translation, *Roland Barthes: A Biography*, by Sarah Wykes, Oxford, Polity Press, 1994.
Champagne, Roland, *Literary History in the Wake of Roland Barthes. Redefining the Myths of Reading*, Birmingham, Alabama, Sumina Publications, 1983.
Collective, *Roland Barthes. Le texte et l'image* (Catalogue, Pavillon des Arts), Paris, Editions Paris Musées, 1986.
Comment, Bernard, *Roland Barthes, vers le neutre*, Paris, Christian Bourgois, 1991.
Coquio, Cathérine and Régis Salado, *Barthes après Barthes: une actualité en questions*, Pau, Publications de l'Université de Pau, 1993.
Culler, Jonathan, *Roland Barthes*, Glasgow, Fontana, 1983.
de la Croix, Arnaud, *Barthes. Pour une éthique des signes*, Brussels, De Boeck-Wesmael, 1987.
Freedman, Sanford and Carole Anne Taylor, *Roland Barthes: A Bibliographical Reader's Guide*, New York/London, Garland, 1983.
Knight, Diana, *Barthes and Utopia. Space, Travel, Writing*, Oxford, Clarendon Press, 1997.
Lavers, Annette, *Roland Barthes: Structuralism and After*, London, Methuen, 1982.
Leak, Andrew, *Mythologies*, London, Grant and Cutler, 1994.
Lombardo, Patricia, *The Three Paradoxes of Roland Barthes*, Athens, Georgia, University of Georgia Press, 1989.
Mauriès, Patrick, *Roland Barthes*, Paris, Gallimard, 1992.
Melkonian, Martin, *Le Corps couché de Roland Barthes*, Paris, Séguier, 1989.
Miller, Deirdre, *Bringing Out Roland Barthes*, Berkeley and Los Angeles, University of California Press, 1992.
Moriarty, Michael, *Roland Barthes*, Oxford, Polity Press, 1991.
Pommier, René, *Roland Barthes ras le bol!*, Paris, Roblot, 1987.
Pommier, René, *Le Sur Racine de Roland Barthes*, Paris, SEDES, 1988.
Rabaté, Jean-Michel (ed.), *Writing the Image after Roland Barthes*, Philadelphia, Philadelphia University Press, 1997.

Roger, Philippe, *Roland Barthes, roman*, Paris, Grasset, 1986.
Rylance, Rick, *Roland Barthes*, Hemel Hempstead, Harvester Wheatsheaf, 1994.
Shawcross, Nancy, *Roland Barthes on Photography. The Critical Tradition in Perspective*, Gainesville, Florida, University Press of Florida, 1997.
Sontag, Susan, *A Barthes Reader*, New York, Hill and Wang, 1982.
Ungar, Steven, *Roland Barthes: The Professor of Desire*, Lincoln, University of Nebraska Press, 1983.
Wasserman, Georges, *Roland Barthes*, Boston, Twayne, 1981.
Wiseman, Mary, *The Ecstasies of Roland Barthes*, London, Routledge, 1989.

(c) Journals devoted to Barthes

L'Arc 56 (1974).
Communications 36 (1982) and 63 (1996).
Critique 423–4 (July 1982).
L'Esprit créateur 22:1 (Spring 1982).
Le Magazine littéraire February 1975 and October 1993.
Nottingham French Studies 36:1 (Spring 1997).
Paragraph 11 (1988).
Poétique 47 (4th term, 1981).
TQ 47 (Autumn 1971).
Textuel 15 (October 1984).

4 *General Bibliography*

Abirached, Robert (ed.), *La Décentralisation théâtrale 1: le premier âge 1945–1958*, Avignon, Actes Sud-Papiers, 1992.
Andréev, Léon, 'Le nouveau roman: école de l'écriture ou école du silence?', *Le Monde*, 9 August 1967.
Anon., 'Le paradoxe contre le comédien', *Humanité*, 29 April 1978.
Arnaud, Alain, *Pierre Klossowski*, Paris, Seuil, 1990.
Aron, Jean-Paul, *Les Modernes*, Paris, Gallimard, 1984.
Attridge, Derek, Geoff Bennington and Robert Young (eds), *Post-Structuralism and the Question of History*, Cambridge, Cambridge University Press, 1987.
Bataille, Georges, *Oeuvres complètes 1*, Paris, Gallimard, 1970.
Béguin, Albert, *Création et Destinée 1*, Paris, Seuil/Editions de la Baconnière, 1973.
Berger, John, *G. A Novel*, London, Weidenfeld and Nicolson, 1972.
Boisdeffre, Pierre de, *La Cafétière est sur la table, ou Contre le nouveau roman*, Paris, Table Ronde, 1967.
Bonzon, André, *La Nouvelle critique et Racine*, Paris, Editions Nizet, 1970.
Bourdieu, Pierre, 'Homo Academicus', *Le Monde aujourd'hui*, 5 November 1984.

Bourdieu, Pierre, *Homo Academicus* (1984), trans. Peter Collier, Oxford, Polity Press, 1988.

Bradby, David, *Modern French Drama 1940–1980*, Cambridge, Cambridge University Press, 1984.

Braudel, Fernand, 'Histoire et sciences sociales', *Annales* 4 (Oct./Dec. 1958), 725–53.

Buin, Yves (ed.), *Que peut la littérature?*, Paris, Union Générale d'Editions, 1965.

Burguière, André, 'Présentation', *Annales*, numéro spécial, 'Histoire et structure' (May/August 1971), 1–7.

Burke, Peter, *Sociology and History*, London, Allen & Unwin, 1981.

Burke, Peter, *The French Historical Revolution: The* Annales *School, 1929–89*, Oxford, Polity Press, 1990.

Burke, Seán, *The Death and Return of the Author*, Edinburgh, Edinburgh University Press, 1992.

Butor, Michel, *La Fascinatrice* IV, Paris, Editions de Minuit, 1974.

Byatt, A. S., *Possession. A Romance*, London, Chatto and Windus, 1990.

Caillois, Roger, *Description du marxisme*, Paris, Gallimard, 1950.

Callinicos, Alex, *Against Postmodernism. A Marxist Critique*, Oxford, Polity Press, 1989.

Callinicos, Alex, *Making History: Agency, Structure and Change in Social Theory*, Oxford, Polity Press, 1989.

Callinicos, Alex, *Trotskyism*, Buckingham, Open University Press, 1990.

Callinicos, Alex, *Theories and Narratives. Reflections on the Philosophy of History*, Oxford, Polity Press, 1995.

Calvino, Italo, *The Literature Machine*, trans. Patrick Creagh, London, Secker and Warburg, 1987.

Cau, Jean, *Croquis de mémoire*, Paris, Julliard, 1985.

Cayrol, Jean, *Le Vent de la mémoire*, Paris, Seuil, 1952.

Cayrol, Jean, *Je vivrai l'amour des autres*, Paris, Seuil, 1972.

Champagne, Roland A., *Beyond the Structuralist Myth of Écriture*, The Hague/Paris, Mouton, 1977.

Champagne, Roland A., *The Structuralists on Myth. An Introduction*, New York, Garland Publishing, 1992.

Collective, *Situation de la critique. Actes du premier colloque international de la critique littéraire*, Paris, Syndicat des Critiques Littéraires, 1964.

Collective, *Structuralisme et marxisme*, Paris, Union Générale d'Editions, 1970.

Combes, Patrick, *La Littérature et le mouvement de mai 68*, Paris, Seghers, 1984.

Copfermann, Emile, *Le Théâtre populaire pourquoi?*, Paris, François Maspéro, 1965.

Corpet, Olivier and Mariateresa Padova (eds), *Arguments, 1956–62*, 2 vols, Toulouse, Privat, 1983.

Cournot, Michel, 'La zuppa Pavese', *Nouvel-Observateur*, 22–28 June 1966.

Diéguez, Manuel, *L'Ecrivain et son langage*, Paris, Gallimard, 1960.

Dort, Bernard, 'Brecht en France', *Les Temps modernes* 171 (June 1960), 1855–74.

Dort, Bernard, *Théâtre public 1953–1966*, Paris, Seuil, 1967.

Dort, Bernard, 'Du combat au constat', *Revue des revues* 1 (March 1986), 54–5.

Dosse, François, *L'Histoire en miettes: des* Annales *à la* nouvelle histoire, Paris, La Découverte, 1987.

Dosse, François, *Histoire du structuralisme*, Paris, La Découverte, 2 vols: *1: le champ du signe, 1945–1966* (1991); *2: le chant du cygne, 1967 à nos jours* (1992).

Doubrovsky, Serge, *Pourquoi la nouvelle critique*, Paris, Mercure de France, 1966.

Duhamel, Georges, 'Le Phénomène Rimbaud', *Les Nouvelles littéraires*, 21 October 1954, 1.

Dumur, Guy, 'Racine à Pigalle', *Nouvel-Observateur*, 6 March 1972, 35.

Dupas, Jean-Claude, 'Situation de Barthes', *La France nouvelle*, 25 August 1975, 19–20.

Durand, Gilbert (1963), *Les Structures anthropologiques de l'imaginaire*, Paris, Bordas, 1969.

Duvignaud, Jean, 'La tragédie en liberté', *TP* 1 (March/April 1953), 7–17.

Duvignaud, Jean, *Anthologie des sociologues français contemporains*, Paris, Presses Universitaires de France, 1970.

Eco, Umberto, *Misreadings*, trans. William Weaver, London, Picador, 1994.

Editorial, *TP* 1 (May/June 1953), 1–6.

Ehrmann, Jacques, 'On Articulation: The Language of History and the Terror of Language', *Yale French Studies* 39, special number, 'Literature and Revolution', 1967, 9–28.

Epstein William H. (ed.), *Contesting the Subject. Essays in the Postmodern Theory and Practice of Biography and Biographical Criticism*, West Lafayette, Indiana, Purdue University Press, 1991.

Estier, Claude, *La Gauche hebdomadaire*, Paris, Armand Colin, 1962.

Etiemble, René, *Le Mythe de Rimbaud. 1. Genèse du mythe 1869–1949*, Paris, Gallimard, 1954.

Febvre, Lucien, *Combats pour l'Histoire*, Paris, Armand Colin, 1992.

Felgine, Odette, *Roger Caillois*, Paris, Stock, 1994.

ffrench, Patrick, *The Time of Theory. A History of* Tel Quel, *1960–1983*, Oxford, Clarendon Press, 1995.

Finkelstein, Joanne, *The Fashioned Self*, Oxford, Polity Press, 1991.

Forest, Philippe, *Histoire de Tel Quel. 1960–1982*, Paris, Seuil, 1995.

Freyre, Gilberto, *Maîtres et esclaves*, trans. Roger Bastide, Paris, Gallimard, 1952.

Fuegi, John, *The Life and Lies of Bertolt Brecht*, London, HarperCollins, 1994.

Gaillard, Françoise, 'Roland Barthes: le biographique sans la biographie', *Revue des Sciences Humaines* 98:4 (Oct./Dec. 1991), 85–103.

Galey, Mathieu, 'Les élans du coeur', *Quotidien de Paris*, 22/3 April 1978.

Gide, André, *Fruits of the Earth*, trans. D. Bussy, London, Camelot Press, 1949.

Gide, André, *Romans. Récits et soties. Oeuvres lyriques*, Paris, Gallimard, 1958.

Goethe, Johann Wolfgang von, *Souffrances du jeune Werther*, Paris, Livre de Poche, 1959.

Goldmann, Lucien, *Le Dieu caché*, Paris, Gallimard, 1955.

Goldmann, Lucien, *Pour une sociologie du roman*, Paris, Gallimard, 1964.
Gontard, Denis, *La Décentralisation théâtrale en France 1895–1952*, Paris, Société d'édition d'enseignement supérieur, 1973.
Guérin, Jean (a.k.a. Jean Paulhan), 'Revues des revues', *NNRF*, January 1955, 167.
Guérin, Jean, 'Notes', *NNRF*, June 1955, 1118–19.
Guérin, Jean, 'M. Barthes se met en colère', *NNRF*, October 1955, 802–4.
Guérin, Jean, 'Histoire du sociologue chinois et des Français bavards', *NNRF*, December 1955, 1182–4.
Gurvitch, Georges, *CNRS: Première semaine sociologique*, Paris, Armand Colin, 1949.
Gurvitch, Georges, *La Vocation actuelle de la Sociologie*, Paris, Presses Universitaires de France, 1964.
Harman, Chris, *The Fire Last Time: 1968 and After*, London, Bookmarks, 1988.
Harvey, David, *The Condition of Postmodernity. An Enquiry into the Conditions of Cultural Change*, Oxford, Blackwell, 1989.
Harvey, Sylvia, *May 68 and Film Culture*, London, British Film Institute, 1978.
Heath, Stephen, *The Nouveau Roman. A Study in the Practice of Writing*, London, Elek Books, 1972.
Hill, Leslie, *Marguerite Duras. Apocalyptic Desires*, London, Routledge 1993.
Hollier, Denis, *Le Collège de Sociologie 1937–1939*, Paris, Gallimard, 1979.
Hook, Sidney, *Pour comprendre Marx*, Paris, Gallimard, 1936.
Hüfner, Agnes, *Brecht in Frankreich 1930–1963*, Stuttgart, J. B. Metzler, 1968.
Hughes, H. Stuart, *The Obstructed Path: French Social Thought in the Years of Desperation 1930–1960*, New York, Harper Torch, 1966.
Ionesco, Eugène, *Les Chaises/L'Impromptu de l'Alma*, Paris, Gallimard, 1973.
Jaurès, Jean, *Histoire socialiste de la Révolution française*, Paris, Éditions Sociales, 1969.
Jones, Robert, *Panorama de la nouvelle critique en France de Gaston Bachelard à Jean-Paul Weber*, Paris, SEDES, 1968.
Josselin, Jean-François, 'Barthes et son double', *Nouvel-Observateur*, 9 May 1977, 38.
Joussain, André, *La Loi des révolutions*, Paris, Flammarion, 1950.
Katz, Barry, *Herbert Marcuse and the Art of Liberation. An Intellectual Biography*, London, Verso, 1982.
Khilnani, Sunhil, *Arguing Revolution. The Intellectual Left in Postwar France*, New Haven, Connecticut, Yale University Press, 1993.
Klein, Richard, 'Images of the Self: New York and Paris', *Partisan Review* 2 (1973), 295–301.
Kleist, Heinrich von, *The Marquise of O-*, London, Penguin, 1995.
Knight, Diana, 'Vie de Barthes', *Modern and Contemporary France*, October 1995, 463–7.
Kofman, Myron, *Edgar Morin. From Big Brother to Fraternity*, London, Pluto, 1996.
Kristeva, Julia, *Les Samouraïs*, Paris, Gallimard, 1990.
Lefebvre, Henri, *L'Idéologie structuraliste*, Paris, Éditions Anthropos, 1975.
Lemarchand, Jacques, 'L'écolier limousin et le petit organon', *NNRF*, May 1955, 897–902.
Lourau, René, *Auto-dissolution des avant-gardes*, Paris, Editions Galilée, 1980.

McAllester, Mary, 'Polemics and Poetics: Bachelard's Conception of the Imagining Consciousness', *Journal of the British Society for Phenomenology* 12:1 (January 1981), 3–13.

Macey, David, *The Lives of Michel Foucault*, London, Vintage, 1994.

Mannoni, Maud, 'Psychoanalysis and the May Revolution', in Charles Posner (ed.), *Reflections on the Revolution in France: 1968*, Harmondsworth, Penguin, 1970.

Marcus, Laura, *Auto/biographical Discourses*, Manchester, Manchester University Press, 1994.

Marty, Éric, *L'Écriture du jour. Le* Journal *d'André Gide*, Paris, Seuil, 1985.

Marx, Karl, *The Eighteenth Brumaire of Louis Bonaparte*, Peking, Foreign Language Press, 1978.

Mauriac, Claude, *L'Alittérature contemporaine*, Paris, Albin Michel, 1958.

Mauriac, François, 'Bloc-notes', *L'Express*, 18 September 1954, 12.

Mazon, Brigitte, *Aux origines de l'École des Hautes Études en Sciences Sociales: le rôle du mécénat américain*, Paris, Cerf, 1988.

Merquior, J. G., *From Prague to Paris. A Critique of Structuralist and Post-Structuralist Thought*, London, Verso, 1986.

Michelet, Jules, *L'Étudiant*, Paris, Seuil, 1970.

Moriarty, Michael, 'Rhetoric, Doxa and Experience in Barthes', *French Studies*, May 1997, 169–82.

Mortier, Daniel, *Celui qui dit oui, celui qui dit non ou la Réception de Brecht en France (1945–56)*, Paris/Geneva, Champion/Slatkine, 1986.

Mounin, Georges, *Introduction à la sémiologie*, Paris, Editions de Minuit, 1970.

Nadeau, Maurice, *Histoire du surréalisme*, Paris, Seuil, 1945.

Nadeau, Maurice, *La Littérature présente*, Paris, Corrêa, 1952.

Nadeau, Maurice, 'Présentation', *LLN* 1 (March 1953), 1–2.

Nadeau, Maurice, *Le Roman français depuis la guerre*, Paris, Gallimard, 1963.

Nadeau, Maurice, *Grâces leur soient rendues*, Paris, Albin Michel, 1990.

Nehamas, Alexander, *Nietzsche. Life as Literature*, Cambridge, Massachusetts, Harvard University Press, 1985.

Nietzsche, Friedrich, *Le Gai savoir*, trans. and pref. Pierre Klossowski, Paris, Club français du livre, 1959.

Orr, Linda, *Jules Michelet. Nature, History, and Language*, Ithaca, New York, and London, Cornell University Press, 1976.

Ostier, Claude, *Jean Cayrol*, Paris, Seghers, 1973.

Palmer, Bryan D., *Descent into Discourse: The Reification of Language and the Writing of Social History*, Philadelphia, Temple University Press, 1990.

Paris, Jean, *Hamlet*, Paris, Seuil, 1953.

Petitjean, Georges, 'Les marginaux de la VIe section', *Nouvel-Observateur*, 9 November 1974.

Petitjean, Georges, 'Les Grands prêtres de l'Université française', *Nouvel-Observateur*, 7 April 1975.

Pinto, Louis, *L'Intelligence en action: le Nouvel-Observateur*, Paris, Métailié, 1984.

Poster, Marc, *Existential Marxism in Postwar France: From Sartre to Althusser*, Princeton, New Jersey, Princeton University Press, 1975.

Poulet, George (ed.), *Les Chemins actuels de la critique*, Paris, Union Générale d'Editions, 1966.

Pyle, Forest, *The Ideology of Imagination. Subject and Society in the Discourse of Romanticism*, Stanford, Stanford University Press, 1995.

Reader, Keith (with K. Wadia), *The May 1968 Events in France. Reproduction and Interpretation*, London, Macmillan, 1993.

Revel, Jean-François 'Le fantasme anonyme', *L'Express*, 19–25 October 1970.

Richard, Jean-Pierre, *Littérature et Sensation. Flaubert, Stendhal*, Paris, Seuil, 1954.

Riffaterre, Michael, *Essais de stylistique structurale*, Paris, Flammarion, 1971.

Rigby, Brian, *Popular Culture in Modern France: A Study of Cultural Discourse*, London, Routledge, 1991.

Robbe-Grillet, Alain, *Pour un nouveau roman*, Paris, Editions de Minuit, 1963.

Robbe-Grillet, Alain, *Le Miroir qui revient*, Paris, Editions de Minuit, 1984.

Ross, Kristin, *Fast Cars, Clean Bodies. Decolonization and the Reordering of French Culture*, Cambridge, Massachusetts, and London, MIT Press, 1996.

Roudinesco, Elisabeth, *La Bataille de cent ans. Histoire de la psychanalyse en France 2*, Paris, Seuil, 1986.

Rousso, Henry, *Le Syndrome de Vichy*, Paris, Seuil, 1987.

Ruscio, Alain, *La Décolonisation tragique: une histoire de la décolonisation française, 1945–1962*, Paris, Messidor/Éditions Sociales, 1987.

Sade, D. A. F. de, *Justine ou Les Malheurs de la vertu*, pref. Béatrice Didier, Paris, Librairie Générale Française, 1973.

Sarrazac, Jean-Pierre, 'L'invention de la théâtralité', *Esprit*, January 1997, 60–73.

Sartre, Jean-Paul, *Qu'est-ce que la littérature?*, Paris, Gallimard, 1948.

Sartre, Jean-Paul, *Situations II*, Paris, Gallimard, 1948.

Seale, Patrick and Maureen McConville, *French Revolution 1968*, Harmondsworth, Penguin/Heinemann, 1968.

Sirinelli, Jean-François, *Intellectuels et passions françaises*, Paris, Fayard, 1990.

Smith, Douglas, *Transvaluations. Nietzsche in France 1872–1972*, Oxford, Clarendon Press, 1996.

Sollers, Philippe, *L'Ecriture et l'expérience des limites*, Paris, Seuil, 1968.

Sombart, Werner, *Le Bourgeois: contribution à l'histoire morale et intellectuelle de l'homme économique moderne*, trans. S. Jankélévitch, Paris, Payot, 1926.

Stafford, Andy, 'Constructing a Radical Popular Theatre: Roland Barthes, Brecht and *Théâtre Populaire*', *French Cultural Studies* 7 (1996), 33–48.

Stafford, Andy, 'Barthes and Michelet: Biography and History', *Nottingham French Studies* 36:1 (Spring 1997), 14–23.

Sturrock, John (ed.), *Structuralism and Since. From Lévi-Strauss to Derrida*, Oxford, Oxford University Press, 1979.

Thibaudeau, Jean, 'Barthes n'est pas Marxiste', *La France nouvelle*, 25 August 1975, 20.

Thomas, Chantal, 'Barthes et Michelet: Homologie de travail, parallèle d'affection', *La Règle du jeu*, January 1995, 73–84.

Thomson, George, *Aeschylus and Athens. A Study in the Social Origins of Drama*, London, Lawrence and Wishart, 1946.

Tilby, Michael (ed.), *Beyond the Nouveau Roman*, London, Berg, 1990.

Todorov, Tzvetan, 'La réflexion sur la littérature dans la France contemporaine', *Poétique* 38 (1979), 131–48.

Trotsky, Leon, *Literature and Revolution*, London, Bookmarks, 1991.

Ulmer, Gregory, 'Fetishism in Roland Barthes's Nietzschean Phase', *Papers on Language and Literature* 14:3 (1978), 334–55.

Valéry, Paul, *Monsieur Teste*, Paris, Gallimard, 1946.

Velan, Yves, 'Barthes', in John K. Simon (ed.), *Modern French Criticism. From Proust and Valéry to Structuralism*, Chicago, University of Chicago Press, 1972.

Venaissin, Gabriel, 'Jean Cayrol, romancier du point zéro', *Critique* 84 (May 1954), 414–20.

Viallaneix, Paul, *Michelet cent ans après*, Grenoble, Presses Universitaires de Grenoble, 1975.

Vilar, Jean, *Le Théâtre, service public*, Paris, Gallimard, 1975.

Villiers, André (ed.), *Théâtre et Collectivité*, Paris, Flammarion, 1953.

Wagener, Francis, 'La rencontre de Erté et Roland Barthes', *Le Monde*, 13 December 1973.

Wald, Alan, *The New York Intellectuals: The Rise and Decline of the Anti-Stalinist Left from the 1930s to the 1980s*, Chapel Hill, University of North Carolina Press, 1987.

White, Hayden, *Metahistory: The Historical Imagination in Nineteenth-Century Europe*, Baltimore, Maryland, Johns Hopkins University Press, 1973.

Wilson, Edmund, *To The Finland Station*, London, Collins/Fontana, 1974.

Wilson, Elizabeth, *Adorned Dreams. Fashion and Modernity*, London, Virago, 1985.

Wintzen, René, 'Le roman et le public', *Documents* 2 (February 1955), 178–9.

Index